# SOCIAL MEDIA MARKET

## 3 BOOKS IN

---

Marketing Made Simple for Beginners with Branding Strategies to Accelerate Your Success in Business and Create Passive Income. Learn Digital Marketing and Algorithms, Become an Influencer Using Facebook, Instagram and YouTube.

# TABLE OF CONTENTS

# FACEBOOK ADVERTISING
# (SOCIAL MEDIA MARKETING STRATEGY)

---

**An Easy Guide For Optimizing Facebook Page And Facebook Advertising And Create A Volume Of New Customers And Income For Your Business**

**By**

**Edward Keller**

for any reparation, damages, or monetary loss due to the information herein, either directly

or indirectly.



The information herein is offered for informational purposes solely and is universal as so.

The presentation of the information is without a contract or any type of guarantee assurance.

The trademarks that are used are without any consent, and the publication of the

trademark is without permission or backing by the trademark owner. All trademarks and

brands within this book are for clarifying purposes only and are owned by the owners

themselves, not affiliated with this document.

# CHAPTER ONE
# INTRODUCTION

Social media marketing is the actual use of social media platforms and websites to promote a product or service. And Although the terms e-marketing and digital marketing are still prevalent in the academic world, social media marketing is becoming increasingly popular among professionals and researchers. Also, Most social media platforms have built-in data analytics that allows companies to track the progress, success, and engagement of their advertising campaigns. Companies reach out to a range of stakeholders through social media marketing, including current and potential customers, current and prospective employees, journalists, bloggers, and the general public. At the strategic level, social media marketing involves managing a marketing campaign, managing it, defining its scope (for example, using it more actively or passively), and establishing a "culture," as well as the social media tone desired by the company.

Informal community promoting isn't equivalent to online life focusing. Online networking focusing on is a technique for upgrading web-based experience publicizing by utilizing profile information to convey commercials legitimately to singular clients. Interpersonal organization advertising alludes to the way toward coordinating informal community clients to target bunches that have been indicated by the promoter.

**Application**

Individuals who utilize long range interpersonal communication locales get their different data about themselves, including their age, sexual orientation, interests, and area put away on the servers of the online networking organizations. This put away data permits sponsors form making explicit objective gatherings and individual sizing their promotions. The favorable position for publicists is that their advertisements can reach to a particular arrangement of the crowd who are keen on the item or administration. The preferred location for clients is that they can see ads that are pertinent to their advantage.

**Facebook**

Facebook, the most well known interpersonal organization, has built up a focusing on innovation which permits promotions to contact a particular crowd. This is inside the Facebook item called Facebook Ads, which is accessible to clients and organizations the same. While posting a promotion through the Facebook Ad Manager, a promoter is given a lot of qualities that will characterize his objective market. Facebook calls this crowd focusing. These qualities incorporate land area, sexual orientation, age, work, relationship status, and interests, for example, music, among others. Facebook claims that sponsors can even modify their intended interest group dependent on their conduct; for example, buying designs, gadget use, and different exercises. This is the reason Facebook clients see notices on their profile page that are significant to their inclinations and interests. This permits the promotions to be not so much meddlesome but somewhat more effective in conveying the fitting substance to the correct crowd. The promotion calculation is likewise fit for checking execution with the goal that sponsors or Facebook advertisers can adjust their circle just as the nature, spending plan, and length of the promotions dependent on its exhibition.

**Instagram**

Instagram is an online networking application that is made as an outlet to share photographs with supporters. While it is, for the most part, utilized for loved ones, and some of the time an expansive after on any off chance that you are an influencer, littler organizations use their foundation to publicize to general society just as utilizing influencers to advance certain items. Web-based life programs, for example, Instagram, utilizes advanced commitment to permit organizations to advertise various items. The program (Instagram) takes the data accumulated about the purchaser and makes a domain for the notice. Since Instagram is primarily utilized by ages 18-24 and on regular is being used by every individual around 72 minutes per day, the manner in which promotions are introduced is critical, supposing that they are not compelling they will be ignored, ed and the notice would not be convincing.

**Activity**

Inside social networks, clients give segment data, interests, and pictures. This data is gotten to by online networking focusing on programming and empowers sponsors to make show promotions with qualities that coordinate those of informal community clients. The significant segment of web-based life concentrate on is the arrangement of the clients' socio-segment and intrigue data. By utilizing this data, online presence focusing on makes it feasible for clients to see commercials that may really intrigue them. The accessibility of client information takes into consideration itemized investigation and detailing, which is a significant piece of web-based social networking focusing on and what makes it more viable than accurate projections alone.

**Socioeconomics**

Around seventy, five percent of Internet clients are individuals from at any rate one informal organization. 49% of U.S. grown-up ladies visit online networking locales a couple of times each day, while just 34% of men visit them. The quickest developing age bunch on Twitter is 55-to 64-year-old, up 79% since 2012. Furthermore, the 45-54 age bunch is the fastest developing on Facebook and Google+. Web-based life use is still increasingly regular among the 89% of Internet clients matured 18–29, versus 43% of the individuals who are 65 and more established.

**Sorts of promoting**

Well known internet-based life destinations, Facebook, Twitter, and YouTube, offer various approaches to promote brands. Facebook gives publicists choices, for example, advanced posts, supported stories, page post advertisements, Facebook object (like) promotions, and external site (standard) promotions. Also, To publicize on the twitter website, there are advertiser tweets, slants, and excellent records that appear on clients newsfeed. For advertising on YouTube, there are marked channels, advanced recordings, and in-video promoting.

In July 2015, during their Q2 profit call, Facebook uncovered that it had accomplished $2.9B in portable income, adding up to over 76% of its worldwide quarterly income. A vast bit of this income was from application introduce advertisements, of which engineers purchase on a Cost for every Install premise.

Another sort of promotion is utilizing an instrument called "purchase catches". A few systems are now engaging with "purchase fastens', or being immediate advertisers for different items a business wishes to advance on their online networking stage. Interpersonal organizations like Facebook and Twitter are now associated with such organizations, and this is still only the start. The "purchase button" is the portal to rash internet shopping. These notices spring up in the news channel of web-based life interfaces and give you the alternative to click a catch and buy the thing at that moment—these record for just shy of 2% of online deals. The "purchase button", which can be followed back to the framework being protected by Amazon in 1997, has an incidental influence in web deals as well as web life.

Although the domain of online networking promoting can be utilized for deals, it very well maybe for something other than that. For instance, online life assumed a critical job in the 2008 presidential race. Recordings that included both Obama and McCain had the option to gather 1.45 billion perspectives. A portion of those perspectives and records could have faltered one's democratic choice. Web-based social networking promoting likewise assumes a gigantic job in a brand's or organization's notoriety and gathering. The manner in which an organization introduces itself can decide its prevalence and crowd. This strategy is even demonstrated in specific investigations to happen on a worldwide scale.

**Advantages**

- Publicists can arrive at clients who are keen on their items.
- Takes into account point by point examination and detailing (counting business intelligence)
- The data assembled is genuine, not from factual projections
- Doesn't get to IP-locations of the client

**Advertising on social media**

Advertising on any social network is a must if you want to reach new audiences quickly.

Of course, it can be daunting to move from an organic social strategy to putting real money on the table. Therefore, it is essential to understand all the options.

**Facebook advertising**

Facebook advertising is available to businesses in many forms. Ads can actually be as simple or sophisticated as they want. Regardless of the scale, the Scope is broad: companies have the potential to market to Facebook to 2 billion people every month.

The process is simple: Facebook allows users to target audiences with self-service tools and provides them with analytics that tracks the performance of each ad. Scope and visibility can help to level the playing field for an independent company that wants to compete with companies with much larger budgets.

Thanks to the Facebook Business Manager platform, businesses have a single point of contact for all their marketing and advertising needs. Additional resources such as access to Instagram and product catalogues are part of the selection.

Conquering Facebook advertising requires continuity and a deep understanding of how the platform works in all its dimensions. Fortunately, we have created the ultimate guide for you to get started.

**A Deep Dive Into Facebook Advertising**

As a canny web client, you may think nobody taps on Facebook advertisements.

Wrong.

Facebook is on target to make over $4 billion in income this year from promoting. Somebody's clicking.

How would you get them to click your advertisements? All the more critically, how would you get them to purchase your item?

Numerous advertisers who have attempted Facebook promotions, particularly in their initial days, concluded that Facebook publicizing doesn't work. Try not to trust them.

In case you're absolutely new to Facebook, start with this Facebook Marketing Guide. At that point, return to this post for a profound jump into promoting.

Right now, realize which organizations are the best fit for Facebook promotions and how to run effective crusades. We'll cover the most widely recognized slip-up advertisers make and the most significant factor in your promotion's prosperity.

### How Do Facebook Ads Work?

Facebook promotions presently come in a few assortments. You can advance your Page, posts on your Page moves clients made, or your site itself. Notwithstanding Facebook's expanding center around local promotions and keeping traffic on its webpage, you can, in any case, be fruitful sending clients to your site.

Facebook advertisements are focused on clients dependent on their area, segment, and profile data. A significant number of these choices are just accessible on Facebook. In the wake of making an advertisement, you set a financial limit and offer for each snap or thousand impressions that your promotion will get.

Clients, at that point, see your advertisements in the sidebar on Facebook.com.

This guide will walk you through the accepted procedures for making CPC promotions that direct people to your site. Facebook's other promotion alternatives are incredible for driving commitment and brand mindfulness, yet developments driving clients off-site are as yet the best choice for direct reaction sponsors hoping to make a deal.

### Who Should Advertise on Facebook?

Numerous organizations fall flat at Facebook publicizing since they are not a solid match. You ought to consistently test new promoting channels, particularly before request drives up costs, yet make a point to consider your plan of action's fit to the system.

Facebook advertisements are more similar to show promotions than search promotions. They ought to be utilized to create request, not satisfy it. Clients are on Facebook to associate with their companions, not to discover items to purchase.

**Low-Friction Conversions**

The organizations that prevail with Facebook promotions request that clients join, not to purchase. You should utilize a low-contact transformation to be effective.

A guest to your site wasn't searching for your item. He clicked your advertisement spontaneously. In case you depend on him to promptly purchase something to make your advertisement ROI positive, you will fall flat.

Facebook clients are whimsical and liable to click back to Facebook on any off chance that you request a significant duty (buy) in advance. Instead, stick to straightforward transformations like pursuing your administration, rounding out a short lead structure, or presenting an email address.

Regardless of whether you sell items, not administrations, you ought to consider concentrating on a middle change like a pamphlet information exchange. At that point, you can upsell later through email advertising.

Day by day bargain destinations like Groupon, AppSumo, and Fab are genuine instances of organizations that can prevail with Facebook publicizing. After you click one of their promotions, they simply request your email address. They'll sell you on an arrangement later.

**Plan of action**

Regardless of whether you just request an email address at first, you'll have to, in the long run, bring in cash from these clients if your promotions are to be gainful.

The best plan of action that fits for Facebook advertisements procures income from their clients after some time, not at the same time. A client may have given you her email. However, you'll have to assemble more trust before she purchases anything.

You shouldn't rely upon one significant buy from her. A few littler purchases are perfect.

Day by day arrangement and membership locales are incredible instances of plans of action that can blossom with Facebook. Both have clients whose lifetime esteem is spread out more than a half year or more.

At Udemy, we center around getting clients to join on their first visit. By meaning to be gainful on advertisement go through in a half year (not one day), we can transform Facebook clients into long haul clients. We focus on a 20% compensation on promotion spend on the very first moment and 100% restitution in a half year. These numbers can fill in as a harsh guide for your business.

# CHAPTER TWO

# INSTRUCTIONS TO TARGET FACEBOOK ADS

---

The #1 botch most advertisers make with Facebook promotions isn't focusing on them effectively.

Facebook's advertisement focusing on choices are unrivaled. On Facebook, you can target clients by:

- Area
- Age
- Sex
- Interests
- Associations
- Relationship Status
- Dialects
- Training
- Work environments

Every decision can be helpful, contingent upon your crowd. Most advertisers should concentrate on the spot, age, sexual orientation, and interests.

Area permits you to targets clients in the nation, state, city, or postal district that your administration.

Age and sexual orientation focusing on ought to be founded on your current clients. In any event that ladies 25-44 are the central part of your clients, begin just concentrate on them. On any off chance that they end up being beneficial, you would then be able to grow your client base.

Enthusiasm focusing on is the most remarkable; however, the abused element of Facebook advertisements. While making a promotion, you have two choices: general classes or specific interests.

**General Category Targeting**

General classes incorporate themes like Gardening, Horror Movies, and Consumer Electronics. As of late, Facebook has included fresher targets like Engaged (1 year), Expecting Parents, Away from Hometown, and Has Birthday in 1 Week.

Broad interests may appear to be a proficient method to contact an enormous crowd. Be that as it may, these clients frequently cost more and spend less. Abstain from utilizing Broad Category focusing.

**Exact Interest Targeting**

Exact Interest Targeting permits you to target clients dependent on data in their profile, including "recorded likes and interests, the Pages they like, applications they use, and other profile (course of events) content they've given" (Facebook). You'll locate the best ROI utilizing Precise Interest focusing.

Facebook has an astounding exhibit of interests to focus from Harry

Potter to submerged rugby. The critical step is picking the correct ones.

While focusing on specific interests, Facebook gives the size of the crowd and other proposed likes and interests. You won't have any severe information. When you select benefits for a promotion, Facebook will show a total proposed offer.

As opposed to targeting broad terms for your specialty like "yoga" or "advanced photography," center around specific interests. On any off chance that you use laser-centered premiums like these, you'll contact the individuals who are generally keen on your subject and the readiest to burn through cash on it.

For instance, when we included another DJ course Udemy, we didn't merely focus on the intrigue "plate racer."

Instead, made promotions focusing on DJ productions like DJ Magazine and Mixmag. At that point made another promotion focusing on DJ brands like Traktor and Vestax. Join littler, related interests into a gathering with a group of people of 50,000 to 1M+. This structure will make advertisements with enormous crowds that are probably going to change over.

Propelled tip: Use Facebook Connect as a signup alternative on your site. At the point when clients interface by means of Facebook, you'll have the option to break down their inclinations. List these interests against the number of fanatics of their particular Facebook Pages. You'll be left with your high-fondness interests. Utilizing this strategy, we made an objective gathering that has been our best entertainer (out of many experimental groups) for about a year.

**Pictures for Facebook Ads**

The most significant piece of your promotion is the picture. You can compose the most beautiful duplicate on the planet, yet In any event that your image doesn't get a client's attention, you won't get any snaps.

Try not to utilize low-quality pictures, nonexclusive stock photography, or any images that you don't reserve the privileges to use. Try not to take anything from Google Images. Except if you're a famous brand, don't utilize your logo.

Since we have them, no's off the beaten path, in what manner should publicists discover pictures to utilize? Get them, make them yourself, or use ones with a Creative Commons permit.

Beneath, you'll realize which sorts of pictures work best and where explicitly to discover them.

**Individuals**

Pictures of individuals work best—ideally their countenances. Utilize close-ups of appealing faces that look like your intended interest group.

More youthful isn't in every case better. In case you're focusing on retirees, test pictures of individuals more than 60. Utilizing a genuinely multi-year old young lady wouldn't bode well.

Facebook promotion pictures are little (100 x 72 pixels). Make a point to concentrate on an individual's face and yield it if necessary. Try not to utilize a blurry or dim picture.

Propelled tip: Use pictures of individuals looking to one side. Clients will follow the headlines of sight and be bound to peruse your advertisement content.

Besides models, you can likewise include the individuals behind your business and grandstand.

**Typography**

Transparent, comprehensible sort can likewise draw in clicks. Splendid hues will enable your promotion to stick out.

Much the same as with content duplicate, utilize an inquiry or express an advantage to the client. Treat the content in the picture as an expansion of your copy.

**Amusing**

Insane or amusing pictures certainly draw in clicks. See I Can Has Cheeseburger, 9GAG, or any public image.

Sadly, even with elucidating advertisement message, these promotions don't generally change over well. On any off chance that you utilize this sort of advertising, set a low spending plan and track the exhibition intently. You'll frequently draw in heaps of interest clicks that won't convert.

**The most effective method to Create Images**

You have three alternatives to discover pictures: get them, find ones that are as of now authorized, or make them yourself.

You can purchase stock photography at numerous destinations, including iStockPhoto or Big Stock. Try not to utilize stock photographs that resemble stock photographs. No nonexclusive businesspeople or unmistakable white foundations, if you don't mind.

Clients perceive stock photographs and will overlook them. Instead, discover remarkable pictures and give them character by trimming or altering them and applying channels. You can utilize Pixlr, an online picture editorial manager, for both.

In any event that you don't have the cash to purchase photographs, you can look for Creative Commons authorized pictures.

The third alternative is to make the pictures yourself. In case you're a visual creator, this is simple. In any event that you aren't, you can, in any case, make typographic pictures or utilize fundamental picture altering to create something unique from existing photographs.

**Pivoting Ads**

Each battle ought to have in any event three advertisements with a similar intrigue target. Utilizing a few promotions will permit you to accumulate information on everyone. For a given crusade, just 1-2 promotions will get a ton of impressions, so try not to run such a large number of on the double.

Following a couple of days, erase the advertisements with the most reduced navigate rates (CTRs) and continue emphasizing on the champs to build your CTR persistently. Focus on 0.1% as a benchmark. You'll likely begin nearer to the normal of 0.04%.

**Composing Facebook Ad Copy**

In the wake of seeing your picture, clients will (ideally) read your promotion content. Here you can sell them on your item or support and win their snap.

In spite of the 25-character feature and 90-character body content cutoff points, we can, in any case, utilize the famous copywriting equation AIDA.

**(A)attention:** Draw clients into the advertisement with an eye-catching feature.

**(I)interest**: Get the client intrigued by your item by quickly depicting the most significant advantage of utilizing it.

**(D)desire**: Create immediate want for your item with a rebate, free preliminary, or restricted time offer.

**(A)auction:** End the advertisement with a source of inspiration.

AIDA is a great deal to fit into 115 characters. Compose 5-10 advertisements until you're ready to provide a brief attempt to close the transaction into the promotion.

Here's a model for a web-based programming course:

**Become a Web Developer**

Get the hang of all that you have to turn into a web designer without any preparation.

**Offering on Facebook Ads**

Like in any advertisement organize, the critical offering can mean the contrast among benefit and a bombed test.

After you make your advertisement, Facebook will give a recommended offer range. At the point when you're merely beginning, set your offer close to the low finish of this range.

Your CTR will rapidly begin to direct the value you'll have to pay for traffic. On any off chance that your CTR is high, your recommended offers will diminish. In any event that your CTR is low, you'll have to offer more for each snap. Enhance your advertisements and focuses on building your CTR continually.

Notwithstanding click volume, your offer will likewise direct the amount of your intended interest group you're ready to reach.

Facebook outline indicating the amount of your intended interest group your battle has come to

Expanding your offer will enable your advertisement to arrive at a more significant amount of your intended interest group. In any event that your promotion is performing high, however, you're coming at under 75% of your intended interest group, you can build your offer to get more snaps.

On any off chance that your crowd entrance is high, expanding your spending will build your promotion's recurrence: how often a focused on the client will see it.

**Points of arrival**

Getting a tick is just the start. You, despite everything, need the guest to change over.

Try to send him to a focused on, high-changing over the point of arrival. You know his age, sex, and interests, so show him a page that will take care of his issues.

The point of arrival ought to likewise contain the enlistment structure or email submit box that you'll follow as a transformation. Concentrate the presentation page on this activity, not the later deal. On any off chance that you need guests to pursue your pamphlet, show them the advantages or offer an unconditional present for their email.

**The most effective method to Track Performance**

Facebook never again offers change following. Facebook Insights are incredible for information inside Facebook yet can't give data on clients who have left the site.

To appropriately follow the presentation of your Facebook crusades, you'll have to utilize an examination program like Google Analytics, or your back end framework. Label your connections using Google's URL developer or your following labels.

**Transformation Tracking**

As referenced above, try to isolate battles by intrigue gatherings with the goal that you can perceive how everyone performs.

You can follow them utilizing the utm_campaign parameter. Utilize the utm_content setting to separate advertisements. Advertisement level following is valuable when testing eye-getting pictures and before you've built up a gauge CTR and change rate.

**Execution Tracking**

You will likewise need to screen your exhibition inside the Facebook interface. The most important measurement to follow is active clicking factor. Your CTR influences both the number of snaps you'll get and the sum you will pay per click.

Advertisements with a low CTR will quit serving or become increasingly costly. Ads with a high CTR will produce the same number of snaps as will fit inside your spending limit. They will likewise cost less. Watch out for CTR by premiums and promotions to realize which crowds work best and which advertisements impact them.

Indeed, even the best advertisement's exhibition will decrease after some time. The littler your intended interest group is, the quicker this will occur. Typically you'll see your traffic begin to drop off in 3-10 days.

At the point when it does, invigorate the promotions with new pictures and duplicate. Copy your current promotions at that point, change the picture and advertisement content. Try not to alter the ongoing development. Erase any current advertisements, not getting clicks. By the following day, you'll see the new promotions accumulating impressions and snaps.

Screen the pictures' presentation after some time to see which ones produce the best CTR and keep up their traffic the longest. You can turn high-performing photos back in at regular intervals until they quit getting clicked by any stretch of the imagination.

Despite the expectation to absorb information, Facebook promoting can be an extraordinary showcasing channel for the right business. The most significant focuses to recall are specific target interests, use eye-getting pictures, give clients a low-contact transformation, and track everything.

Following possibly 14 days of realizing what works for your business, you'll have the option to create a consistent wellspring of transformations from the world's most prominent interpersonal organization.

**How to set up a good Facebook advertising account**

The primary first step is simple: create a Facebook Advertising account. Its a relatively simple process that involves the following four steps:

1. **Install Facebook Business Manager.** Firstly, you create the Facebook page for your business. And From there, you can create a Business Manager account that will allow you to serve ads on this page. Start by accessing the Business Manager page and click on "Create an account" - Then log in with the email address and also password that you used to configure your business page.
2. **Install Facebook Pixel.** Then Go to your website and install the Facebook pixel, which allows Facebook to identify people who have visited your website, create personalized audiences of visitors, and then show them ads.
3. **Create audiences to target users.** Use this tool to create and record the audiences most relevant to your brand. Return to

Business Manager and select the "Audiences" option in the Property column.

4. **Create a Facebook ad from a Facebook message.** You can now try it. First, decide what you want to achieve - do you want more clicks, sales, video views, or leads?

Facebook ads manager can be used for making and dissecting your Facebook advertisement battles. Making the promotion itself just includes choosing "ake Ads," "starting from the drop menu in the upper right of your business page.

At the point when you open the primary menu, you'll see five areas: Plan, Create and Manage, Measure and Report Assets, and Setting. Realizing how each apparatus functions is fundamental to forming your crusade.

- **Plan.** The Plan area contains apparatuses that assist you with learning things about your crowd and give you imaginative thoughts for running your advertisements. With the Audience Insights apparatus, you can discover a great deal of data about many groups on Facebook.
- **Make and Manage.** Here you discover devices for making your advertisement and dealing with your battles.
- **Measure and Report.** At any point when you need to break down how your advertisements are performing, look at the instruments in the Measure and Report segment. For instance, here, you can try and make those custom changes to follow

whether advertisements are meeting your business objectives.

- **Resources.** This segment gives you speedy and straightforward access to critical resources that you' used to fabricate your advertisements, including crowds that you' put something aside for promotion focusing on, pictures you' utilized, your Facebook pixel, and that' just the beginning.
- **Settings.** The settings region is the place the entirety of your record data is put away. Go here to refresh installment data, your email, etc.

The Facebook pixel is an instrument that causes you to run exceptionally focused on crusades, so it' essential to introduce it before running Facebook promotions. Every promotion account gets one default pixel to utilize. The code is comprised of two principal parts: the pixel base code and occasion code. Well, The pixel base code tracks the entirety of the traffic to your site. Occasion codes are extra bits of code you can include under the default pixel code to specific pages of your website that permit you to follow particular activities on those pages.

As you experience this procedure, it's essential to give sharing access to Google Analytics, Facebook, ClickFunnels, and other lead page resources because every stage has its own record arrangement structures and, in some cases, includes different arrangements. The motivation which is behind why this is significant is twofold:

- You can try and evacuate risk under the General Data Protection

Regulation (GDPR), the European Union (EU) law that gives more prominent assurance to a person's very own data and how it' gathered, put away, and utilized. On any off chance that you collect customers' client information in your own record, you can wind up in the situation of being the information processor or information controller and along these lines subject under GDPR.

- You ensure your notoriety. Customers actually may not personally comprehend the stray pieces of information and advanced pipes when they begin working with you, yet in the long run, they will understand. On any off chance that they feel exploited toward the finish of your relationship, they compliment you to their kindred entrepreneurs.
- 

**Instruction on how to Get Started With Facebook Ads**

Understanding the Facebook Ad calculation is significant in light of the fact that it recognizes promotions that give a decent client experience.

In doing such, and the correct settings can help upgrade your spending limit. There is a handy motivation behind why the calculation exists: If sponsors consume the news source, Instagram, the right-hand segment, or whatever you're utilizing to publicize on Facebook, individuals who come back to Facebook. That implies your advertisements need to offer some benefit in light of the fact that

Facebook needs to make a positive client involvement in significant connections.

Promotion straightforwardness is significant for making sense of the calculation. The capacity for a client to see precisely what promotions a Facebook page or also the Twitter account is running a very especially valuable for advertisers and organizations. There are actually three key ways that advertisers can use this data to further their potential benefit:

- **Research contender battles and purchaser markets**. Seeing all the advertisement battles your rivals are running is priceless as you think about your own crusade. Visit their points of arrival and evaluate their source of inspiration. What unique offers would they say they are running? To what extent are their recordings? Is it true that they are attempting to pull in clicks, drive buys, or simply make mindfulness?
- **Get motivation for utilizing new advertisement highlights.** New advertisement highlights regularly reveal on Facebook and Twitter. And Hope to notable brands like Home Depot, Target, or Airbnb to perceive how they 'reutilizing new advertisement includes; it' a decent method to understand what each component does and how it functions without contributing your first dollar.
- **Offer dynamic crusades with clients and possibilities**. Since clients can draw in with the advertisements similarly, they would if the promotion showed up in their news channel, clients and Also prospects currently have an excellent chance to start a buy

or an information exchange they may have passed up.

So how would you construct a successful Facebook publicizing effort? First, you have to have a strategy. Else, you'll fly visually impaired with no away from where you need to go. To see steady outcomes, also recognize where in your business channel, you can use Facebook promotions. Answer the four inquiries to help characterize your system:

- what' your goal for Facebook promoting? For instance, would you actually like to produce new leads for your business, deals for your internet business store, or endorsers of your blog?
- Do you have existing or predictable site traffic?
- Do you have an email list? Provided that this is true, is it dynamic, and what a number of individuals are on your rundown?
- Would you be able to make a novel substance about your business/industry?

In view of your answers, there are three Facebook promoting methodologies you can use to step forward:

**Give let loose substance to warm your crowd.**

Content advertising is one of the best approaches to separate your business and warm up chilly crowds. Give free important substance that engages, teaches, or rouses your optimal client. You could utilize recordings, lead magnets (guides, agendas, coupons, and so on.), or blog entries, for instance.

**Connect with individuals on your email list.**

Conveying your message through your Facebook promotions and email showcasing is twice as compelling. Clients will always see your message in their inbox and when they peruse Facebook.

**Retarget site guests.**

On any off chance that you introduce the Facebook pixel on your site, also you can also target individuals who have as of late visited your main website.

Facebook Marketplace is where you can contact nearby crowds with your item and administrations.

Consider it what might be compared to eBay and Craigslist — Here' where regular individuals can post any amount of things or administrations available to be purchased. Also, As of now, Facebook says it has more than 800 million clients in the Marketplace. The in addition to Facebook Marketplace is that it' where individuals are effectively searching for a particular decent, which implies you have prompt access to a group of people that are searching for you.

1. **Make a battle objective.** The commercial center offers five targets: reach, traffic, transformations, index deals, and video sees. When you pick one, also you can give your battle a name.

2. **Pick position.** Where do you need the promotion to show up? Look down to the Placements area and pick the settings.

3. **Make a video promotio**n. In the Ad Creation segment, you can transfer pictures just as a video. Recordings will, in general,

outflank static images in Marketplace, so that maybe your best alternative.

4. **Break down position results.** Look at how your promotion is acting in contrast with different positions. You can do this by separating your advertisement reports by choosing "placement" "from the Breakdown drop-down menu.

**instructions to Incorporate Facebook Ad Funnels**

You can likewise make a succession of Facebook promotions dependent on your email showcasing channel. Most deals channels incorporate an email follow-up arrangement, which is a progression of pre-composed messages that are consequently conveyed on specific days in the pipe. Every deal channel is unique and can incorporate a grouping of a couple of words to numerous messages. To make a unique promotion grouping, you supplant the messages with Facebook advertisements for every point. Some portion of this procedure is making the sort of promotion. Among your decisions:

- **The Hook Ad.** The objective of the snare promotion is to bring your optimal customer into your locale. Consider what you can offer for nothing to provide some benefit to this crowd. An agenda, also video arrangement, challenge, coupon code, or online course are mostly useful bits of the substance you can elevate to help guide your optimal customer into the agreement you give.
- **The Nurture Ad.** This is the place the dynamic grouping kicks in. The main individuals who 'll see this promotion are the individuals who picked into the snare advertisement. This crowd is presently

gotten used to you since they got your complimentary gift, preparing, or challenge.

- **The Testimonial Ad**. Do you have any customer who has accomplished something incredible with your answer? Is it true that you were remembered for another definitive distribution or digital recording? This is the ideal opportunity to inform your new network regarding it through a tribute advertisement.

The Ask Ad. Since your new leads are prepared with significant substance and a feeling of your aptitude in the field, it' time to make them an offer. This offer should be the following best advance in taking care of the issue that made them select into your lead magnet in any case. This crowd is currently prepared to exploit the new paid techniques you will give.

When setting up, your promotion pipe can target individuals at each phase of the client venture. It takes a unique arrangement that draws in individuals who have brought in with your online life posts inside the most recent three months.

The initial step is serving a site change promotion to individuals who are like the individuals who have actually just bought from your store dependent on their age, also socioeconomics, interests, qualities, and then some. That will require setting up the central Facebook pixel to follow the individuals who made a buy from your online store or visited your site.

From that point, construct brand and item mindfulness by means of advertisements served to individuals who drew in with your online life posts inside the most recent three months. You, at that point, need to make merry go round promotions to target individuals who visited your site inside the previous 30 days.

You can likewise utilize contextual investigations and tributes to make a Facebook pipe battle.

The motivation behind why both are successful is on the grounds that they do not just form mindfulness; they fabricate trust.

- Contextual investigations depend on close to home stories and point by point data that persuade individuals your item has esteem.
- Tributes are firsthand records by individuals like your focused on crowd concerning why your item helped them conquer a test.

After you fabricate crowds that show enthusiasm for your contextual analyses and tributes, you would then be able to offer a preliminary, demo, or rebate that will affirm your item or administration works for your possibilities and, in this way, defeat their outstanding questions.

On any off chance that you have a sizable Facebook following with whom you consistently connect with and share significant substance, you can assemble a Facebook pipe dependent on contextual analyses and tributes with three battles, every one of which focuses on a warm crowd. With this pipe set up, you can amplify the outcomes you accomplish with your Facebook advertisement spend.

**instructions to Improve Facebook Ad Targeting With a Custom Audiences**

The most positive effect of Facebook fans on your business isn't just about the size of your crowd; its show drew in they are with your substance. Beforehand, also the primary way you could focus on your group with promotions was either the overall crowd or by making sections with essential segments.

Since there were no robust focusing on alternatives, your intended interest group would incorporate countless individuals who like your page, yet do not actually connect with any of your posts or advertisements.

With the presentation of page commitment custom crowds, you would now be able to portion and construct congregations dependent on the cooperations individuals have with your Facebook page and promotions. This permits you to target just the most connected with individuals who will be hyper-receptive to your advertisement battles.

Facebook occasions are additionally a decent instrument to target new crowds. Would you like to target Facebook promotion crusades to individuals who really went to your event? On any off chance that you gather data from individuals while they' physically at your occasion, you can actually utilize that information to make a custom crowd dependent on disconnected action. To get somewhat more explicit about the individuals you need to target dependent on their commitment to your Facebook occasion, you can set up a custom crowd for Facebook occasion commitment.

Imagine a scenario where you need to retarget site guests with promotions for items they saw; however, they did not purchase—the appropriate response: dynamic item advertisements.

- Dynamic item promotions let you target clients who have visited your site and perused a scope of your items; however, they left before finishing the buy. This is a sweltering crowd, so it's essential to target them to urge them to change over.
- With dynamic item promotions, you can make a customized advertisement for every individual with the items they've seen on your site and a scope of different things. They'll see these advertisements on their Facebook channels whenever they sign in.

The advantage of dynamic item promotions is that you limit the number of changes lost at the last phase of the business procedure. The advertisements help clients to remember your items and improve the probability of a site guest coming back to your site to purchase something. And you can likewise highlight offers, also show item surveys, and enlighten clients regarding conveyance time or other vital focuses.

Facebook likewise permits organizations to retarget possibilities dependent on their movement with your site, item, or greeting page. The Custom Audiences device allows you to make a rundown of these contacts and target them with profoundly significant promotion battles.

Here are seven kinds of crowds you can target:

**Everybody who visited your site.**

This is the default choice and a decent one for littler organizations that need more site traffic to target individuals by online visits.

**Individuals who visited a particular item page, however, didn't buy.**

This is a propelled site custom crowd that joins a URL condition with an occasional activity.

**Individuals who saw your lead magnet greeting page, however, didn't select in.**

Like the past site custom crowd, you can utilize this next crowd to target Facebook advertisements to individuals who visited your lead magnet greeting page yet haven't selected in yet.

**Individuals who saw your contact page, however, didn't click on it.**

This next crowd is perfect for administration organizations that need to target individuals who are keen on working with them. This crowd bunches individuals who have visited your contact page; however, you haven't finished your contact structure.

**Individuals who began the purchasing procedure, however, didn't finish it.**

This next crowd utilizes your occasion activities and is compelling for internet business organizations. Making this crowd permits you to aggregate individuals who have visited your site and begun the purchasing procedure, for example, adding an item to the crate or starting checkout.

**Individuals who recently bought from you, however, didn't like it.**

Probably the very most ideal approach to build your income is to drive rehash buys from existing clients. You can present new item contributions and elite limits to support further purchases.

**Individuals who actually read your blog, however, didn't share it.**

On any off chance that you have a blog, this site custom crowd is for you. This is a hyper-responsive crowd to which you can run offers or even simply elevate substance increasingly to construct more grounded brand mindfulness and develop your relationship.

**The most effective method to Control Facebook Ad Spend**

When setting up these battles, you have to have a financial limit. However, for what amount? Assessing a Facebook promotion spending plan is significant in light of the fact that it ought to be founded on the measure of income you need to create. To do this requires the following hardly any means.

**Set an objective income objective.**

Characterizing an income objective for your battle appears to be a straightforward move for a growing business or advertising proficient. However, you'd be astonished how frequently individuals skirt this progression. There's nothing amiss with this approach as long as the "perceive how it goes" part is planned, followed, and enhanced.

**Make a custom transformation way in promotions administrator.**

When you have an excellent income objective set up, and design Facebook Ads Manager to show you the information you need.

**Make a two-section advertisement battle.**

At the point when you ascertain cost per lead, your crowd, advertisement inventive, and channel procedure can hugely affect the outcomes.

**Screen your outcomes and change your promotion crusade.**

After you run your promotions for some time, and assemble transformation information, go to the Ads Manager to investigate your expenses. To see the vital information, you'll have to arrange your sections to show custom transformations.

Facebook's Budget Optimization device utilizes a calculation to consequently enhance your spending dissemination across promotion sets so you can discover an approach to set aside cash. Similarly, as with most parts of Facebook promoting, the best method to recognize what's working best for your business is through trying.

The equivalent is valid for recognizing your optimal crowds to set aside cash. By setting up numerous promotion sets, each focusing on the other group, you can accumulate information that will assist you with figuring out which crowd is performing best inside your present crusade.

At the point when you're running advertisement sets with various crowd estimates, it's prescribed to set spending plans relatively dependent on singular crowd sizes. This guarantees your spending limit has equivalent potential with every crowd.

**Need to bring down costs further?**

Building commitment on your presents imparts positive signs on the Facebook calculation, which can help your compass, increment the size of your warm crowd, and at last, lower you're publicizing costs. And here are three hints for building commitment that conveys better advertisement results.

**Reuse effective strategies from posts with high commission rates.**

The commitment rate is the level of individuals who make the most of your substance so much that they interface with it (respond, remark, share, click) in the wake of seeing your posts in their news source.

**Make content in view of the discussion.**

On any off chance that you need better outcomes from your battles, assemble your Facebook page authority while making network. Educate, pose inquiries, and take part in a discourse on your page. The more individuals who cooperate with your Facebook posts, the more pertinent the calculation will locate the substance, at last serving it up to more individuals and developing those warm custom crowds for retargeting.

**Supercharge the transformation with commitment circling.**

To supercharge these tips, attempt a little stunt called "commitment circling." When reacting to remarks on your posts, support more discourse with your Facebook page crowd. At the point when you do this, Facebook will start demonstrating your page content naturally to the loved ones of the individuals connecting with your substance.

One approach to oversee costs is to pick whether you get charged by the expense per click (CPC) or cost per mille (CPM).

At the point when you pick to be charged by interface click, you'll be charged by CPC. This implies you'll possibly get charged when somebody clicks a connection in your promotion. At the point when you pick to be accused by impression, you'll be charged by CPM. This implies you'll get charged each time an idea of your promotion is appeared, with the cost determined per 1,000 impressions.

**Which is directly for you?**

- You possibly get charged when somebody clicks your advertisement, so in principle, if your promotion doesn't get numerous snaps, you'll at first be getting a large number of impressions for nothing. This charge type likewise goes about as a protection against paying bunches of cash if your promotion isn't performing admirably.
- The drawback is that if your promotions perform well and you get a high active clicking factor, you'll pay for each snap. Your CPM will rise, and you'll be following through on a significant expense for that extraordinary presentation.
- In case you're not going through a ton of cash and aren't running

investigations with various crowds, sets, and promotion varieties, and are investing a ton of energy into improvement, picking Link Clicks is likely a decent choice.

Facebook's Automated Rules highlight is another approach to deal with your Facebook advertisement spend all the more adequately.

Facebook's robotized rules highlight is a concealed jewel for improving Facebook advertisement execution without depending on manual advancement. It can spare occupied Facebook publicist's time, vitality, and assets.

By joining distinctive KPI measurements when characterizing rule conditions, you can plan your custom robotization work process on Facebook. It might require any experimentation to locate the privilege of robotized rules, yet it merits the venture.

With computerized rules, you set predefined conditions for crucial execution pointers (KPIs, for example, likes, reach and leads, and advertisement crusade components, promotion sets, promotions, and so forth.) in your Facebook advertisement accounts. Facebook will check the condition you set an exact time interim, and when a battle meets that paradigm, it will make your predefined move, basically setting aside your time and cash.

**instructions to Test Facebook Ads**

The Facebook Dynamic Creative promotion apparatus is a powerful method to test Facebook advertisement varieties, consequently.

The device conveys the best mixes of your imaginative promotion resources. It runs various blends of your promotion segments, for example, pictures, recordings, titles, depictions, and calls to activities, over your intended interest group to figure out which mixes produce the best outcomes.

Prior to the presentation of this component, you needed to make full-grown advertisements separately and test them physically to locate the best promotion inventive and the best promotion to-crowd fit. Dynamic Creative naturally randomizes promotion varieties for you, making it simple to demonstrate the correct advertisements to individuals. Facebook lets you utilize around 30 inventive resources, including:

- Five title/feature varieties.
- Ten pictures or ten recordings.
- Five content varieties.
- Five depictions.
- Five CTA button varieties.

Once in a while, improving your Facebook promotion execution implies ensuring your advertisements don't cover crowds.

A side-effect of this marvel is advertisement weariness — What happens when your crowd has seen your promotion too often, which can lessen its viability. A few responses are as innocuous as advertisement visual impairment, where your advertising basically turns into a steady in their ever-changing news source. On different occasions, clients come to the heart of the matter that they're blocking or leaving negative remarks on your promotions. The three different ways advertisement weariness can happen are:

- Social channels permit you to manufacture particular crowds around specific socioeconomics, interests, etc. In any case, that degree of control can now and then influence execution. It's a lot simpler to oversaturate a crowd of people of 2,000 individuals than a gathering of 200,000 or 2.1 million of every a 1% U.S. carbon copy audience. That's not to state you should see just objective crowds with several thousand or a great many clients. Here and there exceptionally focused on, littler circles can be entirely significant. In any case, it's critical to scale your every day spending plan to relative crowd size.
- Not invigorating inventive is the most significant reason for advertisement exhaustion. Regardless of whether you're advertising to a similar crowd, do a refreshed round of imaginative. It can go far toward safeguarding your crowd's understanding.
- An individual may have visited your site, had the interests you're focusing on and was placed in your copy crowd by Facebook. In any event that you don't make any move, this individual could consider you to be multiple times as frequently as somebody in just one of the crowds. Forestalling crowd cover takes some arranging, a couple of helpful apparatuses, and tolerance, yet it can have a significant effect in battle execution.

**instructions to Establish Facebook Messenger Ads**

Facebook's Messenger application takes into account coordinated informing between clients. I' also another potential stage for your company's advertising. Facebook advertisements can be shown inside the Messenger application on the Home tab, which improves the probability that individuals will cooperate with your image or business.

You can likewise trade client information from your Messenger application endorsers to make custom and carbon copy crowds that you can later use to serve focused on Facebook promotions. These clients are ordinarily profoundly connected with and super-acquainted with your business and substance, making them a perfect crowd for promoting your items. At the point when you target hotter masses, you'll find you convert at a higher rate, and your advertisements cost less.

You can likewise make a carbon copy crowd dependent on your custom crowd. While the custom crowd is a close imitation of your supporters, the copy crowd is comprised of individuals who are fundamentally the same as your endorsers. Focusing on this copy crowd can assist you in developing your endorser base with similar clients.

**Instructions on how to Combine Facebook Ads with Facebook Video** most Likely Facebook Messenger and Facebook video is another stage inside Facebook to have to promote for your organization. Facebook Live permits clients to communicate spilling video as it occurs progressively to different clients inside their system. A decent methodology resembles this:

- **Start with at any rate four Facebook Live recordings.**

These Facebook Live recordings need to give important substance that enables your objective to advertise. First, you have to look into what individuals need to watch by means of a Facebook survey.

- **Build up a warm crowd by boosting live video posts.**

It costs about $1 every day. Remember that these ease advertisements will set aside you considerably more cash when the compass of your recordings permits you to retarget warm leads later right now.

- **Drive original videos to see from different channels to expand your warm crowd.**

Advancing a post helps, yet you ought to extend your compass through natural strategies as well. Extend the range of your live video by posting it in Facebook gatherings and other informal communities.

- **Make a lead magnet greeting page.**

After you post a few Facebook Live recordings and follow the means to advance those recordings on Facebook and past, you ought to have a set up (or warm) crowd. Your following stage is to change over them.

- **Make free substance, for example, a digital book, manage, online course, or another bit of insurance.**

Ensure the insurance you make relates back to the Facebook Live recordings. Doing so improves your odds of trapping leads intrigued by your offer. At that point, make a greeting page where anybody interested enters their name and email address to get a record, clicks a catch to pursue an online class, or in any case, makes a move to acknowledge your complimentary gift.

- **Convey your offer by means of a Facebook advertisement that retargets your warm crowd.**

The last advance is to make a retargeted Facebook advertisement that directs people to your greeting page. The individuals you need to retarget are the individuals who saw your past Facebook Live recordings.

Obviously, your video has no effect if watchers do not watch it right through. Among the approaches to ensure seeing arrives at finishing each time is to advance your video' text and thumbnail characteristics and decide the correct day and time when you discharge the footage to the general population.

Facebook In-Stream Video Ads may very well speak to the most significant type of video promoting. This sort of advertisement position lets you show mid-move video promotions to watchers who are watching video content from select makers and distributors, for example, ESPN, VICE, CNN, The New York Times, and others. The advertisements can be 5-15 seconds long and not skippable by watchers.

Your promotions are conveyed to a focused on the crowd that has been seeing a video for in any event 60 seconds, which means they reconnected and bound to focus on your message. On any off chance that you join this component with all around looked into and concentrate on crowds, it could be a compelling promotion type for you.

Notwithstanding the Facebook news channel, you can choose the Audience Network arrangement to contact a focused on a crowd outside of Facebook.

**Instructions to Analyze and Improve Facebook Advertising**

The examination is critical to understanding which advertisements work and which ones don't Facebook Analytics is a reliable device that lets advertisers investigate client connection with cutting edge objective ways and deals pipes for Facebook promotions.

Facebook Analytics is a free device. However, it' designed to work with Facebook Ads, which do have a cost connected to them.

Previously, Facebook permitted you to see just the last touchpoint in your channels. For instance, on any off chance that somebody collaborated with seven of your posts yet bought on the eighth cooperation, just the last association would be given acknowledgement for the change. Presently you can see the full connection way to the change, as opposed to merely the last touchpoint.

Google Analytics works with Facebook to quantify transformations from your Facebook advertisements. As such, following where individuals are coming from before they land on your site. You can likewise utilize Google Analytics to follow the moves individuals make while they are on your website. Those activities can include:

- Buying into an email list.

- Review item pages.
- They are adding to their shopping basket.
- Review your presentation page.

The objective is to apply these bits of knowledge into your promotion through Facebook and to follow your arrival on speculation for the advertisements themselves.

Google Data Studio is a decent method to give an account of and imagine your online networking effort. You can utilize this device to make simple to-refresh gives an account of your site, Facebook, or other internet-based life-promoting efforts. Google Data Studio is free. You can impart reports to customers and colleagues, and import information from numerous sources to increase a comprehensive, 360-degree perspective on your advanced exercises.

To begin with Facebook Analytics itself, you should simply choose your Facebook pixel, which will start giving you information. At that point, you have to make an occasion source gathering, or ESG, which interfaces your Facebook business page and Facebook pixel, so you can draw from more information sources like a Messenger bot. The dashboard shows ongoing total information of every one of your sources, and you can perceive how they cooperate.

During this procedure, it' necessary to see how Facebook Attribution functions. At the point when individuals collaborate with your Facebook advertisements, their activities — viewing a video, visiting your site, and so forth — are recorded. Each time your promotion prompts a transformation, Facebook will credit, or quality, the advertisement in Ads Manager so you can perceive how well your crusade is getting along and decide whether you are arriving at your objectives.

The best approach to do that is to set up your Ads Manager dashboard to guarantee you reviewing the most state-of-the-art information. The best time window is in the course of the most recent seven days. From that point, you can see which promotion sets have high client obtaining costs. Interruption any advertisement sets with an expense for every outcome that 'sat least twofold your reasonable fees.

The ideal approach to screen execution of your Facebook promotions is to produce reports through Facebook Ads Manager. The stories will uncover which advertisements are working best in arriving at your objectives and which ones are falling behind. By breaking down your battle execution on a reliable premise, you'll ready to rapidly spot changes in crusade measurements that signal a requirement for testing invigorates or uncover winning Facebook promotions you should scale.

Examining four center measurements — cost, pertinence, recurrence, and cost per mille, or CPR — causes you to recognize and evaluate the exhibition of your battles and the promotions inside them.

**Cost per Result**

This cost measurement is your general spend or sum spent on every one of your crusades; it's your cost per result dependent on your battle goal and promotion set streamlining. On any off chance that you set an every day spending plan and aren't scaling your battles, and you see your expense per result diminishing, your crusade results will be expanding.

**Pertinence Score**

The following measurement to take a gander at is pertinence. A pertinence score is a rating from 1–10 that Facebook provides for every one of your advertisements. This score mirrors the advertisement to-crowd fit and how well individuals are reacting to your promotion. This measurement can be seen distinctly at the advertisement level of your crusades.

On the flip side, when your significance score is diminishing, you'll find your expense per result expanding, demonstrating your battle execution is diminishing.

**Recurrence**

The third measurement to take a gander at is recurrence. Repetition is a conveyance metric that reveals to you how often on regular somebody has seen your advertisement. Your recurrence will consistently begin at one and increment after some time as you spend a higher amount of your battle spending plan and arrive at a higher amount of your intended interest group.

As your recurrence increments to 2, 3, 4, 5, etc., you'll notice that it impacts your expense per result and importance score. The higher your recurrence, the more individuals are seeing the equivalent Facebook promotions.

**CPM**

At long last, take a gander at CPM, which is an abbreviation for the cost for each mile. This is your expense per 1,000 impressions. As your recurrence increments and you arrive at a higher amount of your intended interest group, your CPM will begin to increment. This implies it currently costs you more for 1,000 impressions than it recently did. This will affect the cost, importance, and recurrence measurements.

**Internet-based life publicizing: receiving the correct methodology**

Informal communities possess a significant spot in people's daily lives. In 2018, 83% of grown-up Quebecers utilized at any rate one interpersonal organization. Furthermore, almost certainly, they are presented to web-based promoting. We enlightened you concerning the significance of informal organizations in your business, in a past article. So as to make your essence and all the more especially your ads on friendly communities compelling, embrace a decent technique.

**Here are three hints to enhance your web-based publicizing.**

**Identify the correct targets**

So as to arrive at the objective which will be generally disposed to be keen on your business. We should distinguish their persona s (anecdotal character having the attributes of target clients ).

To do this, you have to ask yourself the correct inquiries:

- Who is your persona: average age, salary
- What position does he hold?

- What are its targets, its issues, its difficulties to be met?
- What device does he use?

Furthermore, some more, the objective here is to accumulate; however, much data as could reasonably be expected about your objective clients.

The most significant inquiry is, without a doubt, the reference to its issues (corresponding to your offer, obviously). On account of this data, you will have the option to carry your skill to it through your notices.

Cautioning !! Realize that your persona isn't solidified. It must develop after some time.

**Define the stages you need to utilize**

The setting up of publicizing efforts on interpersonal organizations is finished by your particular goals. When your targets have been characterized, you can pick the stage on which you wish to continue.

Facebook is perceived for its presentation on crusades with exceptionally exact focusing on criteria and the securing of new guests. The administration of Facebook promotions is anything but difficult to utilize and successful.

LinkedIn promotions have for some, points of interest like its progressed focusing on highlights, the full Scope of commercials, spending plan adaptable administration, lead age instrument lastly the checking device and estimation investigation of battle execution. Clearly, consider this stage to incorporate it into your B2B promoting technique.

Instagram is vital for meeting specific destinations as a result of its continually developing and youthful client base. The informal community shows the quickest development on the planet. The social stage offers to target battles through criteria of reach, promotion update, and reputation. Supported campaigns on Instagram have appeared, notwithstanding, that they are more proper for B2C brands than B2B.

**Creativity and enhancement are the watchwords**

Web-based life stages are loaded with a vast number of online promotions; you will probably stand apart from the group. For that, be inventive. The more your promoting is customized, intuitive, and offers genuine enhanced the individual uncovered, the almost certain you are that the client will tap on it.

Web-based promoting efforts require genuine upstream work, so they directly affect the customer.

When your commercial is done, test it. To comprehend what works and what doesn't watch your diverse KPIs: Key Performance Indicator (click rate, number of sharing and remarks, number of guests, new endorsers, and so forth ).

**IN SHORT**

An all-around run crusade makes it a lot simpler to construct and manufacture a network. Likewise, web-based promoting brings about expanded traffic to your webpage, notwithstanding creating deals and deals openings (leads).

For more data, don't spare a moment to get in touch with one of our pros in internet-based life.

# CHAPTER THREE
# FACEBOOK ADVERTISING: A COMPLETE GUIDE

---

Facebook ads allow you to interact with your audience on the world's largest social network.

It can be challenging to connect with your fans the natural way due to the continually evolving Facebook algorithm. Fortunately, the micro-targeting features offered by the platform allow you to reach your target audience precisely. Facebook thus ensures that your advertisements reach the users most likely to buy your products or services.

This is a remarkable asset in terms of budget, conversion rate and return on investment because you only pay to reach the prospects who have the most potential.

To get good results, you must understand the different types of Facebook ads and the targeting options available before you start using them. We'll explain everything you actually need to know in this guide, from planning your first ad to developing advanced ad campaigns.

## Types of Facebook Ads

### Advertisements with images

These simple ads are an effective way to start promoting your brand on Facebook. You can create one in a few clicks, only by boosting an existing publication using an image from your Facebook page.

Ads with images may be simple, but they should not be boring. For example, do you think socks aren't the most exciting product out there? Think again: Happy Socks stages them in surprising contexts to create fun photo ads on Facebook.

### Video ads

Video ads can appear in the newsfeed and Stories or appear as in-stream video ads, which are longer than others. They will allow you to present the work of your team or the functioning of your product, like this short demo published by We Are Knitters.

Please be aware that you do not have to incorporate film footage into your video ads. You can also compose GIF-like graphic elements or other animations to capture the attention of users or present your offer, such as this New York Times advertisement.

Take a closer look at the targeting of this advertisement: it is specifically an offer for Europe (where I live). I can also see my friends who have already liked the NYT Facebook page in my newsfeed, which makes advertising much more enjoyable.

### Survey advertisements

This Facebook advertising format for mobile offers an interactive experience to users through video surveys. If it is a new type of paid advertising, the first data from Facebook have revealed that these kinds of ads can increase brand awareness more effectively than no full video advertising.

### Carousel ads

In a carousel ad, you can include up to ten images or videos to showcase your product or service. You can use this format to highlight the different advantages of the same product, present various offers or even use all the photos together to create a large panoramic image, like this one:

### Slideshow advertisements

Slide show ads make it easy to create short video ads from a collection of existing static photos text, or video clips. If you don't have images yourself, you can choose from the royalty-free pictures available in the Ad Manager.

As with videos, the movement of slideshow ads draws attention, but they require five times less bandwidth. Charging is optimal, even for people with a slower Internet connection, making it an easy way to get attention with less impact.

### Collection advertisements

These paid ads, dedicated only to mobile devices, allow you to showcase five products customers can click to buy them directly.

Collection format ads go hand in hand with Instant Experiences (we'll come back to that shortly) to also allow people to buy your products without ever leaving Facebook. Thus, purchases are made easier for users who are on the move and do not necessarily have an optimal Internet connection.

### Instant Experience Ads

Instant Experience ads were previously called Canvas. It's a full-screen ad format that loads 15 times faster than a mobile website outside of Facebook, like this example from American Express.

You can also add a link to other Instant Experiences so that users can access even more instant mobile content.

## Form advertisements

Form ads are only available for mobile devices because they are specifically designed to make it easier for users to give you their contact information, without requiring a lot of typing. They are ideal for collecting new subscriptions to your newsletter, offering Internet users a free trial of your product or even allowing them to ask you for more information.

The insurance company Tokio Marine managed to generate 11,000 leads in just 17 days thanks to the form advertisements. The latter not only offered an easy-to-fill contact form but also included a Messenger bot in qualifying other prospects. The campaign thus reduced the cost of lead generation by 60%.

These ads constitute a fantastic way to feed your sales funnel; we have compiled a guide to using Facebook form ads (in English) which details everything you need to know to take full advantage of this type of Facebook advertising campaign.

## Dynamic advertisements

Dynamic ads will always allow you to promote your products to targeted customers who are most likely to be interested.

For example, if a user visited a product page or placed a product in their cart on your actual website but then abandoned the purchase, and dynamic ads for that specific product will appear in their Facebook feed.

This will remind the potential customer to complete the purchase, which can be a profitable Facebook marketing strategy.

The French online store Smallable has, for example, used dynamic advertising with the carousel, collection, image and Stories formats to retarget its potential customers. Smallable thus offered Facebook users advertisements displaying products they had already expressed interest in, which multiplied its return on advertising investment by 124.

## Messenger ads

Messenger ads allow you to reach 1.3 billion people, the number of Messenger users each month. When you create your ad, all you have to do is choose Messenger as the placement you want. You will also need to select the Facebook news feed.

Here's what all ad looks like in the Messenger app:

You can also create "click-to-Messenger ads" in the Facebook news feed. These include a call-to-action button that opens a Messenger conversation with your Facebook Page so that users can have an individual discussion with one of your sales or customer service representatives.

## Stories ads

Scientific American magazine found that 72% of millennials don't turn their phones on to watch full-screen videos. Fortunately, Stories ads appear in a vertical video format that allows you to maximize screen space without the need for rotation.

These advertisements have proven to be very useful. According to an Ipsos survey commissioned by Facebook, more than half of the users said they make more online purchases because of Stories ads.

### Stories ads in augmented reality

Augmented reality ads make features such as filters and animations available to users to allow them to interact with your brand. This format is brand new on Facebook, but 63% of American internet users claim to have already tested augmented reality as part of a brand experience. The augmented reality Facebook Stories ads will be available in open beta this fall.

### Playable ads

This is another new format for interactive advertising. It involves creating a game that will encourage users to interact with your content.

Vans, for example, used playable advertising to increase brand awareness.

## How to create an advertisement on Facebook

If you already have a good Facebook page for your business (which should be the case), you can go directly to Facebook Ad Manager or to Business Manager to create your Facebook advertising campaign. If your business does not actually have a Page, you will first need to create one.

In this book, we will outline the steps to follow on the Ad Manager. If you prefer to use Business Manager, you can find more information in our Business Manager user guide on Facebook.

**Step 1: Choose a goal**

Log into the Facebook Ad Manager and select the Campaigns tab. Then click Create to start a new Facebook advertising campaign.

Facebook offers 11 marketing goals based on the results you expect from your advertising. They correspond to corporate objectives:

- Brand awareness: present your brand to a new audience.
- Coverage: expose your advertisement to as many members of your audience as possible.
- Traffic: feed traffic to a specific Facebook Messenger web page, application or conversation.
- Interaction: reach a broader audience to increase the number of interactions on your publication or likes on your Page, increase the number of participants in your event, or even encourage users to take advantage of a special offer.
- Application installations: have users install your application.
- Video views: Getting more people to watch your videos.
- Lead generation: get new leads in your sales funnel.
- Messages: encourage users to contact your business through

Facebook Messenger.

- Conversions: getting people to take a specific action on your website (for example, sign up for your newsletter or buy your product), through your app, or on Facebook Messenger.
- Catalogue Sales: Connect your Facebook ads to your product catalogue to show users of the product ads they are most likely to buy.
- Point of sale traffic: encourage customers near your stores to go there.

Choose a campaign goal based on your expectations for this specific ad. Keep in mind that for conversion goals (like sales) you can pay for each action, but for exposure goals (like traffic and number of views) you will pay for the impressions.

For the main purpose of this example, we will choose the Interaction objective. Some of the options that you will see in the following steps will vary slightly depending on the lens selected.

**Step 2: Name your campaign**

Scroll down to give a name to your Facebook advertising campaign and choose whether to configure an A / B split test or not. You will also need to actually decide whether to turn on campaign budget optimization. This option can be useful if you use different advertising formats, but you can leave it disabled for now.

Regarding the Interaction objective, you will also have to choose whether you want to focus on the engagement generated by the publications, the number of likes on your Page or the number of responses to an event. For this example, we will select the number of likes on the Page.

### Step 3: Configure your advertising account

If you have created an account, simply click on the button that appears.

If you've never created Facebook ads before, you'll see the Configure an advertising account button instead. After clicking on it, then you will be prompted to enter some essential information to create your advertising account. Enter your country, currency and time zone, then click Continue.

Pay attention to your choices, because if you want to change them later, you will have to create a different advertising account.

### Step 4: Target your audience

At the top of this screen, also you can give a name to your advertising campaign and choose which Page you want to promote.

Scroll down to start defining the target audience for your ads.

The first option you will see is to add a personalized audience, made up of people who have previous interaction with your business on or outside Facebook. We have written a guide to help you master the art custom audiences on Facebook (in English), so we focus here on the targeting options.

Start by selecting your targets by location, age, gender and language. As you make your choice, also keep an eye on the audience size indicator on the right of the screen, which gives you an idea of the potential reach of your advertising.

You'll also see an estimate of the number of likes the Page could get. It will be more precise if you have already created campaigns because Facebook will have more data at its disposal. Always keep in mind that this is an estimate and not a guaranteed figure.

Now is the time for detailed targeting. Remember: effective targeting is the key to optimal ROI, and there is no shortage of options for targeting your audience using Facebook's Ad Manager. Here you have two fields that allow you to target your audience with as much precision as you want:

- Advanced targeting: Use this field to include or exclude certain people based on their demographics, interests and behaviors. You can be particularly precise here. For example, you have the option of choosing to target users who are interested in both meditation and also yoga but exclude people who are interested in hot yoga.
- Connections: you can also target or exclude people who already have a link with your Facebook page, your application or an event that you have managed. For example, then if you want to reach a new audience, you need to select "Exclude people who like your Page". Then If you're going to promote an offer or a new product to existing fans, choose "People who like your Page" to reach users who already know your brand. You can also choose to target the friends of people who have previously interacted with your brand.

### Step 5: Choose the placements of your Facebook ads

Scroll down to choose where your actual ads will appear. If the mechanisms of Facebook advertising are still unknown to you, the most comfortable choice is to use Automatic Placements. Also When you select this option, Facebook automatically places your advertisements on Facebook, Instagram, Messenger and Audience Network when they are likely to generate the best results.

When you gain experience, you may want to display your ads in specific places. the following options are available to you:

- Device types: mobile, computer or both
- Platforms: Facebook, Instagram, Audience Network or Messenger
- Placements: newsfeeds, Stories, in-stream (for videos), messages, article, applications and (external) sites
- Mobile devices and specific operating systems: iOS, Android, classic mobile or all mobile devices

### Step 6: Determine your budget and program

Next, you then need to decide how much you want to allocate to your Facebook advertising campaign. You can choose a daily or global budget, then configure the start and end dates if you're going to schedule your ad for later. You also have the main option of making it public immediately.

You can also control fees and bids if you wish. This option will allow you to cap the amounts based on the action instead of limiting the overall budget of your campaign.

The advanced budget options allow you to express how you want to spend your money accurately.

Remember: optimize your budget, your paid ads on Facebook must follow a delivery schedule, allowing you to run your ad only when your target audience is most likely to be connected to Facebook. It is possible to configure a delivery program only if you have allocated a global budget for your advertising.

Once you have actully made your selection and are satisfied with the audience size indicator, click Continue.

### Step 7: Create your ad

First, choose the format of your advertisement. Then enter the text and add the media of your choice. The forms available will vary depending on the campaign goal you set at the start of the process.

Then Use the preview tool at the bottom of the page to check that your advertisement is displayed correctly on all of the chosen placements (mobile, computer, a news feed, right column, etc.). Once you are actually satisfied with your choices, click on the green Confirm button to submit your request, then wait for an email from Facebook notifying you that your advertisement has been approved.

## Characteristics of Facebook Ads

so there are a lot of details to keep in mind when preparing your images and videos for inclusion in Facebook ads. Since these criteria change very often, we have compiled them in another regularly updated article on the sizes of Facebook ads (in English).

We also offer 16 Facebook ad mockups that you can use for free to create your ads in minutes.

## Technical characteristics of the text and objectives of Facebook ads

To create effective Facebook ads, you need to keep in mind the maximum number of recommended characters. Any text exceeding this limit will be truncated.

You also need to understand the types of Facebook ads that work with each of the campaign objectives described above.

### Ads with Images

- Title: 25 characters
- Description of the link: 30 characters
- Body text: 125 characters
- Campaign goals: all except Video views

### Video ads

- Title: 25 characters
- Description of the link: 30 characters
- Body text: 125 characters
- Campaign objectives: all except Catalog sales

**Stories Ads**

- Text: no character limit set, but do not add text in the 250 pixels at the top and bottom of the ad
- Campaign objectives: Interaction, Messages, Catalog sales, Point of sale traffic

**Carousel Advertisements**

- Title: 25 characters
- Description of the link: 20 characters
- Body text: 125 characters
- Campaign objectives: all except Interaction and Video views

**Slide show commercials**

- Title: 25 characters
- Description of the link: 30 characters
- Body text: 125 characters
- Campaign objectives: all

**Collection advertisements**

- Title: 25 characters
- Description of the link: not applicable
- Body text: 90 characters
- Campaign objectives: Traffic, Conversions, Catalog sales, Point-of-sale traffic

**Instant Experience Ads**

- Text: text blocks of 500 words maximum each
- Campaign objectives: all except Lead generation, also Catalog sales and Messages

**Ads in the Messenger inbox**

- Title: not applicable
- Description of the link: not applicable
- Body text: 125 characters
- Campaign objectives: Traffic, Application installations, Conversions, Catalog sales, Messages

## Five tips to help you advertise on Facebook

### 1. Experiment with targeting your audience

Start with a small audience, then gradually expand it by adding one focus at a time. For example, you can get started with an audience specifically interested in "visiting Bordeaux wine estates" and also then broaden it after a few weeks.

You can then add "wine tasting", then "food and wine", etc. Thus, you will get a somewhat representative idea of how your results may be affected by the widening of your target audience.

You can also use targeting to create different advertisements dedicated to various groups, corresponding to different objectives. For example, you can address your existing customers in a certain way and use different speech with people who have never heard of your business. You can also offer promotions based on the relationship you already have.

If your business is local, and you can target your audience by postal code. Use this same option if you know a city or neighborhood with high conversion rates.

Pro tip: Be careful not to jump to too hasty conclusions about your audience when selecting your targeting options. Since I live in Europe, I see a lot of very relevant Facebook ads when you consider my place of residence. However, they are in Dutch, a language I don't speak (yet).

Advertisers are therefore spending money to show me advertisements that I don't understand, which they could easily avoid by using language targeting.

## 2. Use the Facebook pixel

The Facebook pixel is a piece of computer code that can have a significant impact on your advertising campaign. Once the system is integrated into your website, you will be able to track conversions, retarget consumers who have seen a product on your site, and create similar audiences.

It is essential that you install the Facebook pixel now, even if you are not yet ready to invest in some of the most advanced strategies that it can implement. So when you want to start optimizing your Facebook ads, its tracking and retargeting data will be directly available to you.

Use our step-by-step Facebook pixel user guide to set it up on your site now.

### 3. Use excellent quality photos and videos

Nothing more prohibitive than blurry or pixelated images, or even amateur videos that move so much that they make you dizzy. Indeed, your words are important, but what will grab the attention of your targets in the first place and give them the best impression is your visuals.

These royalty-free image banks can help you find high-quality images for use in your advertisements.

### 4. Test everything

it's essential that you do not make assumptions about what may or may not work in your Facebook ads. Whenever you modify an advertisement by trying something new, compare the latest version to the old one to see if you have improved the indicators that matter most to you.

Best practices for Facebook ads are continually evolving. You are the only one who actually knows what works with your specific audience. The best way to keep this accurate is to test regularly.

Knowing that this is a most important topic, we have compiled a comprehensive guide explaining how to do A / B testing on social media.

### 5. Track and optimize performance

Closely monitor the actual performance of your campaigns in the Facebook Ad Manager dashboard. If a campaign does not generate conclusive results, instead inject money into a proven advertisement.

If you're just getting started, running a variety of campaigns with smaller audiences and on a lower budget can be helpful. Once you know what works best, make the best performing ad your primary advertising campaign.

Here are some additional resources on this topic:

- How to boost the conversions through your Facebook ads (in English)
- Eight advertising-related indicators on social media you need to follow (in English)

There are tools that will simplify or even automate this process.

For solo marketers, agencies and SMEs, AdEspresso make creating, managing and optimizing advertisements quick and easy.

If you work for a larger company, of course, we recommend Hootsuite Ads. From a single dashboard, you can monitor all of your social media channels and create and test hundreds of Facebook ads in minutes. In addition, thanks to intuitive analyzes, you will know at a glance which is your best performing advertisements.

You can also transfer the money allocated to your less successful ads to those that work best (even if they appear on another social network). Optimize your budgets or start new campaigns based on predefined performance thresholds. Then, improve your results even more with daily automatic recommendations.

## Facebook ad ideas

Are you ready to get started, but you don't know what content to include in your advertisements? We've put together three campaign strategies to help you get started on Facebook. If you're looking for good inspiration, check out the examples of Facebook ads we've put together.

## Advertising strategy # 1: transform a successful publication into video advertising

Each brand has content items that drive the majority of traffic each month. Adapting this content into a short video can be a great way to create sensational Facebook advertising with a proven post.

To create your video, find short texts and images that could translate the main messages of your content. Then use one of these social media video tools to design your video. You can also create a slideshow ad in the Facebook Ad Manager.

At Hootsuite, using the content of a remarkable blog article is one of our favourite strategies. So you will see many examples of this type on the Hootsuite Facebook page. Our team responsible for making our videos used this blog article on applications that can help you create Instagram Stories to transform it into the Facebook video.

Pro Tip: Check out our Guide to Social Media Video Strategy for Marketers, which has lots of information on the types of videos that work best on social media.

## Advertising strategy n ° 2: trigger a direct sale

If your brand is recognized, and you have a quality product, in a reasonably affordable price range, there is no reason why Facebook cannot generate direct sales.

Thinx uses this method to sell their menstrual underwear. Since the company has received a lot of media attention and offers a product at a low price, it is an excellent candidate for this type of advertising strategy.

Pro tip: One of the more effective ways to generate sales directly from Facebook advertising is to target a group of people who have already considered buying your product.

You can make targeted offers, recommend products, or send reminders to complete a purchase.

## Advertising strategy # 3: don't just look at the Internet

Nothing forces you to limit your Facebook advertising strategy to online sales. By opting for the Point of Sale Traffic objective, you can also promote offline purchases.

It is also possible to encourage users to participate in a physical event. Use the Interaction objective to increase the number of responses to events on Facebook or opt for the Traffic and Conversions objectives to sell more tickets.

Use the Lead Generation goal to invite users to come and try your product in person at your store or dealer, for example, by trying a car.

Louis Vuitton, for example, used the Point of Sale Traffic target in Italy to target adult buyers located at a certain distance from one of its eight stores in that country. The products were highlighted in carousel advertisements which also included a map to find the nearest store. These ads have generated 13,000 visits in stores for $ 1.32 per visit.

Pro tip: Facebook actually allows you to track offline conversions, and thus understand the effectiveness of the advertisements that drive your offline sales. You can also use this information to create personalized audiences made up of people who interact with your brand offline so that you can target them more effectively in future campaigns.

# 15 WAYS TO OPTIMIZE YOUR FACEBOOK ADS

Our Facebook promotions working for you? Is it true that you are hoping to show signs of improvement return on your Facebook promotion speculation?

To get the best execution from promotions, you have to ensure they contact the correct crowd. Right now discover 15 different ways to set up and advance your Facebook advertisements.

**#1: Keep Mobile and Desktop Ads Separate**

Utilize separate advertisement sets for portable and work area so you can enhance your promotions, offers and changes depending on the gadget. Developments and suggestions to take action are probably going to perform distinctively on work area versus portable, and any advertisement arrangement should consider.

In case you're utilizing Power Editor, you can choose the gadget focusing on legitimately from the Ad Set menu.

**#2: Optimize the Desktop News Feed and Right-Column Ads Separately**

Perhaps the best practice in advertising is to set up exceptionally sectioned promotions. Isolating work area news source and right-segment promotions are essential for advancing efforts by the gadget, position and some other focusing on an alternative. Work area news channel promotions have a lot of bigger pictures than right-segment advertisements.

On any off chance that you need to expand your exhibition, you have to upgrade news source and right-section promotions independently.

Facebook permits you to tweak your focusing for work areas in a submenu of the Placement menu at the Ad Set level.

**#3: Test Different Images**

Pictures are the most significant component of your promotions and the main factor when individuals conclude whether to click a post. Test out various views and locate the ones that amplify your active clicking factor and changes.

When you distinguish the best pictures, discover business as usual style and continue testing. Beneath, take a gander at the navigate rates to perceive how enormous a distinction an image can make.

**#4: Choose a Call to Action**

Facebook permits you to choose a source of inspiration in your promotions. Suggestions to take action can significantly affect your active visitor clicking percentage, just as your transformation rate, and you should part test them entirely after some time.

You can discover the source of inspiration alternatives in the Ad Setup menu. Right now, the decisions are Book Now, Download, Learn More, Shop Now and Sign Up.

**#5: Segment Audiences Into Ad Sets**

Various interests will perform diversely inside a similar arrangement of promotions. When in doubt, you should gather your real advantages into subjects and make one Advertisement set for each theme.

For example, assume that your real advantages are:

- AdWords
- AdWords master
- Google Certification Program
- Facebook advertisements
- Facebook promoting
- Facebook promoting arrangements
- Facebook showcasing hour day
- Web-based promoting
- Advanced promoting
- Showcasing on the web

You can distinguish three subjects of intrigue and along these lines, three advertisement sets for your Facebook crusade, as demonstrated as follows.

This division permits you to advance dependent on various interests and make advertisements concentrated on subjects identified with the promotion set you're focusing.

**#6: Install a Conversion Pixel**

This is a conspicuous tip, yet shockingly numerous organizations disregard to introduce transformation pixels.

- To make a transformation pixel, sign in to your advertisement supervisor and snap-on Conversion Tracking.
- Snap-on Conversion Tracking to make a transformation pixel.
- On the following page that shows up, click the green Create Pixel button in the top-right piece of the screen.
- Snap the Create Pixel button.

Follow the guided arrangement to wrap up your change pixel. When you get the code, ensure you introduce the system in the footer of your thank-you page.

Presently you can all the more likely track the aftereffects of your advertising endeavours on Facebook.

**#7: Specify a Conversion Code**

Facebook permits you to make numerous change codes since you might need to follow a few objectives on your site; for example, visiting the shopping basket page and the thank-you page. Or then again, and you may necessarily need to promote for various spaces.

Facebook has to recognize what code your advertisement should use for transformation following purposes. Henceforth, you have to supply one for every promotion in your advertisement sets.

In Power Editor (or the live record on any off chance that you incline toward that), then click on Use a Conversion Tracking Pixel at the base of your promotion arrangement.

Next, conclude whether to utilize a current code or make another one. You can likewise look over existing transformation following pixels (see the red bolt in the picture beneath) or pick a current pixel to enhance for changes.

To utilize existing transformation following pixels, click the catch showed by the red bolt.

The last choice is valuable on any off chance that you have a transformation pixel introduced and need Facebook to enhance promotions dependent on that specific change pixel.

For instance, say you introduced transformation pixels on both the shopping basket page and the thank-you page. Usually, you would need to enhance promotions, so you get more visits to the thank-you page.

Except if you need to upgrade by clicks, I suggest setting up both of these alternatives: the superior choice (the one with the red bolt) to tally your changes, and the subsequent opportunity to improve for one explicit sort of transformation, for example, finished checkouts.

**#8: Target by Behaviors**

Numerous organizations use Facebook promotions to target interests only. In any case, remember that focusing on practices takes care of as a general rule.

Instances of practices you can focus on Facebook are Training and Publications (individuals who purchase things identifying with business preparing and productions), Console Gamers and Primary

Browser: Internet Explorer (individuals who basically interface with Facebook utilizing Internet Explorer).

To target practices, you have to choose them in the promotion set menu either in the live record or in Power Editor, as demonstrated as follows.

Make separate promotion sets for every conduct point correspondingly to what you saw before for advantages.

**#9: Target by Income**

A few organizations sell items that are more costly than their rivals' or mainly focus on the most extravagant part of the populace. Facebook can be a gold dig for these organizations since you can target individuals dependent on their yearly salary.

To focus by salary, you have to go into the live record or Power Editor and enter the settings of your advertisement set. Snap-on More Demographics and afterwards click on Income to choose your ideal salary focus, as demonstrated as follows.

As should be evident in any screen capture on the left, there are numerous other focusing on choices you can utilize. Test the ones that bode well for your business and make sure to keep your advertisement set structure as portioned as could reasonably be expected.

**#10: Set Up a Remarketing Pixel**

Potential clients who visited your site by means of any traffic source (counting Google AdWords) yet didn't change over are in all likelihood looking at costs and suppliers. When they're set, they may have overlooked your business inside and out.

This is the place remarketing on Facebook comes in. What's more, honestly, this is probably the ideal approaches to connect with traffic that initially came by means of Google AdWords.

To set up a remarketing pixel, sign in to your promoting director and snap-on Audiences, as demonstrated as follows.

Snap Audiences to set up a remarketing pixel.

Next, click on Create Audience, and afterwards, click Custom Audience and Website Traffic in the upper right corner of your screen to begin a bit by bit procedure to make the remarketing pixel.

When you introduce the code in the footer of the site, return to the Website Traffic drop-down menu and also select People Who Visit Specific Web Pages, as appeared here.

You would then be able to make arrangements of individuals visiting a particular page of your site and target or prohibit them from your crusade. A valuable best practice is to create a rundown of individuals visiting your thank-you page and afterwards not promote to them since they previously changed over.

### #11: Identify Profitable Age Groups and Genders

Not all age gatherings and sexual orientations play out the equivalent. You may find that you're squandering your cash on unfruitful age classifications or that you're passing up on chances by not committing enough spending plan to sex that is producing most of the deals for a given objective strategy.

The ideal approach to examine age gathering and sexual orientation execution is to sign in to your promotion supervisor and snap-on Reports.

On the report page, then set up the date run you need to break down. At that point, click on Customize Columns to choose what esteems to cover. Under Breakdown, also select Age, Gender or Age and Gender, as demonstrated as follows.

You can settle on important vital choices dependent on the bits of knowledge you gather right now. Look at it for you now.

### #12: Test Lookalike Audiences

A carbon copy crowd is a rundown of clients whose qualities are like clients of a site custom crowd. This opens up a lot of chances, for example, promoting to clients like the individuals who previously visited your site, publicizing to clients like the individuals who visited a particular page or promoting to clients like the ones who prior changed over on your website.

To make a carbon copy crowd, sign in to your publicizing director and snap Audiences. When you enter your Audiences page, click on Create Audience and select Lookalike Audience starting from the drop menu, as appeared here.

Next, select the source crowd of your copy crowd and the objective nation. At that point pick a group of people size—the littler the size you choose, the more focused on it will be.

Select the objective nation and crowd size.

**#13: Target an Email List**

Facebook permits you to make a custom promoting crowd dependent on email records. You should try simply to make a .csv or .txt record that incorporates one email for every column and avoids some other information.

When you have that document, click Audiences. At that point click Create Audience and select Custom Audience starting from the drop menu.

Next, click on the Customer List, as demonstrated as follows. From here, it's anything but difficult to transfer your rundown.

Remember that you can likewise transfer a rundown of telephone numbers and afterward focus on those individuals in Facebook advertisements. The procedure is substantially equivalent to the one I simply portrayed. Also, you have the alternative to make a copy crowd of your recently made client list.

**#14: Test Bidding Strategies**

Offering procedures altogether impact the accomplishment of Facebook promotions.

The three principle classifications for the offering are cost per click, cost per thousand impressions and transformation streamlining agent (which requires the establishment of a change code).

Test distinctive offering techniques to discover what lessens the expense per change yet at the same time gets enough volume. I prescribe beginning with CPC and transformation streamlining agent.

You can set up your offering technique at the Ad Set level in the Optimization and Pricing area, appeared here.

At whatever point you offer per snap or utilize the transformation analyzer, you can choose your most extreme expense per catch or target cost per obtaining or let Facebook pick an incentive for you.

**#15: Schedule Ads**

Facebook permits you to section your promotions by days and hours. This choice is accessible just with a lifetime spending plan and not with the day by day spending choice. This essential is the motivation behind why most organizations, despite everything, don't utilize this element.

Lifetime spending alludes to the complete spending plan of an advertisement set and actually doesn't have a day by day limit. In any event that the crusade doesn't have a dependable execution design that has been demonstrated fruitful after some time, this isn't the correct setting for you. In any event that you choose to utilize day and hour separating, you can set it up in the Budget and Schedule area of the advertisement set, as appeared here.

# CHAPTER FOUR

# INSTRUCTIONS TO CREATE A SOCIAL MEDIA MARKETING STRATEGY

---

The key element for doing internet-based life-promoting excellent has a methodology.

Without a methodology, you may be posting via web-based networking media stages for posting. And Without understanding what your objectives are, who your intended interest group is, and what they need, it'll be challenging to accomplish results via web-based networking media.

Regardless of whether you need to develop your image through internet based life or to step up as an online networking advertiser, building up web-based social networking promoting procedure is essential.

Here's a single direction to do it.

**The most effective method to make online networking showcasing procedure**

It's intriguing to take note of that an online networking showcasing process, and an internet-based life advertising plan have a lot of hybrids.

You can consider it thusly: A methodology is a place you're going. An arrangement is a manner by which you'll arrive.

Perhaps the least complicated approaches to make your online networking advertising methodology is to ask yourself the 5Ws:

For what actually reason would you like to be via web-based networking media?

- Who is your intended interest group?
- What are you going to share?
- Where are you going to offer?
- When are you going to offer?

To assist you with making your procedure, I have made a straightforward web-based life advertising methodology layout. Don't hesitate to utilize, adjust, or change it as you see fit (in the wake of making a duplicate of it).

Here's another fascinating point about the procedure (or systems): You can likewise have a technique for every one of your online networking channels, for example, a Facebook showcasing methodology, an Instagram promoting methodology, etc., which all lead up to your general internet based life advertising procedure.

However, how about we start with your general methodology.

**For what reason does your business need to be via web-based networking media?**

The absolute first inquiry to answer is the Why.

This identifies with your online networking objectives. It's safe to say that you are via web-based networking media to advance your items?

As a rule, there are nine online networking objectives you can have:

1. Increment brand mindfulness
2. Direct people to your site
3. Create new leads
4. Develop income (by expanding information exchanges or deals)
5. Lift brand commitment
6. Construct a network around your business
7. Give social client care.
8. Increment specifies in the press.
9. Tune in to discussions about your image

You'll likely have more than one online networking objective, and that is fine.

For the most part, it's incredible to concentrate on only a bunch of objectives except if you have a group, where various individuals or gatherings inside the group can take on multiple purposes.

For instance, at Buffer, the promoting group utilizes web-based life both to expand our image mindfulness and direct people to our substance while our Advocacy group uses online experience to give timely client assistance.

**Who is your intended interest group?**

When you have made sense of your Why, the following interesting point is your intended interest group.

Understanding your intended interest group will help you all the more effectively answer the accompanying inquiries on what, where, and also when you are going to share.

For example, if a movement and way of life brand (like Away) realize that its intended interest group wants to find out about new places and travel tips, it could share such substance on its web-based life profiles.

An incredible exercise to attempt here is to manufacture advertising personas.

There is a wide range of methods for building advertising personas. My undisputed top choice methodology is to, once more, utilize the 5Ws and 1H.

- **Who right?** (For example work title, age, sexual orientation, compensation, area, and so forth.)
- **What are they inspired by that you can give?** (For example, amusement, instructive substance, contextual analyses, data on new items, and so forth.)
- **Where do they generally hang out on the web?** (For example Facebook, Instagram, and so on or specialty stages)
- **When do they search for the sort of substance you can give?** (For example, ends of the week, during their everyday drive, and so on.)

- For what reason do they devour the substance? (For example, to show signs of improvement at their specific employment, to get reliable, to keep awake to date with something, and so on.)
- **How would they expend the substance?** (For example, peruse internet based life posts, watch recordings, and so forth.)

You likely don't need to begin without any preparation. In any event that your business has been running for some time, you most presumably as of now have a decent feeling of your intended interest group. What may be useful is to record it so you can impart it to the group or use for your future reference.

To assist you with building up your advertising persona, Kevan Lee, our Director of Marketing, have composed a total manual for showcasing personas.

1. **What are you going to share?**

At the point when you see this inquiry, you may be pondering the kinds of substance to share. For instance, would you like to share recordings or pictures?

However, hang on for a second!

We're discussing your online networking showcasing methodology here so we should make a stride back and think on a more elevated level. Rather than the kinds of substance to share, "topic" may be a superior word.

Here are a couple of brands and their theme(s):

- MeUndies, a clothing brand, shares photographs from their

clients and pictures of their items on their Instagram profile.

- Huckberry, an open-air and experience brand, shares their article substance and great photographs of the outside on their Facebook profile.
- Tunnel, an extravagance love seat brand, for the most part, shares images on their Instagram profile.

In any event that you look through the online life profiles referenced above, you may have seen that the brands have more than one primary topic. Having a bunch of subjects is superbly beautiful as it gives you the space to share the scope of substance to keep your crowd connected with without being apparently unfocused.

This is the place a decent comprehension of your intended interest group will be useful. Take a gander at your showcasing personas and think about the accompanying inquiries:

- What objectives and difficulties do they have?
- How might you help settle them?

For a wellness attire and adornments brand (like Gymshark), an objective of its intended interest group may be to keep awake-to-date with the most recent wellness gears. All things considered, it can share its most recent items on its web-based life profiles.

(Would that be excessively special? Perhaps not. Venture bank Piper Jaffray studied in excess of 8,600 American young people and found that 70 per cent of them favoured brands to get in touch with them about new items through Instagram. The key returns to understanding your intended interest group.)

**Where are you going to offer?**

The following stage which is to figure out where you are going to share your substance. At the end of the day.

Before we go any further, recollect that your image doesn't need to be on each web-based life stages. We have committed that error previously. Being on fewer steps gives you a superior concentration and more opportunity to make a better substance.

A quick tip: That being stated, it'll be insightful to in any event have a complete profile on the Big Four which are— Facebook, Instagram, Twitter, and LinkedIn — as they would regularly appear on the main page of Google query items when individuals scan for your image.

Once more, the comprehension of your intended interest group will prove to be useful here. Which stages are your intended interest group generally dynamic? What makes them visit that stage? For instance, adolescents and youthful grown-ups may like looking through Instagram when they are exhausted to perceive what their companions are doing or whether their preferred brands have new items.

Another, though littler, the interesting point is, what is your image's "X factor"? Is it true that you are extraordinary at photography, recordings, or composing? Certain stages loan itself well to certain substance types. For instance, photographs are incredible on Instagram, long-structure records on YouTube, articles on Medium. Yet, this is a minor point since web-based life stages are advancing to give pretty much every sort of substance these days.

At long last, think about littler, specialty stages, as well. For instance, Zwift, multiplayer web-based cycling preparing programming organization, has begun a club on Strava, an informal community for competitors. Their club has in excess of 57,000 cyclists, and thousands draw in with their posts on Strava.

**When are you going to offer?**

The last key piece of your methodology is making sense of when you need to share your substance. You may be enticed to hop into an examination for the best time(s) to post.

Respite. What's more, relax.

We should always make a stride back and take a gander at this from a more significant level once more. Before choosing precisely which time and days of the week, you need to post, think about the practices of your intended interest group.

**When do they, for the most part, utilize online networking to discover the sort of substance that you'll share?**

Here are a few guides to consider:

- Avid supporters are likely via web-based networking media not long previously, during, and soon after games to discover and collaborate with content about the occasion.
- Competitors may be on Instagram while they are chilling off after

their morning or night exercises.

- Individuals who love to travel may be increasingly dynamic via web-based networking media during the ends of the week when they are making arrangements for their next outing (or during their work breaks when they are actually dreaming about their next excursion).
- Moms of infants may be looking through web-based social networking when they are breastfeeding in the night.

You may have construed from these couple of models that there probably won't be a widespread best time to post. It indeed relies upon your crowd. So for this progression, centre around the general personal conduct standards of your intended interest group.

At the point when you have made your web-based life advertising procedure, you would then be able to discover your image's best time to post through experimentation.

**At long last, how are you going to execute this technique?**

What's more, there you have it — your online networking advertising methodology!

In any case, that is not the end. As referenced over, a technique is a place you're going; an arrangement is a manner by which you'll arrive. You have chosen where to make a beeline for; presently, you need an agreement.

In what manner would it be a good idea for you to round out your internet based life profiles? What should your tone and voice resemble? What posts type (for example, picture, connect, video, and so on.) would it be advisable for you to utilize?

To assist you with the following stage and your web-based life achievement, we have a bit by bit control for making an internet based life promoting plan. Here's a sneak look of the infographic you'll discover in that manage:

## Concentrate on the 10,000-foot view

Building up a web-based life advertising system is most likely perhaps the most laborious activity since it expects you to step back and take a gander at the comprehensive view. You need to move your outlook away from your day-by-day undertakings like planning and to answer to remarks to more significant level reasoning.

Yet, it's extraordinarily fulfilling and supportive of having an internet-based life showcasing technique with the goal that you aren't merely posting content only for posting content. It'll assist you with accomplishing your internet-based life and business objectives.

# NINE SOCIAL MEDIA GOALS YOU CAN SET FOR YOUR BUSINESS (AND HOW TO TRACK THEM)

The thing we actually love most at Buffer is to assist you with prevailing at internet-based life. What's more, a key piece of web-based life achievement is knowing which objectives and focuses on setting for your group.

Without objectives, well, it's difficult to know precisely how well your online networking procedure is performing and where you have to emphasize to keep moving advances.

Today I'd love to impart to you a lot of super-noteworthy web-based life objectives you can use to enable your group to accomplish incredible things. Altogether, we'll stroll through 9 totally different, however powerful online life objectives and for every purpose we additionally applicable measurements to track and offer how-to gauge your outcomes.

How about we begin

**Nine internet-based life objectives for your group (and how to follow them)**

Internet-based life isn't just a promoting device, and it can influence pretty much every territory of business – for instance, as we found in our State of Social 2016 report, web-based life is a crucial channel for brand mindfulness, commitment, lead age, client assistance and significantly more.

All in all, in 2017, we realize that internet-based life can help organizations from various perspectives, however, how might we guarantee we're getting however much incentive as could reasonably be expected from the time and assets we placed into online networking?

In 2010, a gathering of scientists in Canada examined the impact of objective setting on the scholastic execution of 85 understudies. Following four months, they found that the crowd that experienced an escalated unbiased setting program accomplished necessarily preferred outcomes and over the benchmark group.

In any event that you need to remain inspired and accomplish more outcomes for your organization through web-based social networking, science suggests defining objectives. In any case, which purposes would it be a good idea for you to set?

The following is a rundown of 9 ultra-compelling web-based social networking objectives to assist you with expanding your profits from online life:

**Increment brand mindfulness**

As indicated by our State of Social Media 2016 study, brand mindfulness is the top explanation advertisers utilize web-based experience. It's straightforward why: The healthy individual goes through almost two hours via web-based networking media consistently, and in this manner, web-based social networking is perhaps the best spot to catch purchasers' eye.

Internet-based life has likewise empowered advertisers to have an increasingly quantitative comprehension of their image's essence and reach in the online world. Furthermore, presently most web-based life stages give information on the scope of your substance, permitting you to report your online nearness all the more precisely.

**Potential measurements to quantify brand mindfulness:**

- Supporters tally – "What number of individuals can you possibly reach?"
- Reach of your web-based life posts – "What number of individuals have do arrive at every day/week/month?"
- Notices, offers, and RTs – "What number of individuals are discussing your image or sharing your web-based life posts?"

**instructions to follow brand mindfulness:**

While most internet-based life stages give local examination, outsider administration instruments make following and revealing brand mindfulness measurements a lot simpler. For instance, utilizing Buffer Analyze, you can discover your adherents development and reach on the different stages.

To do this in Buffer Analyze, also select the social profile you are keen on and head to the Metric breakdown graph under the Overview tab. There, you can choose your all-out devotees or reach starting from the drop menu.

**Direct people to your site**

Above and beyond from having a brand nearness via web-based networking media is driving guests to your website or blog, who may transform into your clients.

Three out of five advertisers utilize internet based life to disperse their substance and direct people to their locales. A group at HubSpot, for example, developed their month to month blog traffic by 241% more than eight months through online networking tests.

**Potential measurements to quantify traffic:**

- Traffic from internet-based life – "What number of guests are originating from your online life channels?"
- The portion of by and significant traffic – "What amount of your general traffic does online life represent?"
- Bob pace of web-based life traffic – "What is the nature of the traffic from online life?"
- Taps on your web-based life posts – "How well is the informing of your web-based life posts?"

**The most effective method to quantify traffic to your site:**

Google Analytics is most likely, perhaps the least demanding device for following web traffic. It gives you data about your site or blog traffic from different traffic sources, including online networking.

To comprehend the traffic from your online networking channels, go to Acquisition > All Traffic > Channel.

This view actually shows you the Number of visits from each channel, the portion of generally speaking traffic (the rate in sections), the ricochet rate, and that's just the beginning. For example, in the picture above, you can see that internet based life drove around 46,000 visits, which represents approximately 4 per cent of the traffic.

You can separate this information considerably further in Google Analytics by tapping on the 'Social' connection and seeing which stages were driving that traffic:

**Produce new leads**

Lead age is regularly utilized by organizations with the process of a great deal, for example, venture programming organizations.

This "way" is basically your business channel. With the immense number of individuals, you can reach, web-based life can be an incredible apparatus for getting individuals to the highest point of your pipe (or warming them up to your business).

The meaning of a lead is extensive, however, it, as a rule, implies that the individual has given your organization some type of data about themselves, for example, their name, email address, and comparative. There are numerous approaches to follow your web-based life first age endeavors, and the rundown underneath incorporates a couple of the more typical measurements to track to quantify your online life leads.

**Potential measurements to follow lead age:**

- Individual data (for the most part email addresses) gathered through internet-based life – "What number of leads have you gathered through online networking?"

- Downloads of your gated content – "What number of individuals visited from internet-based life and downloaded your gated content?"
- Support – "What number of individuals took an interest in your internet-based life challenge or occasions and imparted their data to you?"
- Taps on your lead-age web-based life posts – "How well is your informing on those posts?"
- Transformations of leads from online life – "How great are the leads from internet-based life?"

**The most effective method to follow internet-based life lead age:**

Google Analytics is amazingly incredible, and on any off chance that you have some transformation objectives set up, you can adequately follow your internet-based life lead age utilizing Google Analytics reports. (In any event that you haven't precisely define up any change objectives in Google Analytics, here's a far-reaching guide on the actual best way to do as such.)

When you have a change objective set up, to see reports, go to Acquisition > Social > Conversions inside Google Analytics and guarantee you select the transformation objective you're hoping to gauge. You should then observe a screen this way:

The change report will, at that point give you what Number of leads your internet-based life directs are getting or which divert is acquiring the most leads.

Different examination instruments like KISSmetrics and Mixpanel can likewise disclose to you such data (and maybe in more prominent detail).

**Develop income (by expanding information exchanges or deals)**

In any event that you don't have the process of a significant contract, you can utilize web-based life to transform your crowd into paying clients straightforwardly. For instance, internet-based life-promoting, for example, Facebook advertisements, is a turning into an inexorably mainstream methodology to help deals.

**Potential measurements to gauge income development:**

- Information exchanges/Revenue – "What number of recruits or what amount of income is your internet-based life diverts acquiring?"
- Income from advertisements – "What amount of income is your online life promoting getting?"

**The most effective method to follow income development:**

Once more, you could follow income in Google Analytics by defining up another physical transformation. Be that as it may, this time, you'd have to relegate a dollar incentive to every conversion:

In any event that you are a web-based business webpage, Google

Analytics' Ecommerce Tracking may be increasingly proper. What's more, in any event, that you are utilizing Facebook promotions, you can likewise set up change following the Facebook Pixel and ascribe qualities to the transformations. Here's an incredible apprentice's manual for the Facebook Pixel by Shopify.

**Lift brand commitment**

Commitment is the subsequent top motivation behind why advertisers utilize web-based social networking. What's more, look into has discovered that web-based social networking associations improve brand discernment, dependability, and simple suggestions.

Besides, internet-based life stage's calculations, for example, those on Facebook and Instagram, are organizing posts with a higher commission on their channels because of the conviction that clients will be progressively keen on observing profoundly captivating substance.

To condense, on any off chance that you need individuals to see your internet based life posts, you need to deliver engaging substance and react to your locale.

**Potential measurements to gauge commitment:**

- Likes, offers, and remarks per post – "What number of individuals are associating with your online networking posts?"
- Notices and answers – "What number of individuals are referencing your image, and what number of have you answered to?"

**The most effective method to follow commitment:**

Much the same as brand mindfulness measurements, you can physically follow commitment measurements through the online life stages themselves (Facebook Insights or Twitter examination, for instance) or you could utilize a web-based life investigation apparatus to support you.

In Buffer Analyze, you have the measurements breakdown outline referenced previously. You can likewise sort your posts by preferences, remarks, or commission rate. For instance, here's our most-loved Instagram post from the previous 30 days:

**Manufacture a network around your business**

Following crowd numbers, for example, all-out devotees and fans are extraordinary. However, we've additionally seen an ascent in the quantity of shut networks and visits business has been concentrating on over the previous year or something like that. For instance, we run #Bufferchat consistently on Twitter, and we additionally have a Slack Community (and a few organizations are in any event, exploring different avenues regarding Facebook gatherings, as well.)

The kinds of objectives you need to set for these networks may feel totally different to your general fan/devotee development objectives, and obviously, the sort of system you decide to construct will affect the measurements you choose to quantify accomplishment.

Here's a rundown to kick you off:

**Potential measurements to follow network building:**

- For Facebook gatherings: Number of posts, likes, and remarks – "How drawn in is your locale?"
- For Twitter visits Number of members and tweets per member – "What number of individuals are associated with your Twitter talks, and how drawn in the right?"
- For Slack people group: Number of days by day dynamic clients – "What number of individuals are effectively associated with your Slack people group?"

**instructions to follow network building:**

There are numerous extraordinary devices that can assist you with developing such information consequently. For Facebook gatherings, there are Grytics and Community Analytics. For Twitter talks, there are Keyhole and Hashtracking. While the vast majority of these apparatuses aren't free, they give free preliminaries to you to check whether they suit your necessities before you pay for them.

In any event that you don't have the monetary allowance to pay for such apparatuses right now, physically including and recording the numbers in a spreadsheet is totally conceivable, as well! I likewise locate that manual following causes me to comprehend the information better in the first place (however, it may get too dull inevitably).

**Viable social client assistance**

Having decent client care via web-based networking media can assist with expanding income, consumer loyalty score, and maintenance. In any case, in our State of Social Media study, just one of every five respondents (21%) said that they utilize web-based life for client assistance.

The pattern of individuals going to web-based social networking for client care will probably proceed, and we believe there's as yet an immense open door for organizations to separate themselves from their rivals with incredible web-based life client support.

**Measurements to follow your client care viability:**

- The Number of help questions – "Is there an interest in online networking client service for your organization?"
- Reaction time – "How quick would you say you are returning to your clients?"
- Consumer loyalty Score (CSAT) – "How fulfilled are your clients with your administration?"

**instructions to quantify your client assistance adequacy**:

On any off chance that you have a low volume of client assistance requests on your internet based life channels, you could physically follow the Number of help questions and your reaction time. Something else, utilizing an online networking client care device will probably be progressively effective. For instance, in Respond, our social client support programming for help groups, you can access to information, for example, Average Time To First Reply.

**Increment specifies in the press**

In spite of the way that internet-based life has empowered organizations to claim their news and offer stories legitimately with their fans and devotees across online experience, the press and media can at present drive critical outcomes PR despite everything assumes a crucial job in numerous organizations' promoting methodologies.

This makes it simpler to manufacture relations with famous production writers for getting press makes reference to and to construct thought authority in the business.

**Potential measurements to quantify your PR achievement:**

- Possible reach – "What number of individuals did a PR battle conceivably reach through web-based life?"
- Offers and notices – "What number of individuals are sharing or discussing your idea initiative articles?"
- Influencers – "What Number of and who are the influencers or columnists discussing your articles? What's the size of their following?"
- Effort – "What Number of individuals are asking your organization about industry-related inquiries? What Number of columnists are posing inquiries about your organization through online networking?"

**The most effective method to follow your PR makes reference to:**

In any event that you are merely beginning, it may be conceivable to physically follow all the social and press notices of your organization. With regards to hard to stay aware of the opinions (congratulations!), Mention is an incredible apparatus for following beliefs via web-based networking media.

there are three straightforward advances:

**Rundown the watchwords you need to follow**

- Set up your need (pages that you wish to be told about when they are shared via web-based networking media)
- Select spots where you need Mention to follow (for example Twitter, Instagram, and Pinterest)
- On any off chance that you go to Dashboards > Listening, you can see the information of the notices. From here, you can start to find and channel the most significant and farthest arriving at opinions of your image.

**Never miss a notice through social tuning in**

Online networking has brought organizations and their clients closer, and now it is a lot simpler for clients to impart their criticism to organizations than it ever has been previously. It has become a typical pattern for clients to air their musings about items and organizations via web-based networking media. By getting and answering to these posts, your clients will feel heard.

**Potential measurements to gauge social tuning in:**

- Client discussions – "What number of discussions have you had with your clients via web-based networking media?"

- Proposals or criticism from online life – "What number of recommendations would you say you are getting from your clients through internet-based life?"
- Item/content upgrades produced using those proposals – "What number of the recommendations affected your item improvement or substance creation?"

**instructions to viably tune in to online life discussions:**

TweetDeck is an extraordinary, free device for social tuning in and examines on Twitter. By setting up the correct catchphrase look, you can catch and react to the relevant tweets from your clients.

For instance, in any event, that you have tweeted us about our iOS application, you may have gotten an answer from Andy, one of our iOS designers. He utilizes TweetDeck to "tune in" for and answer any tweets about our iOS application.

Top tip: As most social listening apparatuses permit you to follow watchwords, you could make even astonishment and enjoyment your clients when they didn't label you in their online networking posts. For instance, at Buffer was watch out for all Tweets referencing 'Support' just as those that notice our handle '@Buffer'.

**What are your web-based life objectives?**

With the web-based life scene rushing, new objectives and approaches to quantify achievement usually are rising, and I'd love to hear what objectives you're at present centered around:

- What web-based social networking objectives do you use?

- What new web-based social networking objectives or use cases do you think will develop in 2017, and why?

# CHAPTER FIVE

# INSTRUCTIONS TO BREAK DOWN YOUR SOCIAL MEDIA GOALS INTO TACTICS AND PLANS

---

Creating a successful web-based social networking procedure to assist you with accomplishing your objectives can be a genuine test.

Like we referenced before in a post about objective setting procedures, thinking of web-based social networking objectives for our showcasing group here at Buffer has frequently been somewhat aimless for us.

There are such vast numbers of objectives we might concentrate on – like brand mindfulness, commitment, traffic, and information exchanges, to give some examples. There's additionally the test of making sense of how to ensure your web-based life objectives are lined up with your worldwide organization objectives.

So how would we choose what to focus on for the coming year?

Right now, love to share a structure you can use to put forth sure your internet-based life promoting attempts are going the correct way and having the most significant effect this year (roused by our companions at Moz).

Also, we're continually hoping to discover better approaches to improve our objective setting process. So don't hesitate to share any contemplations and thoughts you may have about how you may make a web-based life plan.

From online life objectives to noteworthy strategies and plans

**Stage 1: Set web-based social networking objectives that line up with your general organization objectives**

In any event that we need our online life showcasing endeavors to have the most excellent effect, it's very significant that they're lined up with our global organization objectives and qualities.

In case we're all paddling in various ways, it's tough to gain any significant ground toward where we need to go.

"Not money. Not a methodology. Not innovation. It is cooperation that remaining parts a definitive upper hand.

In any event that you could get all the individuals in an association paddling a similar way, you could overwhelm any industry, in any market, against any opposition, whenever."

In light of that, as you're defining your internet-based life objectives, it's imperative to zoom out and take a gander at the 10,000-foot view: by what method can web-based life sway your entire business, as opposed to merely online life objectives?

At that point, map your organization's important objectives to how your web-based life endeavors can best help. Here's a guide to get a feeling of what that could resemble practically speaking

**Model: Setting objectives for Campfire, Inc.**

Envision we run web-based life for an (anecdotal) organization called Campfire, Inc.

Open-air fire's best three organization objectives for 2017 are to:

- Venture into another market fragment
- Boat 3 new essential item includes
- Improve the NPS score with their SMB clients

The key here is to take the objectives that the authors, administrators, or board care most about achieving, and show that online networking can help accomplish them in an essential manner.

**Things being what they are, in what manner can internet-based life assist us with achieving our organization objectives?**

- So as to assist Campfire with venturing into another market section, we could:
- Find and manufacture associations with influencers who can intensify our message inside the new objective market
- Join forces with influencers and brands to use and develop our crowd inside the new accurate market

Make and advance marked substance that drives top-of-the-pipe development in the new market and positions our organization as a head alternative.

Also, to help the organization's drive to dispatch three new essential item includes, we could:

- Run online networking efforts to advance item dispatches
- Bring issues to light around and drive the commitment of new highlights.

Basically, what this procedure is doing is taking the objectives that are generally essential to your association and adjusting your web-based life objectives to show that you're assisting with achieving them.

So as opposed to stating, "we're concentrating on an influencer outreach technique this quarter." You could report, "So as to help us [accomplish our top-level organization goal], we're fabricating an influencer outreach methodology." Imagine a scenario where your organization doesn't have essential objectives that you can legitimately affect with web-based social networking.

For instance, here are a couple of thoughts for web-based life objectives and measurements you could concentrate on that would almost certainly be lined up with your promoting endeavors:

1. **Increment brand mindfulness** — Follower means your social profiles, reach of your online life posts, notices, shares, and retweets
2. **Direct people to your site** — Referral traffic from internet-based life, portions of in general rush hour gridlock, bob pace of web-based life traffic, and taps on your online life posts
3. **Create new leads** — New leads gathered through online life, downloads of your gated content, click on your lead-gen web-based life posts, and change pace of points from web-based experience.
4. **Develop income** — Signups deals income or income from social

promotions.

5. **Lift brand commitment** — Likes, shares, remarks per post, notices, and answers
6. **Fabricate a network around your business** — Number of posts, likes, and comments for Facebook gatherings. A number of members and tweets per member for Twitter visits. Number of every day dynamic clients for Slack people group
7. **Increment makes reference to in the press** — Potential reach, offers and notices, influencers discussing your substance, and a number of individuals contacting ask about industry-related inquiries.
8. **Research and find out about your clients** — Number of discussions with clients via web-based networking media, proposals or input, and item/content enhancements produced using those recommendations.

What's more, in any event, that you need to figure out how to follow the objectives in the model above, just as the best devices to utilize, look at our guide on the kinds of web-based social networking objectives you can set.

### Stage 2: Break down your objectives into explicit strategies

When you've made an interpretation of your organization objectives into internet-based life objectives, the subsequent step is to outline the particular moves you have to make to achieve the goals you've set.

We should hop again into our model from the past advance.

On any off chance that our organization objective at Campfire is to venture into another market portion, and we've defined a web-based social networking objective to find and fabricate associations with influencers and brands in that advertise – how might we separate that into explicit strategies we can make a move?

Here's the single direction we might move toward it:

- Make a rundown of 100 influencers in the objective specialty which may be available to supported posts
- A direct message every one of them to check whether they'd be keen on joining forces with us
- Set up a supported post with one brand or influencer consistently

Presently we can legitimately perceive how online networking can impact the general organization objectives:

The particular strategies you'll utilize will be distinctive, relying upon your goals, clients, market, item, and various different factors.

Furthermore, you can alter your arrangement after some time as you begin getting criticism and seeing the aftereffects of your strategies. Will we speak increasingly about that soon?

**Stage 3: Prioritize your arrangement**

Each advertising group, regardless of its size, has limited assets. So it's essential to organize your strategies and make a web-based life showcasing plan from them.

**How would you pick what to organize?**

One methodology I've discovered overly helpful and instinctive is Product Plan's worth versus intricacy model. Here are the means by which it works:

1. Assess how much value I expect every strategy will bring to the business
2. Contrast that with how much exertion every approach will probably require and how complex it will be to actualize
3. Organize the most elevated worth strategies that need the least exertion/unpredictability

It is highly unlikely to anticipate precisely how much time and exertion every strategy will take or how much worth they'll bring to the business! So give a valiant effort to make an informed theory and make an effort not to get too hung up on flawlessness here.

You can not be right about this. It's alright to be, "Hello, we're speculating, thumb noticeable all around. We don't generally know without a doubt. However, we're going to attempt."

**Assessing esteem versus intricacy**

So take a gander at the diagram beneath, the web-based social networking strategies that fall into area 1 of the model (high worth, low complication) would be our top needs to handle first.

The strategies that fall into segment 2 (high worth, high multifaceted nature) would be next on our rundown In any event that we have the assets. Also, the remainder of the strategies that fall into the other two segments most likely do not merit centering a lot of our consideration on – assuming any.

Here's the manner by which ProductPlan's originator, Jim Semick, portrays this way to deal with prioritization:

In the Value versus Complexity model, you assess each open-door dependent on its business worth and its relative multifaceted nature to actualize.

The grid is straightforward: The activities that have the most elevated worth and the least exertion will be the low-hanging organic product.

**Stage 4: Assign errands and set ETAs**

When you've organized the particular strategies, you plan on utilizing to achieve your online networking objectives; the subsequent step is to add two components to every policy:

1. **Dole out individuals** – Who will chip away at and be answerable for every one of them?
2. **Set an ETA** – When might you like every one of them to be to finished?

Returning to our past model with Campfire Inc, this is what that may look like in real life:

- Connect with 100 influencers by Feb first [Assigned to Brian]

- Direct message 100 influencers by Feb twentieth [Assigned to Brian]
- Set up one supported post by the 30th of every month [Assigned to Brian, Hailley]

**Stage 5: Analyze and adjust the arrangement as you go,**

it's too critical to make modifications and adjust your objectives and strategies as you go.

At any rate that is the means by which we will in general handle objective setting on our showcasing group here at Buffer – if something doesn't feel right, we can generally transform it to something that is a superior fit.

Our promoting executive Kevan summarized it well when he stated:

I like to think about this arrangement as an excursion. Begin by pointing yourself the correct way, at that point pick the manner in which you will arrive, check-in regularly to ensure you're on target, and have a ton of fun en route.

**Over to you!**

**How would you set your internet-based life objectives?**

At the point when we're defining our internet-based life objectives, we generally attempt to adjust them to our vast organization objectives – in light of the fact that we've seen that getting everybody paddling a similar way can be a colossal bit of leeway for us.

We're continually testing and searching for approaches to improve our objective setting process, and I'd love to hear how you set online networking objectives at your organization!

**Do you utilize an alternate procedure?**

**How would you guarantee your web-based life endeavors advantage the business?**

I'd love to hear your musings and gain more from you in the remarks underneath. Furthermore, I'd be glad to respond to any inquiries you may have about our procedure too.

# 22 FACEBOOK ADVERTISING TIPS TO MAXIMIZE CONVERSIONS

Facebook publicizing is similarly as amazing as it's at any point been. Maybe considerably more so. The sheer volume of clients alone makes it an advanced advertiser's play area.

With regards to Facebook publicizing, I could gush off a clothing rundown of done-to-death traditional procedures.

What's more, most are still very viable.

Be that as it may, be, what I need to do here is dig somewhat more profound and genuinely analyze Facebook Ads.

I need you to comprehend its maximum capacity.

Here are 22 Facebook promoting procedures and techniques to expand changes that. You should without a doubt, try different things.

**Focus on the correct customers**

Here's the arrangement. It doesn't make a difference how astonishing your Facebook promotions are. In any event that the opportune individuals are not seeing them, they won't convert. That is all.

Consider it.

On any off chance that the UFC ran an advertisement for the ongoing McGregor versus Diaz battle focusing on soccer mothers and enthusiasts of futureswithoutviolence.org, do you figure it would change over?

Presumably not.

Regardless of whether the promotion was very much planned, streamlined for shading brain research, and contained world-class duplicate, there would be zero deals if the perfect individuals didn't see it.

For instance, in any event, that you are running a Facebook promotion battle to sell your new item on wellbeing and health, you presumably wouldn't target Facebook clients who are aficionados of McDonald's and Wendy's.

Fortunately for you, Facebook focusing on is the undisputed heavyweight boss of client concentrate.

The initial step to running high changing over Facebook advertisements is to target clients dependent on their inclinations.

Discover clients who have comparable interests to the items you are selling, and you'll have the option to develop a large fan base you can later change over into paying clients.

**2. Utilizing "Pages to Watch"**

Facebook has a genuinely cool element called "Pages to Watch." It's not something I use for promoting legitimately, yet it can give some supportive bits of knowledge to help me in my advertising. Long story short, you can accumulate a rundown of pages you're keen on alongside investigation. This is what I mean: Simply include pages from brands that are important to your industry and have a robust Facebook nearness.

This is useful on the grounds that you can see which posts are the most and least captivating. Thusly, you can utilize this data when choosing what to post on your own page.

**3. Post pictures through Instagram**

Here's a slippery little strategy I discovered. Instead of posting pictures legitimately on Facebook, post them by means of Instagram.

Why? An investigation from Buzzsumo found that "pictures posted through Instagram get 23% greater commitment." Also, this bodes well, considering the crazy degree of commitment Instagram gets. As indicated by Brand Watch, "Commitment with brands on Instagram is multiple times higher than Facebook, multiple times higher than Pinterest and multiple times higher than Twitter." Genuineness!

In principle, following this essential advance can net you about a quarter more commitment than basically posting legitimately on Facebook.

**4. Disregard the hashtags**

OK, hashtags are high in specific circumstances. Indeed, they're very advantageous on systems, for example, Instagram and Twitter. Be that as it may, less on Facebook. A similar report from Buzzsumo found that posts with hashtags got less commitment than jobs without.

In addition to the fact that this saves time, however, you'll likewise get all the more value for your money with each bit of substance you post. Consider it a scaled-down hack.

**5. Post between 10 p.m. furthermore, 12 p.m. neighborhood time**

I'm sure you definitely realize that planning is essential via web-based networking media.

Regardless of whether you post a perfect work of art, it'll have just a negligible effect if your crowd never really observes it. It'll get rearranged to the base of their feeds. From my experience and reliable information from Buzzsumo, the perfect time to post is between 10 p.m. what's more, 12 p.m. nearby time. There are two principal reasons why.

There are fewer individuals posting content, which implies not so much rivalry but rather more permeability.

Second, there are sufficient individuals despite everything alert and dynamic on Facebook to make it worth your time.

This diagram from Buzzsumo delineates this marvel: Stick with this two-hour window, and you ought to be brilliant.

**6. Utilizing "Crowd Insights"**

You should know I'm a sucker for cool internet-based life highlights. Particularly those that are profoundly information-driven.

The "Crowd Insights" highlight is ideal for helping me get a nitty-gritty preview of my crowd so I can oblige them all the more productively and make important substance based around their inclinations.

What's more, the significance is essential since it, at last, amplifies your effect and builds your ROI.

You can get data on:

- Age
- Sex
- Way of life
- Instruction level
- Employment title

However, that is only a hint of something more substantial.

The information you create from this can overflow into different components of your general promoting effort.

**7. Work video into your center technique**

I figure we could all be able to concur that video is gigantic right now. Some may even think about 2016 as the time of the video. Interestingly, video represents just 3% of all substance on Facebook. I saw that number as incredibly low. However, it likewise presents an extraordinary chance. Posting a lot of excellent video content permits you to snatch the low-hanging natural product a large number of your rivals give off an impression of being passing up. This leads me to my next point.

**8. Legitimately implant recordings**

Considering YouTube is so enormous, your fundamental nature might be to install YouTube recordings into your posts. Be that as it may, be, that is an inappropriate move. That is on the grounds that "legitimately implanted Facebook recordings get more commitment than YouTube installed recordings."

Significantly more!

Simply take a gander at how much the complete number of connections from direct implanting smaller people the quantity of those installed with YouTube.

Remember this pushing ahead, and your commitment levels should increment extensively.

**9. "Publicly support" your business choices**

You're presumably acquainted with the expression "crowdfunding," where capital is raised with commitments from countless individuals. You can apply a comparable idea to Facebook with "publicly supporting" critical choices. Here is a few models: Request that your crowd pick your fresh out of the box new's logo An approach which new foundation to use for your Facebook profile This is cool on the grounds that:

1. it tells your crowd you're really keen on their suppositions, and
2. it's a great characteristic impetus for commitment.

The most effortless approach to public support is to do surveys in which individuals can cast a ballot.

**10. Hold posts under 150 characters long**

Less is best as far as Facebook character tally. Indeed, I prescribe treating it like Twitter—utilize a maximum of 150 characters.

Why?

It's straightforward. Shorter Facebook posts get unquestionably more commitment than longer ones. Here's information to demonstrate it: As should be visible, posts with 50 characters or less get the most connections, and the quantity of communications step by step decreases as more characters are included. At the end of the day, keep it quick and painless.

### 11. Add CTA catches to your Facebook advertisements

Here's a fascinating truth: "The normal promoting active clicking factor on Facebook is 0.9%." In any case, "including a CTA catch can lift your active clicking factor by 2.85 occasions." Simply think about the long-haul sway this can have on your battle. A droll even made a brief infographic that makes reference to the "huge outcomes from a little catch."

### 12. Utilizing "Facebook Groups" for network building

You may have heard Seth Godin talk about the significance of gatherings or "clans" as he calls them. It's a fundamental part of brand building. In any case, one asset I believe that numerous advertisers are neglecting to exploit is "Facebook Groups." It's a great deal like LinkedIn Groups where you make a particular gathering based around a critical subject of intrigue (typically your specialty).

- This is advantageous for a few different reasons:
- It reinforces your connections
- It causes you to fabricate new ones.
- It manufactures brand value.

- It encourages collaboration
- You can increase significant intel.

**13. Pin your most epic post**

Another element I love is the choice to "pin" jobs at the highest point of your course of events. That way, Facebook clients see your best substance once they land on your page. It's sort of like doing your absolute best, which notices back to the radiance impact. I propose investigating your course of events and finding the most excellent post that got the most commitment and "sticking" it to the top.

**14. A/B test your promotions with Qwaya**

I won't dispatch into an indulgent conversation of the amount I love A/B testing. You most likely definitely realize that. I will say, notwithstanding, that it's your pass to most extreme transformations and for tidying up any wasteful aspects when all is said in done.

In any case, also how precisely would you be able to play out A/B testing on Facebook? I propose utilizing Qwaya. It's an extraordinary Facebook promotion chief that will assist you in taking things to the following level. Here's a screen capture:

In case you're channeling a lot of cash into Facebook promotions, this instrument is an absolute necessity.

**15. Be fascinating**

This is the most exceedingly terrible thing you can do at whatever point you are making a promotion is to be nonexclusive.

It doesn't actually make a difference whether you are starting contention or being somewhat restless insofar as individuals recall you.

Keep in mind "St. Rooney," the Nike promotion depicting a recovered Wayne Rooney with a dark red cross on his chest? It's difficult to overlook.

I can't address your specialty, however, figure out how to separate yourself from the opposition through one of a kind promotions, and you will begin changing over like there's no tomorrow.

**16. Flash feeling**

Individuals are passionate animals, not legitimate ones.

- Educate individuals regarding the advantages they will get.
- Inform them concerning how your item or administration will transform them.
- Discover the torment point they are battling with and press on it until they are eager to fork out the cash to purchase whatever you are selling.

Another point to recall with respect to starting feeling is that individuals relate more emphatically to human countenances than they do to some other picture.

Rather than utilizing scenes or item pictures in your advertisement, use photographs that contain outward appearances passing on the feeling you are attempting to summon.

**17. Ace shading brain science**

Something else that can totally change the transformation paces of your advertisements is the hues you use. Because of transformative brain science, individuals partner certain tones with specific feelings. Red catches our eye.

Do some examination into how various hues influence the human cerebrum, and utilize that information to make the human mind work for you rather than against you.

**18. Use a lot of "inquiry" posts**

In a past article on Quick Sprout, I inspected which kinds of jobs got the most associations on Facebook.

This is what I found:

It doesn't actually take a scientific genius to make sense of that "question" posts are perfect as far as producing connections.

It's presumably in light of the main fact that individuals like to get in on the activity and have their voices heard, so I propose utilizing this a considerable amount.

**19. Stick with articles somewhere in the range of 1k and 3k words**

I trust you wouldn't fret, yet I'm going on a snappy long-structure content tirade. Indeed, as per Buzzsumo's discoveries, long-structure content performs best on Facebook. Specifically, posts somewhere in the range of 1,000 and 3,000 words are perfect. In any case, also you would prefer not to go any farther than 3,000, considering the reality there's a critical drop off in the number of collaborations.

### 20. Make an essential and convincing lead magnet

What is your opinion about remuneration? All things considered; I trust you can grapple with it in light of the fact that a lead magnet is fundamentally a moral fix intended to assist you with accumulating a rundown of contacts. At the point when you are making a lead magnet, the objective is to "influence" your potential clients, offering them something of significant worth in return for their messages or some other contact strategy. This will permit you to develop a colossal rundown of leads who are keen on purchasing your item or administration later on. The most significant key to recollect at whatever point you are creating your lead magnet is this is the primary "example" of your work your leads are accepting.

It doesn't make any difference in any event that you have unusual items or administrations.

In any event that your lead magnet is low quality, individuals will pass judgment on your business in like manner.

This implies it's significant that you create a kick-ass lead magnet.

I don't mean anything significant.

I mean something that you could charge $100 or more for in great inner voice.

The absolute most normal lead magnets are:

- digital books or articles
- Video preparing

- Email arrangement
- Free devices

The configuration you decide for your lead magnet is up to you. However, settle on sure you base your choice on your crowd.

For instance, and on any off chance that you have a large YouTube following, you'll need to decide on a video preparing arrangement.

In any event that you have a colossal blog following with gigantic measures of commitment, composing an incredible digital book is most likely the route forward.

**21. Make a stellar greeting page**

Despite the fact that this isn't actually a piece of your Facebook advertisements, it's as yet one of the essential parts of producing a high transformation rate.

Your point of arrival is the contrast between a Facebook advertisement that creates a large number of snaps and a Facebook promotion that produces a vast amount of deals.

Making an actual point of arrival that changes over isn't simple. Be that as it may, it's fundamental to Facebook advertisement dominance. Moreover, no good thing ever comes simple, isn't that so?

How would you approach making a high changing over presentation page for your Facebook promotions? By acing these three basics.

**Fundamental 1: The heading**

Let me try and disclose to you something you definitely know.

Individuals have the capacity to focus on roughly 9 seconds (no, indeed).

There is such a vast significant number of interruptions in the advanced world that individuals seldom have the regard for really kick back and read a greeting page. Regardless of whether the item could completely change them, they, in all likelihood, won't be eager to devote any piece of their day to your page—except if you give them motivation. This is the place features come in. The initial step to composing amazing greeting pages is to produce breathtaking features. Your features need to catch your crowd's eye. They have to start intrigue, clarify the advantages of your item, and let them know what you are selling—all inside a couple of short words. Simple, isn't that so?

When composing features, you need to keep things as straightforward as could be expected under the circumstances while as yet catching individuals' eye and clarifying your item adequately.

Here are some incredible guides to get your creative energies pumping.

**Basic 2: Customer benefits**

The following thing you have to concentrate on with your greeting page is obviously disclosing the advantages to the client.

What are they escaping this exchange?

Your client couldn't care less about your item—they just consideration around a specific something.

"How might this benefit me?"

That is it.

In any event that you can viably respond to this inquiry in the body of your greeting page, your change rates will soar.

Try not to concentrate on the highlights of your item or administration; instead, center around how those highlights will change your client's life.

For instance, having this move is the effect between duplicate that peruses this way:

"12 video modules are clarifying the mechanics of activity physiology."

furthermore, this:

"12 extraordinary modules on practice brain science that will assist you with finding the wellness mysteries you have to shred pounds of fat and open your hereditary potential… in 8 short weeks!"

I don't think about you. However, I am almost certain I know which visual cue would make me click that "purchase presently" button.

**Basic 3: Build validity**

The third essential piece of your presentation page is the believability you assemble.

Am I not catching my meaning by this?

Individuals purchase from individuals they trust.

What's more, if a client has just discovered you through a lead magnet and a Facebook promotion, chances are you haven't yet manufactured enough trust to change over them into a paying client.

In this way, you have to develop your believability. You can achieve this in a few different ways. The first is by "acquiring" validity from various sources.

For instance, if an industry head supported your item, including their profile picture and underwriting on your presentation page would hugely influence your transformation rate.

Alternately, In any event, that you have been supported by massive brand names like Forbes, Entrepreneur, or Inc, you could remember their identification for your point of arrival to help your believability.

Lastly, you need to ensure you incorporate bunches of inside and out customer tributes.

What's more, I don't mean tributes like:

I mean a few hundred-word tributes that clarify what your customer's life resembled before they discovered your item/administration, and what it resembles now.

In any event that you can collect enough veritable tributes, you will in a split second have the option to construct trust and compatibility and sell your items quickly.

**22. Track, track, and afterwards track some more**

Since you've connected with your internal fur garment wearing pimp, it's an ideal opportunity to communicate with you inward mountain man (or lady).

The last—and generally necessary—the key is to keep tabs on your development.

You have to know what's working and so forth.

This implies you have to set up singular presentation pages with the following pixels so you can see precisely which advertisements are producing snaps and which points of arrival are bringing about transformations. You have to follow all that you can. Evaluate advertisements with various duplicate, various hues, directed at multiple socioeconomics, and offering distinctive lead magnets. When you have found which components bring about the best, you can additionally streamline your advertisements for changes.

One significant thing to recall is that you have to ensure you run your promotions for an adequate measure of time before you roll out any improvements.

# CHAPTER SIX
# 11 TIPS TO IMPROVE YOUR FACEBOOK AD CONVERSIONS

---

The progressions Facebook made to its News Feed calculation prior this year imply that web-based life advertisers need to up their promotion game on the stage. Similar holds particularly valid for web-based social networking groups with little spending plans who have likely observed natural arrive at figures declining.

One of the most critical measurements social advertisers track on Facebook are transformation rates. Ordinarily, a transformation alludes to where a client changes over from being a program to a purchaser.

For some advertisers, changes are a top need. A decent change rate is perhaps the best proportion of progress and is critical to conveying a solid R.O.I.

Transformations are not just about driving buys. They are additionally about driving activities. Maybe the objective of a crusade is to expand pamphlet memberships or for customers to add items to a list of things to get. These activities can be viewed as transformation occasions.

Facebook positions as the main web-based life website for driving transformations, which makes making successful Facebook advertisements even more significant.

Follow these 11 hints to change over your next Facebook battle into a triumph.

**1. Characterize your transformation occasion**

Before you attempt to change over anybody, you ought to have an away from what activity you need individuals to take in the wake of seeing your promotion.

Sorts of transformations upheld by Facebook include see content, add to list of things to get, start checkout, and buy. You can likewise make custom change occasions on any off chance that you have different objectives as a main priority.

Try not to anticipate that one promotion should serve the entirety of your change objectives. Make separate advertisements for every goal, consider where these objectives fit into the buyer excursion and target likewise.

**2. Keep the goal in front of the psyche**

Promotion is just in the same class as its greeting page. At the point when you're figuring out where you'd like the transformation to occur, ensure you have everything set up to convey on your advertisement's guarantee.

Here are a couple of steps you should take to set up your point of arrival:

Execute the Pixel. When you've recognized the page where you'd like the change occasion to happen, you'll have to add the Facebook Pixel code to the page so as to follow the event. For additional on this, read Hootsuite's manual for utilizing the Facebook Pixel.

Focus on Continuity. In any event that your advertisement guarantees a specific something, ensure the greeting page conveys. You would prefer not to have a client searching for shoe land on a jeans item page. Plan and language should help through here, as well.

Streamline for Apps. Since an expanding number of individuals are available to buy on portable, you might need to drive individuals to your application. All things considered, ensure you register your request and coordinate with Facebook SDK.

**3. Make eye-getting visuals**

It takes just 2.6 seconds for a client's eye to pick where to arrive on a page. The utilization of eye-getting symbolism expands the odds their eyeballs will reach in your advertisement. Most initial introductions are educated by configuration, so treat visuals as you would a handshake.

Try not to over-burden pictures with content. Truth be told, Facebook prescribes you use message sparingly in movies, if by any means. Rather than swarming visuals with content, think about moving duplicate to the assigned content territory. In any event that you should incorporate content, utilize Facebook's Image Text Check device to get a rating.

Size to spec. Low-res visuals consider your image inadequately. Look at Hootsuite's convenient picture size manual to ensure your benefits meet the correct size determinations.

Use GIFs or recordings. Choose development over static symbolism to grab clients' consideration. Remember to test vertical records for cell phones.

**4. Keep duplicate quick and painless**

Fresh duplicate is frequently the second component of a substantial promotion, however on any off chance that there's something over the top, a client probably won't try to understand it.

Get individual. Utilizing individual pronouns like you and you recommend a connection among brand and crowd. Be that as it may, be, be cautious with "we." An ongoing report discovered "we" is better utilized with bringing customers back.

Keep away from language. Communicate in your crowd's writing, not a specialized vernacular nobody will comprehend.

Keep it brief. An excessive amount of content can be scary, so center around the fundamentals and scrap the rest—the Hemingway application assists with this.

**5. Incorporate an immediate source of inspiration**

Since changes are tied in with stimulating activities, a stable source of inspiration is fundamental. Trustworthy action words like the beginning, find, find, and investigate are incredible if your change objective is to have clients visit an item page or find out about your organization.

In any event that you will likely drive buys or memberships, be immediate with phrases like "purchase now" or "sign up."

Peruse more pointers on viable C.T.A.s.

**6. Widen your crowd**

While making an advertisement, select in to "focusing on extension," and Facebook will discover more clients like those you have indicated in the "enthusiasm focusing on the segment." Not just does this permit you to contact more individuals, it additionally can possibly drive more transformations at a lower cost for every change.

Remember that you can likewise make Custom Audiences. In any event that you have informational indexes, for example, an email endorser show, you can transfer it to Facebook to discover prior clients on Facebook.

Go above and beyond and utilize your custom crowds to recognize Lookalike Audiences, which are new clients that have similar profiles to your client base.

**7. Streamline for changes**

At this point you have a ton confirmed on your improved changes agenda, however, remember indeed to mark off the "transformations" box on Facebook. You'll discover this choice under the "Improvement for Delivery" area in the Budget and Schedule structure.

Choosing this streamlining strategy is discretionary. However, a couple of contextual investigations have demonstrated its viability. For instance, Save the Children tried both change enhanced advertisements and traffic-advanced promotions to decide the best method to empower gifts. Toward the finish of its time for testing the association found that

Advertisement improved for change created multiple times more gifts.

**8. Pick the correct advertisement position**

Contingent upon your battle objectives, specific Facebook promotion organizations may serve your requirements superior to other people.

For instance, Adidas discovered that utilizing video with Facebook's assortment highlight would be a decent organization to grandstand the numerous highlights of its Z.N.E. Road Trip Hoodie. Therefore, Adidas had the option to diminish cost-per-change by 43 per cent.

Here are some couple of interesting points while picking the correct organization:

Merry go round, and assortment advertisements are perfect when you have numerous items or different highlights to feature.

Facebook Offer advertisements permit you to communicate unique arrangements or limits you may use as buy impetuses. In any event that somebody visits the promotion, Facebook will send notices reminding them to recover.

Facebook Canvas advertisements are most appropriate for high-sway visuals and encounters that live well on full screen.

Get familiar with various Facebook advertisement types.

**9. Track over numerous gadgets**

Notwithstanding where you've decided your change occasion will happen, you should make a point to follow snaps and transformations from versatile to the work area. Regardless of whether your crusade is just proposed to run on the work area, Facebook suggests you introduce Facebook Software Development Kit on your versatile application (In any event that you have one). This will permit Facebook to catch more crowd information and grow the intended interest group.

**10. Consider interface click streamlining**

In case your promotion isn't driving enough transformations in the initial scarcely any days, Facebook might not have enough information to convey your advertisement appropriately. Facebook needs roughly 50 changes for every ad inside the initial seven days to carry the promotion viably.

To perceive what number of transformations you've counted, check the Ads Manager. On any off chance that you find that your advertisement has less than 50 changes, Facebook prescribes that you streamline for interface clicks rather than transformations.

**11. Convert your investigation into experiences**

Likewise, with any online life crusade, it's critical to painstakingly screen execution investigation and change as needs are. What worked and what didn't work? Observe for your next promotion battle and attempt to recreate your prosperity.

Become familiar with working with the Facebook investigation and the most critical measurements for social advertisers to follow.

Since you realize how to make a Facebook promotion upgraded for changes, you're prepared to find out about different techniques for web-based social networking publicizing. Whatever stage you're on, the standards of transformation are the equivalent: keep the experience transparent, immediate, steady, and luring.

# INSTRUCTIONS TO USE FACEBOOK LOOKALIKE AUDIENCES

Facebook Lookalike Audiences can assist you in finding your new best clients. It's an integral asset for better Facebook advertisement focusing on—drawing learnings about your best clients to see unique individuals who are likely as acceptable clients, as well.

Consider it a modern crowd relational arranger for advertisers. You reveal to Facebook what you like in a client, and Facebook a conveys another crowd fragment loaded up with possibilities that meet your criteria.

Prepared to discover the crowd you had always wanted? Peruse on to actually figure out how to make a Lookalike Audience for your Facebook advertisements, in addition to tips that will assist you with finding the best match.

Reward: Download a free guide that tells you the best way to set aside time and cash on your Facebook promotions. Discover how to arrive at the correct clients, bring down your expense pre-snap, and the sky is the limit from there.

**What are Facebook Lookalike Audiences?**

Facebook Lookalike Audiences can be utilized to contact individuals who are like your present clients. They increment the likelihood of producing great leads and offer more an incentive for advertisement spend.

Carbon copy Audiences are shaped dependent on source crowds. You can make a source crowd (otherwise called a seed crowd) utilizing information from:

- **Client Information.** A pamphlet membership list or a client record list. You can either transfer a .txt or .csv record or reorder your data.
- **Site Visitors**. To make a custom crowd dependent on-site guests, you have to have Facebook pixel introduced. With Pixel, you make a crowd of people of individuals who have visited your site, took a gander at an item page, finished a buy, and so forth.
- **Application action.** With dynamic Facebook SDK occasion following, application executives can gather information on the individuals who have introduced your application. There are 14 pre-characterized occasions that can be developed, for example, "added to the container" for retails applications, or "level accomplished" for game applications.
- **Commitment.** A commitment crowd is involved individuals who connected with your substance on Facebook or Instagram. Commitment occasions include video, first structure, canvas and assortment, Facebook page, Instagram business profile, and event.
- **Disconnected action.** You can make a rundown of individuals who collaborated with your business face to face, by telephone, or another detached station.

Various Lookalike Audiences can be utilized simultaneously for a similar advertisement crusade. You can likewise match Lookalike

Audiences with other promotion focusing on parameters, for example, age and sexual orientation or interests and practices.

**Instructions to utilize Facebook Lookalike Audiences**

**Stage 1:** From the Facebook Ads Manager, go to Audiences.

**Stage 2:** Click Create crowd and pick Lookalike Audience.

**Stage 3:** Choose your source crowd. Keep in mind, and this will be a custom crowd you've made from client data, Pixel or application information, or devotees of your page.

Note: Your source crowds need to contain at any rate of 100 individuals from a similar nation.

**Stage 4:** Select the nations or areas you might want to target. The countries you pick will figure out where individuals in your Lookalike Audience are based, including a geo-channel onto your Lookalike Audience.

Note: You don't must have anybody from the nation you need to focus on your source.

**Stage 5:** Choose your ideal crowd size. Size is communicated on a scale of 1-10. Littler numbers have a high likeness, and more significant amounts have a high reach. Facebook will furnish you with an expected range for the size you pick.

Note: It can take somewhere in the range of six and 24 hours for your Lookalike Audience to be done, yet you can even now continue to advertisement creation.

**Stage 6:** Create your advertisement. Go to the Adverts Manager and snap Tools, at that point Audiences, to check whether your Lookalike Audience is prepared. In any event that it is, select it and snap Create Advert.

Have a feeling that you have an idea about Lookalike Audiences? The video underneath broadly expounds.

**Nine hints for utilizing Facebook Lookalike Audiences**

Locate the correct source crowd and use these tips to contact new individuals on Facebook.

**1. Utilize the correct source crowd for your objectives**

Diverse custom crowds coordinate various goals.

For instance, if you will likely drive consciousness of your business, a Lookalike Audience dependent on your Page Fans might be a smart thought.

In any event that you will likely increment online deals, at that point, a Lookalike Audience dependent on-site guests will be a superior decision.

**2. Get innovative with Custom Audiences**

You can make custom crowds around an assortment of parameters. Drill down on the alternatives. that best line up with your battle objectives.

Thoughts for Custom Audiences include:

Video crowd. In case you're propelling a video-based battle, make a crowd of people dependent on individuals who have connected with your recordings previously.

Late site guests. All site guests might be excessively expansive of a rundown, mainly if transformations are your goal. Target individuals who may have visited your site in the previous 30 days, or guests who have placed something in their truck.

Email crowd. Pamphlet supporters are keen on getting news and arrangements for your business. Utilize this crowd to get more endorsers, or in case you're arranging a crusade with comparative substance.

**3. Test your Lookalike Audience size**

Consider distinctive crowd sizes for various battle objectives.

Littler crowds (1-5 on the scale) will most intently coordinate your custom crowd, while enormous crowds (6-10 on the size) will expand your possible capacity reach, however, decline the degree of likeness with your custom crowd. In case you're improving for similarity, focus on a little group. For range, go huge.

**4. Pick top notch information**

The better the information you give, the better the outcomes.

Facebook prescribes somewhere in the range of 1,000 and 50,000 individuals. In any case, a group of people of 500 steadfast clients with consistently perform superior to a crowd of people of 50,000 great, terrible, and regular clients.

Stay away from vast crowds like "all site guests" or "all application installers." These enormous crowds will incorporate incredible clients alongside the individuals who ricochet a little while later.

Focus on the measurements that decide your best clients. Frequently these are further down the change or commitment pipe.

**5. Stay up with the latest**

In case you're giving your own client data, ensure it's as present as could reasonably be expected. In case you're making a custom crowd with Facebook information, include date extend parameters.

For instance, in case you include a custom crowd-based site guests, you may just need to focus on the individuals who have visited your site in the last 30 to 90 days.

Clone crowds update progressively every three to seven days, so anybody new who visits will be added to your Lookalike Audience.

**6. Use Lookalike Audiences in the mix with different highlights**

Improve your carbon copy crowd focusing by including all the more focusing on parameters, for example, age, sexual orientation, or interests.

To dispatch its home theatre speaker, PLAYBASE, Sonos built up a multi-level battle that utilized Lookalike Audiences in blend with video advertisements, interface promotions, and Facebook dynamic advertisements. Stage one of the crusades focused on existing clients and new ones dependent on their inclinations, and stage two retargeted video watchers and Lookalike Audiences dependent on stage one commitment.

The one-two punch battle conveyed multiple times the arrival on promotion spend.

Make a point to exploit the hyper-focusing on capacities of Lookalike Audiences with great advertisements. Peruse our full manual for Facebook advertisement configurations and best practices.

**7. Streamline offers a lot of Lookalike Audiences**

Utilize your best crowd to portion Lookalike Audiences into non-covering levels.

To do this, click Advanced Options while choosing your crowd size. You can make up to 500 Lookalike Audiences from only one source crowd.

For instance, you could section a crowd of people dependent on the most comparative, second generally comparable, and least relative copies, and offer in like manner on each.

**8. Pinpoint the correct areas**

Carbon copy Audiences are an incredible method to target extension in new worldwide markets.

Regularly advertisers realize where they're searching for new acquisitions. On any off chance that worldwide mastery is your point (or you don't know where to center), consider making a Lookalike Audience in application store nations or developing markets.

Facebook will consistently organize similitude over the area. That implies your Lookalike Audience may not be equitably dispersed between your regions.

Shades retailer 9FIVE needed to stretch out their US battle to Canada and Australia, so it made a universal Lookalike Audiences dependent on current clients in the two nations. Advertisements were likewise fragmented per district and focused with one of a kind great promotions. They brought down expense per procurement by 40 per cent and accomplished 3.8 occasions the arrival on advertisement spend.

**9. Attempt the Customer Lifetime Value Option**

On any off chance that your business includes client exchanges and commitment that occur over a more drawn out timeframe, consider making a client lifetime esteem (LTV) custom crowd. Yet, regardless of whether not, Value-based Lookalike Audiences can help separate your large spenders from the not really enormous spenders since they factor in shopper CRM information.

To improve for its The Walking Dead: No Man's Land discharge, Next Games made a standard Lookalike Audience of paying application clients and a worth based Lookalike Audience. By correlation, the worth based crowd conveyed a 30 per cent better yield on promotion spend.

"We saw a deliberate inspire in execution when contrasting worth based Lookalike Audiences and standard Lookalike Audiences constructed utilizing indistinguishable seed crowds and would prescribe testing esteem based Lookalike Audiences," said Next Games

CMO, Saara Bergström.

# INSTRUCTIONS TO USE FACEBOOK LEAD ADS TO GROW YOUR BUSINESS

Facebook lead promotions can achieve an assortment of advertising targets, yet they're best at assisting with one of showcasing's brilliant guidelines: Know thy crowd.

Numerous advertisers think they know their crowd, however frequently mistake client information for client examination. In a generally online environment, it's anything but difficult to overlook that occasionally the ideal approach to find out about clients is to pose inquiries simply.

On any off chance that your targets incorporate statistical surveying, client criticism, or in any event, expanding transformations, Facebook lead promotions might be the correct arrangement. This guide will respond to the entirety of your inquiries concerning the advertisement group, including how to make a crusade and how to streamline for progress.

**What are Facebook lead promotions?**

Facebook lead advertisements are basically advanced structures. These structures permit advertisers to catch subtleties from clients while offering chances to the interface, for example, pamphlet memberships, demo demands, or challenge enlistment.

At any point when somebody taps on a lead advertisement, they gave a structure that is pre-populated with data from their Facebook profile. The rest can be finished in a couple of simple taps.

A significant property about lead promotions is that they are upgraded for versatile. That is key for Facebook's 88 per cent portion of versatile clients, mainly since it ordinarily takes 40 per cent longer to finish frames on the work area.

Another bit of leeway Facebook lead age advertisements offers is that produced leads can be synchronized legitimately with your organization's client relationship the executive's framework or downloaded as a.CSV document. This permits advertisers to catch up more productively, which is essential for finalizing the negotiations.

**The most effective method to make a Facebook lead advertisement in 10 stages**

Here are the main means by which to set up Facebook first age advertisements, bit by bit.

1. Go to Ads Manager.
2. In Ads, Manager click Create in the upper left corner.
3. Pick Lead age as your goal and name your battle.
4. Pick the Page you intend to use for the lead promotion. Snap View Terms and afterwards consent to the Facebook Lead Ads terms and conditions after you've understood them.
5. Pick your intended interest group, arrangements, spending plan, and timetable. Note: Lead promotions can't be focused on individuals younger than 18.

6. Select your lead promotion designs. You can choose merry go round, a single picture, video, or slideshow.
7. Include your feature, body duplicate, and a source of inspiration. A window on the correct offers a review of your advertisement as you make it.
8. Look down and click Contact Form. Here you can include a structure title, include an introduction, questions, your organization's protection approach, and a thank you screen.

- **Introduction:** Use this segment to clarify why individuals should round out your structure plainly.
- **Custom inquiries:** There are two kinds of surveys you can pick: Standard questions (i.e. sexual orientation, work title) and custom inquiries. Pose custom inquiries that relate to your business, for instance: "When are you hoping to purchase another vehicle?" Up to 15 surveys can be incorporated. A few governments bar sponsors from mentioning specific data
- **Structure type:** Under Form Type, you can choose: More volume or higher purpose. Pick more quantity if your battle objective is to get the structure finished by whatever number individuals as could be allowed. Choosing a higher aim adds a stage to your structure that permits individuals to survey and affirm their information before they hit submit. This is a decent choice if your goal is to do what needs to be done.
- **Protection approach:** Facebook lead promotions require a

connection to your organization's security strategy. Ensure you have a page on your business site.

- **Much obliged to your screen**: This screen will show up after the structure is submitted. You can likewise incorporate a source of inspiration or download interface here.

**9**. Snap Settings under the name of your structure and watch that you might want to gather natural leads. This propelled step is discretionary, however, prescribed. You can likewise change the language of your structure here.

**10.** Snap Finish in the upper right corner. Survey your promotion from Ads Manager, and when you're prepared to distribute, click Confirm.

When you've made an advertisement, you can get to leads through client framework reconciliation, usage of the Facebook Marketing API, or by manual download.

Facebook likewise permits promoters to gather drives utilizing Facebook Instant Experience structures.

**Tips for making Facebook lead promotions that convert**

**Offer a motivating force.**

Individuals are all the more ready to impart their own data to you on any off chance that you offer something consequently. Regardless of whether it's a promotion code or a free download, a great motivation shows clients you esteem their data.

- Famous motivating force models include:
- Get arrangements and offers
- Participate in sweepstakes and challenges
- Get item tests
- Go to an occasion
- Pre-request items
- Download studies and whitepapers

**Be clear about your offer.**

Offer your incentive forthright with the goal that individuals comprehend what they are pursuing. While discretionary, Facebook suggests you remember this data for your limited time duplicate and in the presentation toward the start of your structure. Additionally, include marking all through the experience, so there isn't any uncertainty about who individuals are offering their information.

It's additionally essential to pick symbolism that bolsters your informing. For example, the purpose of-deals frameworks supplier Revel Systems tried diverse inventive for its lead promotion battle and discovered pictures with the item as a point of convergence were significantly more powerful.

**Utilize convincing substance and arrangements**

Much the same as some many other Facebook advertisements, lead promotions best served when the medium fits the message. For example, In any event, that you need to grandstand various items or highlights, maybe a merry go round configuration is the best decision. A short video, then again, is a decent organization for narrating and expanding brand mindfulness.

Try not to expect that since you're offering a motivator innovative doesn't make a difference. Incorporate great pictures and recordings, sharp duplicate, and a CTA button for best outcomes. You can discover lead promotion structure specs here.

**Keep your structure straightforward.**

It's straightforward: The simpler your structure is to round out, the higher your finishing rate will be as indicated by Facebook, with each question you include, the possibility of somebody deserting the structure increments.

Just request the most critical data. In any event that your structure incorporates numerous decision questions, limit the number of decisions somewhere in the range of three and four.

**Pose the correct inquiries**

On any off chance that Facebook's given questions don't address your issues, you can make custom inquiries for your structure. Pick between short answer, different decision and contingent questions, which change depending on how a past inquiry was replied.

Your structure can likewise incorporate Store Locator and Appointment Scheduling fields which let individuals scan for a close-by area or calendar visits.

Need assistance conceptualizing questions? Facebook's rubric of business objectives and models is a decent spot to begin.

**Focus on the correct crowd**

Your intended interest group ought to line up with your lead advertisement's goals. There are three essential crowd types you can browse:

- **Carbon copy crowds:** If you likely grow your client base, make a Lookalike Audience displayed off of your most critical clients so as to discover comparative clients. Become familiar with how to utilize carbon copy crowds.
- **Individuals close to you:** If you have at least one areas and your record is overseen by a Facebook delegate, you can utilize the business locator highlight and target promotions to individuals in the scope of your stores. This crowd section is perfect if your point is to plan arrangements, demos, or basically urge clients to visit.
- **Custom crowds**: Examples of custom crowds can incorporate individuals who are bought into your pamphlet, late site and application guests, or individuals in your CRM.

**Plan to development**

A quick follow-up can fundamentally improve the odds of a transformation. Also, the faster you do it, the better. A milestone study distributed in Harvard Business Review found that organizations that reach clients inside an hour are multiple times bound to make sure about qualified leads.

Remember that informing applications are currently buyers' favored method to associate with brands. 66% of clients rank telling in front of the telephone, live visit, and up close and personal correspondences. Possibly it's the ideal opportunity for your business to jump onto Facebook Messenger. Also, obviously, in any event, that you need to know your client's favored time and methods for correspondence, remember to inquire.

**Test and streamline**

The best lead promotions are regularly the consequence of A/B testing and calibrating. Consider running two lead promotions with various symbolism or duplicate. Or then again have a go at running lead promotions with different structure lengths to gauge finishing rates.

**Six effective Facebook lead advertisement models from brands**

Here are some Facebook lead promotion guides to move your next battle

**LA Auto Show: Fueling pass deals**

The LA Auto Show ran numerous Facebook advertisement battles to advance its marquee occasion. However, lead promotions were essential for firing up interests. To discover auto lovers and increment ticket deals, LA Auto Show made a lead promotion crusade focused on a carbon copy crowd like the individuals who had just bought tickets on the web.

The lead advertisements offered a ticket rebate motivating force for the individuals who presented the structure. Furthermore, basically, LA Auto Show agents followed up to finish the business, adding to a 37 percent expansion in online ticket deals contrasted and the earlier year.

**Hubble Contacts: Clear market bits of knowledge**

To advertise enthusiasm for moderate expendable, contact focal points, Hubble Contacts utilized lead promotions to make a straightforward signup structure. All the organization requested was for individuals to present their pre-populated email address In any event that they were keen on finding out additional.

While the organization hadn't propelled at this point, these bits of knowledge assumed an essential job in raising financing. "The information from this crusade was vital to raising a USD 3.7 million seed connect before dispatch, which gave us the cash-flow to lean intensely into showcasing from the very beginning," said Co-CEO Jesse Horowitz.

At the point when Hubble propelled had the option to utilize its email rundown to make advertisements upgraded for transformations.

**Revel Systems: Optimizing pays off**

With the objective of creating more client leads for its place of-deals framework, Revel Systems tried lead advertisements against interface promotions that guided individuals to a crusade point of arrival.

Early outcomes indicated that the in-application lead advertisement design prompted multiple times the measure of leads and a 74 per cent lower cost for each point. The organization likewise tried various pictures, finding that movies that concentrated on the item performed better.

**Generali Thailand: Ensuring better reactions**

To improve its reaction time to new client inquiries, individual insurance agency Generali Thailand ran a first advertisement battle that coordinated leads with its CRM the executive's framework.

The pre-populated structures and mechanized assortment of client data helped remove the weight from deals group specialists, helping them recognize and react to new inquiries quicker. By following up on Facebook leads inside 24 hours, Generali Thailand saw a 2.5x increment in deals transformations.

**Myra: Slimming down testing costs**

The UL Skin Sciences brand Myra is a significant brand in the Philippines and had the option to develop its national client base through contribution tests disconnected. To build its business on the web and diminish costs, Myra went to Facebook lead promotions.

Utilizing clone and custom crowds, the magnificence brand focused on a current client base and another certified client portion. The crusade had the option to make sure about 110,000 recruits at a 71 per cent lower cost for each signup rate.

**Genuine Madrid: Scoring leads in new markets**

Champions League soccer group Real Madrid has a devoted fan base on Facebook, and a significantly more grounded one disconnected. To overcome any issues and develop its base in nations with low commitment, the club propelled a progression of lead promotions.

It was streamlining assumed a significant job in the three-month crusade through a progression of A/B tests that analyzed crowds, imaginative, and positions. Toward the finish of the apportioned period, the club created an astounding 2.4 million leads and had the option to accomplish a 70 per cent decline in cost per lead.

# TOP 25 BENEFITS OF FACEBOOK ADVERTISING AND WHY YOU SHOULD BE USING FACEBOOK ADVERTISING

---

**Need to know the advantages of Facebook publicizing?**

This rundown of Facebook promoting advantages will take your breath away. You will be appreciative you understood this.

This is your admonition to take care of your promoting system to obtain clients. You are committing a colossal error In any event that you are not utilizing the entirety of the advantages of Facebook publicizing. In any event that you're as of now persuaded you to need Facebook advertising for your business, at that point, get in touch with us here. On any off chance that not, at that point, continue perusing and most likely, you'll understand the main advantages Facebook publicizing can have for your business.

You are losing cash each day if your business isn't promoting on Facebook. Here's the reason:

**1. Your clients invest the vast majority of their energy on Facebook**

We should begin with the realities. 80% of all Internet clients use Facebook. And Indeed, even 65% of grown-ups beyond 65 years old use Facebook. Its has billions of clients, and a large portion of them check their Facebook page on various occasions every day. Also, despite who your clients are, they are utilizing Facebook. What's more, they use it consistently. Consequently, also one of the most significant advantages of Facebook publicizing is that your clients use it day by day.

**2. Facebook publicizing is the most focused on the type of promoting**

A significant advantage of Facebook advertising is its capacity to contact your accurate crowd. Facebook is actually the most concentrate on the kind of advertising. And You can publicize to individuals by age, interests, conduct, and area. On any off chance that you truly know your clients, and you can also utilize Facebook promoting to connect with them.

**3. Facebook Advertising which is the least expensive type of promoting** well Another significant advantage of Facebook advertising, is that it is perhaps the least costly type of publicizing. Also, You can actually burn through $5 and contact 1,000 individuals. And It doesn't bode well to spend more in radio promotions, TV plugs, bulletins, and other conventional media to reach a similar crowd.

**4. Facebook publicizing is quick**

Facebook advertising is immediate. It drives quick outcomes. You can begin arriving at a large number of individuals today. So on any off chance that you are searching for a fast method to drive traffic and changes, Facebook promoting is the best arrangement.

**5. Facebook promoting expands brand mindfulness**

Facebook promoting will fundamentally assemble your image mindfulness. It is an incredible method to make individuals mindful of what you bring to the table. Also, the more comfortable individuals are with your image. Also, it is almost certain they will buy most of your items when the time has come to settle on a choice.

**6. Facebook publicizing expands site traffic**

Facebook publicizing will actually help your site traffic. Also, you can run a site click crusade to focus on your crowd and send them to your site. While you can build your site traffic through various sources, the exactness and cost-adequacy of Facebook publicizing make it more advantageous than different sources.

**7. Facebook promoting builds income, deals, and leads**

Facebook advertising isn't a legend. It really drives revenue, sales, and leads. The following is a screen capture of a business that burned through $519.87 in Facebook promotions and produced $1,557.50 in deals. All things considered, they burned through $3.42 per transformation. Peruse how web-based life can expand sales here.

Looks great right? The appalling part is that it is challenging to build deals through Facebook publicizing. It requires some investment and experience. You sometimes can without much of a stretch waste a large number of dollars and not perceive any arrival on your speculation. Along these lines, we emphatically prescribe putting resources into a web-based life promoting administration or contract a Facebook publicizing expert. Internet-based life-promoting costs for proficient administration ordinarily run from $400-$800/month. Along these lines, it is more practical to enlist an expert organization than to procure a representative.

**8. Facebook promoting is quantifiable**

There is no speculating with Facebook advertising. The outcomes are measurable. Also, the numbers will represent itself with no issue. You will have the option to perceive what number of impressions, snaps, and changes you are getting. So as to follow transformations, also you should introduce change pixels on your site to support the movement. And This is something that your Facebook publicizing pro will assist you.

**9. Facebook promoting expands your client attribution**

Facebook developing will expand your client attribution. Attribution is on various occasions your crowd sees your image. The more times they collaborate with your business, the more probable they will change over. Facebook publicizing will assist you with expanding your touch focuses with your crowd and prompts more changes later on.

**10. Facebook publicizing can bring down your expense per securing**

In any event that you can get Facebook publicizing to work for your business, it will probably diminish you're ensuring costs. Since Facebook promoting is so modest, you can remove a portion of the other costly publicizing efforts you are put resources.

**11. Facebook promoting can drive disconnected deals**

Facebook promoting can, likewise drive disjointed sales. Vast numbers of our customers who are running Facebook advertisements see higher in-store traffic subsequent to working with us. Also, A portion of your clients will probably observe your ads on Facebook, visit your site, and visit your area on any off chance that they trust your answer.

**12. Facebook promoting can draw in your site guests**

Have you at any point try and visited a site and saw their Facebook promotion not long after? Also, this is a promoting strategy called remarketing. Remarketing permits you to promote to late site guests. This implies In any event that somebody visits your site, and doesn't buy or get in touch with you, also you can reconnect them with Facebook promoting. This is an immense advantage that can significantly support your transformations.

**13. Facebook publicizing can drive rehash business**

Facebook promoting can actually drive rehash business from clients who have bought from you previously. Utilizing their crowds include, you can import your client messages into your Facebook publicizing effort. This will permit you to advertise straightforwardly to the group that is well on the way to purchase from you.

**14. Facebook promoting constructs commitment**

Facebook supports the constructs commitment with your intended interest group. Determination comprises of the preferences, remarks, and collaborations on your promotions. Commitment is significant in light of the fact that it connotes a more grounded association with your intended interest group. Also As individuals draw in with your image, a roundabout association is being created. The more drew in your crowd is, the more grounded your association is with them. And The more associated they are to your business, the almost certain they will change over. Putting into online networking, the executives can likewise significantly build your commitment.

**15. Facebook publicizing expands verbal exchange and referrals**

well, The social part of Facebook advertising improves it than some that another type of promoting that exists. Facebook notices can circulate around the web. On any off chance that your promotions are contacting the opportune individuals, and they will probably impart it to a companion. Also, the capacity to spread verbal exchange and referrals will be a vast advantage your business can profit by utilizing Facebook publicizing.

**16. Facebook promoting can assist you with building your email list**

Facebook promoting can fuel your email showcasing endeavors. You can also use Facebook's "lead promotion" structures to catch email contacts through Facebook advertisements. Also, you can likewise guide traffic to an outside structure on your site to construct your email list.

**17. Facebook publicizing can develop your blog traffic**

A blog moves no place without traffic. You can utilize Facebook promoting to open your blog to the majority and produce moment traffic. And Through promoting your blog, you can acquire trust and believability with your crowd. Online journals are an extraordinary method to assemble a more profound association with your group. What's more, you can utilize Facebook promoting to connect the association between your blog and traffic.

**18. Facebook promoting can expand your SEO rankings**

Web crawlers depend on common signs to rank sites. Common symptoms comprise of the action on your online networking content. This movement incorporates offers, likes, and remarks on your posts. Facebook promoting can assist you with expanding your social signs, which will, by implication, impact your SEO rankings.

**19. Facebook promoting can assist you with breaking into new markets**

Facebook promoting can help you with venturing into new markets. In any event that you are putting up another item or administration for sale to the public, also you can utilize Facebook publicizing to build its introduction. Facebook promoting will assist you in testing the market at your own pace.

**20. Facebook publicizing is ongoing**

Facebook advertising is continuing. You can also take a gander at your battle constant. Also, on any off chance that you are discontent with the outcomes, you can make acclimations to your crusade right away.

This is preposterous with different types of promoting. In any event that you put resources into radio promotions, TV advertisements, or print media, you can't change your ad quickly. In any event that you don't get results. Also, You should do what needs to be done and assume the misfortune. Facebook promoting can assist you in cutting your mishaps promptly and make changes in accordance with acquiring transformations.

**21. Your rivals are utilizing Facebook promoting**

Your competitors are actually using Facebook encouraging to develop their business. You are making it more straightforward for them by not utilizing Facebook promoting to contact your crowd. In any event that you are not using internet publicizing to develop your business, you won't have a company soon. In any event that your clients invest the majority of their energy in online life.

**22. Facebook promoting can give you an edge on more prominent organizations**

Facebook promoting can be the secondary passage you use to squash the more significant rivalry. You don't need to stress over enormous contenders driving up the expense of publicizing as you would with Google AdWords. It is merely you and your crowd. For whatever length any time that your advertisements are pertinent, your promotions will probably perform proficiently with Facebook publicizing.

**23. Facebook promoting is versatile.**

Versatile is the fate of on the web. And Half of all Internet clients are portable. Also, over 84% of Facebook clients get to Facebook from a cell phone. Also, Truth be told, Facebook is one of the most prominent portable applications that exist today. In any event that you are following the patterns of publicizing, Facebook promoting won't bomb you. You can help your crowd on the gadgets they utilize each day.

As per the most recent figures discharged this last quarter of 2019, it has been declared that Facebook has again accomplished another achievement. This monster online life arrange has now over 2.7 billion months to month clients.

The reality half of these clients sign in with their cell phones. Honestly, that is in excess of a billion-potential crowd and purchasers for your business.

**24. Facebook publicizing is more viable than (natural Facebook is practically dead)**

The times of natural Facebook advertising are finished. There is nothing of the sort as natural Facebook advertising. To be effective, and you should utilize Facebook publicizing. Also, regardless of whether you are building a network of devotees, you will probably need to use Facebook publicizing to develop your locale. On any off chance that you are posting content, you will possibly use elevated presents on contact more individuals. Facebook advertising is an unquestionable requirement if your field-tested strategies to adjust a standard procedure.

**25. Facebook promoting is spending plan inviting (set your financial limit)**

Facebook publicizing is spending plan agreeable. You are in charge of your predetermination. You can set a day by day or lifetime spending plan.

In any case, here and there this through and through freedom can cause issues down the road for you. In any event that you underspend, you may not get enough presentation to really spend. Also, On any off chance that you overspend on an inappropriate promotion crusade, you can squander a large number of dollars. Utilize a Facebook publicizing administration to abstain from burning through valuable cash and time to acquire deals.

**26. Facebook promoting is most savvy publicizing speculation you can make**

Facebook is the savviest developing venture any business can make. The advantages of Facebook supporting are perpetual. Also, You can twofold, triple, or fourfold your business development with Facebook publicizing. It's less expensive than pretty much every elective wellspring of promoting. Focusing on choices are more exact than the rest. And You can target past clients, site guests, and explicit socioeconomics. Also, you can expand your touch focuses with your crowd, increase mindfulness, and ascribe to changes later on.

In any event that you have confidence in the advantages of Facebook promoting, at that point, begin putting resources into an expert Facebook publicizing effort today. Timetable a call to talk about your promoting needs.

**Conclusion**

You likely need to begin immediately, since you've perused this guide on the most proficient method to advance your advertisements on Facebook Ads. I think Facebook gets neglected some of the time nowadays since it's become the older adult of web-based life. By this I mean there are consistently more up to date, more cooling, hotter systems springing up.

In any case, Facebook isn't going anyplace at any point in the near future. What's more, by following the exact recipe, you can capitalize on an enormous level of those leads and convert them into clients. This procedure isn't simple. Your eagerness to apply every one of these tips will be essential in your excursion to the highest point of your Facebook item advertisements venture. It's everything about giving new things and calculating a shot what works best for you when you oversee Facebook Ads for max results. Make a point to recall that your objectives should manage you. What's more, your goals can vary from the purposes of different distributors That is superbly fine. Try not to attempt to purchase an equation or a formula from another person since you may not get similar outcomes and neglect to get extraordinary Facebook Ads which convert like enchantment. You simply need to get the traffic, break down it, split, overcome, and scale-up. Try not to be reluctant to test! Draw out the thrill-seeker in you.

**Learn, study, be committed and consistently check the most recent instances of Facebook Ads with the goal that you receive present and demonstrated strategies for super focused on Facebook Ads! Intensive streamlining is the contrast among**

**beginners and professionals.**

**Thank you again buying this book!**

**I hope you liked it.**

# INSTAGRAM MARKETING

**Discover Instagram Secrets To Build Your Personal Brand, Create Thousands Of Followers, Find Tons Of New Customers And Expand Your Business To A New Level**

**Edward Keller**

assurance.

The trademarks that are used are without any consent, and the publication of the trademark is without permission or backing by the trademark owner. All trademarks and

brands within this book are for clarifying purposes only and are the owned by the owners

themselves, not affiliated with this document

# INTRODUCTION

Instagram marketing strategy is the first step for anyone who wants to use this network to promote a company or even their personal brand. With the growth of this network many brands have been looking for Instagram as an alternative for the promotion of their products and services.

For example, fashion, health, beauty and tourism are sectors that cannot be left out of Instagram, since they are the "heart" of this network and therefore consider a perfect way to get leads.

Therefore it is necessary for the company to brace itself first of all by creating a marketing plan on Instagram, before running around publishing something and hoping for any response. We both realize it doesn't work this way.

The first step in building an Instagram marketing strategy is to understand the very concept of social media marketing, which has very different characteristics from other digital marketing strategies.

Social media marketing is relationship-based, meaning you first build rapport with your followers and fans, and then subtly present your business proposition. So this is a medium strategy and so you need to start now and then reap the rewards later. There is no immediate result in social media marketing.

The marketing on Instagram , whether personal or corporate, subject to its own rules and understand these rules and network characteristics is essential to your marketing strategy.

Instagram is by definition an entertainment medium. Therefore, your business approach should be to display, that is, to be in the right place for the right people, without interfering with the natural conversation of the network.

As with any other social media platform, when designing an Instagram marketing strategy you must clearly determine what your main goals are with your brand presence on this channel.

The marketing on Instagram does not work or works very little in some situations, such as direct selling, for example. Therefore, your proposal should be to create an alternative to your other online marketing strategies.

By clearly determining your goals, you will be able to select your metrics and make a really technical measurement of the results. It is not for any other reason that in our Instagram Course, we put this issue right between the first training modules.

Another interesting feature of Instagram is that it is extremely demanding in terms of content. In our social media marketing course, I always say that content is the main tool in this area, and Instagram would be no different.

A marketing strategy on Instagram differs greatly from people using the tool. While in private use, we do not have much concern with the sequence of actions, in the case of corporate use, everything needs to be thought of.

This is why it is important that you study the posts of companies in your area that stand out on Instagram to understand your competition and also to see how your audience reacts to these posts.

Images - Always work with unique and innovative images. No need to go around taking beaten images to put in your publications, because they don't work, just because they are already "part of the landscape".

Texts - Invest heavily in creating interaction-generating text, with thought-provoking link baits and strong call-to-action, so that your posts can achieve their goal of building rapport with their followers.

Hastags - Hashtags play a major role within an Instagram marketing strategy, so create your own to achieve greater reach and also monitor the most popular hastags.

Content is largely responsible for interactions on Instagram, so believing that the brand can succeed in this area without proper care in pre-preparing this content is a waste of time.

Instagram, even more so than other social media like Facebook and Twitter, is a conversation environment, so you will need to have an interaction structure, otherwise all the attempts to create a marketing campaign for Instagram would be lost.

People comment and ask questions in your publications, and it is very important for you to create the relationship ties we mentioned in the first item of this article that you are ready to interact with these comments and questions.

The person responsible for these interactions will need to be fully aligned with the Instagram Marketing strategy designed by your team, otherwise the conversion potential of these interactions may be lost, or worse the brand may end up in a social media crisis.

We all realize that Facebook is completely integrated with Instagram, and it makes complete sense to combine your marketing plan with your Facebook marketing strategy to build a connection between them in digital marketing.

Not because you are trying to duplicate everything you do on Instagram, on the Facebook app, which would be a huge mistake, but to have these two resources communicate with each other, with the intention of improving each.

As for every other form of online advertisement, there is only one way for you to evaluate the effectiveness of an Instagram marketing plan: creating a successful conversion monitoring system.

One of Instagram's big issues is precisely the absence of ties in paying articles, they're only included in advertising. As a consequence, most traffic management strategies focused on Google Analytics, such as UTM Tagging, are significantly compromised.

Therefore, via similar Landing Pages sent in response to your experiences, you will need to build a differentiated tracking framework so you can monitor incoming leads created on Instagram in your Conversion funnel.

Instagram is not only a way of sharing pretty pictures. It can be used creatively and can become a really powerful communication device.

You will recognize future customers as the main visual medium, and create a more interactive partnership through photos, videos and stories.

Instagram's focus is turning even further into advertisement, as seen by the platform's new releases. In September 2017 Instagram revealed it had hit 800 million followers, a landmark recognizing there were 200 million users only three years earlier. More than 52 million photographs and videos are released per day, while 300 million people utilize stories per day.

Single month 11.8 million users sign into France (statistics for 2018). According to figures, 41 percent of consumers are between the ages of 16 and 24, 35 percent are between the ages of 25 and 34, 17 percent are between the ages of 35 and 44 and 8 percent are aged 45 and above.

In short, Instagram can be an incredibly effective platform for your brand to grow. More than 60% of app consumers claim they have found a new product or service on this social network already.

These numbers are quite impressive, I've always been questioned about Instagram's importance to your company. So, I decided to write this article to address the question: do you really need an Instagram account to expand your company?

Instagram expanded quite rapidly. Founded in 2010, in February 2013, it exceeded 100 million active users, and in March 2014, 200 million. In September 2017, it developed steadily hitting more than 800 million active users every month. Among such people, 500 million make regular use of their account. During 2017, this number experienced stratospheric growth: from 150 million average users in January 2017 to 200 million in April and 500 million in Sep.

31 per cent of Americans making more than $75,000 are on Instagram According to 2016 survey statistics from Pew Poll, almost a third of rich Americans use Instagram.

In particular, it is calculated that: 38 percent of those earning less than $30,000 use Instagram 32 percent of those earning between $30,000 and $74,999 use Instagram 31 percent of those earning more than $75,000 use Instagram This number is quite important for businesses marketing medium profile items. In reality, the most active age group on Instagram is between the ages of 18 and 29. Many of these people are minors, or new staff. They might not yet have a large salary, of course, but this is the category most likely to invest on posts sponsored by influencers in Instagram.

Marketing Instagram utilized by 70.7 per cent of businesses. This is another statistic that indicates the speed with which Instagram is growing. In 2013, 11.5% of US companies used Instagram for marketing purposes. This percentage rose to 18.4% in 2014, 32.3% in 2015 and 48.8% in 2016. In 2017, this statistic reached 70.7%, surpassing Twitter, which was present in 2017 of 67, 2%.

From children to companies, hipsters, models and football players, everyone uses Instagram. It's the social network of the moment. Anyone using it may wish to expand their account and often organic traffic is no longer enough.

By removing the unorthodox methods available (for example, the use of bots or the purchase of subscribers), sponsoring its publications with the platform can be the most effective and sustainable strategy in terms of costs.

Instagram has become a kind of "golden egg hen" for Mark Zuckerberg and his company. Over the last 24 months, changes on this platform and especially on the advertising side have improved the system to make it consistent with the business needs of users.

As with Facebook, companies have the ability to target audiences very precisely to provide advertising. In addition, Instagram provides highly accurate management statistics to better control campaigns and achieve better results.

In short, Instagram advertising is a very effective way to show your products in front of people who do not know you yet and who are likely to like your products and therefore, to buy them.

How does advertising work on Instagram?

Unlike simple use, the Instagram advertising world at first is not intuitive. Especially for those who have never had to do with Facebook ads or online advertising in general

Advertising on social networks follows different logic of traditional advertising. First, after creating and publishing a sponsored post, the platform must approve it. It may decide to refuse it at any time if it does not comply with the rules on online advertising.

Then, the appearance of the ads is based on an auction system, for which the price, performance, or type of action you want to get from the recipient of the ad may vary over time. In general, for the sponsored publication to function properly, it must be as close as possible to those displayed on social media in an organic context far removed from a conventional print poster or page.

On Instagram, it is possible to sponsor content using several tools and many types of ads. As far as the tools are concerned, the photographic social network offers the possibility of creating advertisements both via its official application and via advanced tools such as Facebook Ads. Instagram also offers different types of ads, some more interesting than others, for those who need to promote their business.

If you already downloaded the application to your smartphone and got your Facebook account as registration data, or if you generated new credentials to access your new profile, stop here and see how to optimize please.

Basics about Instagram accounts

What everyone doesn't know when they decide to follow a sales strategy with a presence on Instagram is that this social network was originally designed to share images, and text has a place.

This doesn't mean it's impossible to implement a sales strategy on Instagram, but in that case you need to know tricks and practices to attract traffic that not everyone knows.

For example, to attract traffic to a website or a specific URL, you must do the following:

See the highlighted links you have in bios in your publication so that your followers can visit it.

Be sure to use the Instagram links correctly because you use dedicated

Use #hashtags mostly to indicate your brands to increase visibility and reach more people.

Share a mini video introducing news on the website.

Unleash your imagination and share a clickable Instagram story that hooks the community from the start.

Instagram offers many possibilities for optimization and content creation in various formats, but you should be aware of the following restrictions:

Characters: The career limit is 29-150, but you can write a maximum of 2,200 for comments and text accompanying a post.

Tags: You cannot tag more than 20 people per post.

Hashtag: Up to 30 per post (never from a third party).

Follow-up: 200 follow and unfollow per hour.

Comments: 60 per hour.

Like: I like 100 other posts per hour.

Automation: Until very recently, this was not possible with external tools. Well, you may schedule publications from some of the most famous tools such as Hootsuite and SocialFlow in a somewhat less restrictive way.

Tag people you don't know or comment and like using an automated application! Please respect the restrictions that may cause you to lose your Instagram account labeled as a spammer.

Do not abuse the hashtag of each publication. Also, do not combine this practice with including additional comments.

Never forcibly get followers in a short time, like buying followers or following / unfollowing.

For developing organizations, it's essential to use the majority of the amazing advertising channels accessible without extending your financial limit excessively far, and web-based social networking is turning into a go-to. As the quickest developing online life stage, Instagram offers a broad scope of promoting apparatuses that can be used to target specific gatherings with profoundly viable advertisement types.

https://www.audible.co.uk/pd/B08BPHQNNR/?source_code=AUKFrDlWS02231890H6-BK-ACX0-202801&ref=acx_bty_BK_ACX0_202801_rh_uk

# CHAPTER ONE

## LEARN ABOUT YOUR COMPETITION AND ATTRACT THEIR FOLLOWERS TO YOUR BRAND

---

Competitive research is the foundation of a solid marketing strategy. All things considered, if you can't identify your competitors and their marketing strategies, you'll fight to differentiate yourself and your item from the group.

In any case, how do advertisers identify their essential competitors and their techniques? Here is our five-advance strategy for how to identify your competitors, inquire about your opposition and channel it into amazing marketing that meets your client's needs.

Step by step instructions to Find Your Competitors

Observing your competitors doesn't need to charge or be confounded. The initial step to finding your competitors is to differentiate between your immediate and roundabout challenges.

What's the difference between immediate and backhanded competitors?

Your immediate competitors are organizations or distributers who sell, or market similar items being provided through your business. Your clients will often assess both you and your immediate competitors before settling on a buy choice or when deciding to change over.

Conversely, your aberrant competitors are those organizations or distributers that don't sell or market similar items, yet are in rivalry with your business nonetheless. They may compose a similar kind of substance as you and be viewing for similar watchwords. To put it plainly, they are going after your clients' attention.

The key to figuring out how to identify your competitors is having the option to recognize your roundabout and direct challenge.

As you create your marketing strategy, you should know about both your backhanded and your immediate challenge. How about we talk about three different ways to identify both your immediate and backhanded competitors

The most effective method to Identify Direct Competitors

When identifying competitors who are in direct challenge to your business, you'll need to begin with your item. An intensive comprehension of your item and the worth it gives to your group of spectators or clients is crucial to identifying your immediate challenge.

If you work for a tennis shoe brand, for instance, you are not just in rivalry with other tennis shoe brands. You're additionally in rivalry with enormous shoe retailers, and some other brands or businesses that are making footwear. Just by taking a look at your item and assessing its worth, you will then understand the full extent of your opposition.

A couple of powerful methods for identifying direct competitors:

1. Statistical surveying

Investigate the market for your item and assess which different organizations are selling an item that would rival yours. Converse with your business group and discover which competitors they see come up often in their business analysis. From that point, you'll have the option to investigate those organizations, their item and marketing endeavors, and develop plans to beat them.

2. Request Customer Feedback

Once more, your clients are the way to identify your immediate competitors. When they've settled on your business and item, you can ask them which different businesses/items they were assessing. Clients often uncover sudden competitors that weren't even on your radar.

Likewise, during the business planning, your business group can likewise ask your potential clients which businesses they are thinking about. If they haven't settled on your item yet, your group will have the option to address their needs better if you know which businesses or items they are thinking about.

3. Check Online Communities on Social Media or Community Forums

Nowadays, your potential clients will often search out counsel and suggestions via web-based networking media destinations and applications or on network discussions like Quora or Reddit. By researching the discussions your clients have on these sites, you'll have the option to further identify your competitors.

This is particularly valid for advertisers addressing millennial spectators. Research by Deloitte demonstrates that half of twenty to thirty years old report that a suggestion from a companion or relative impacts their purchasing choice. Also, 27% of both recent college grads and Gen Z feel an online suggestion from somebody in their web-based life circle affects their purchasing choices.

Contingent upon your intended interest group, internet-based life can help as you figure out how to identify your competitors.

Be that you already know enough about your immediate competitors. Shouldn't something be said about the competitors you don't think about yet? How would you identify your circuitous competitors?

Step by step instructions to Identify Indirect Competitors

Your backhanded competitors have the same amount of impact on your selling procedure as your immediate competitors. Because your backhanded competitors are often composing substance that rivals yours, they have a considerably more prominent impact on potential clients in the beginning times of the purchaser's adventure. So how would you find them?

1. Catchphrase Research

Catchphrase research is the most ideal approach to identify your challenge. By directing an aggressive SEO investigation, you can figure out which businesses or distributers are viewing for space on Google. All things considered, a significant number of your clients are searching for your items and arrangements by composing them into web crawlers. For the present advertiser, it implies that you're in rivalry with your immediate competitors as well as with other sites going after catchphrases significant to your business.

If you are at present utilizing a SEO stage or innovation, you may find that your SEO innovation can enable you to identify competitors with information and bits of knowledge. For instance, Conductor Searchlight can allow you to take a look at the watchwords your immediate challenge is focusing on. It additionally can disclose to you which sites are positioning for a watchword related to your business. These speak to your circuitous competitors.

How can you attract them to your brand and products?

Competitors: Regardless of whether you need to let it be known or not, they're out there and they're eager for your clients. While it may appear to be unreasonable given everything else you have to focus on in your business, you should consider dedicating the time and effort into monitoring your opposition. "By checking competitors on an ongoing premise, you become more acquainted with their conduct thus can begin to foresee what they will probably do straightaway," says Arthur Weiss, overseeing chief of UK-based Aware, which helps businesses increase aggressive insight. "You would then be able to design your own methodologies with the goal that you keep your clients and win (not take) clients from competitors." At the end of the day, monitoring your opposition is an extraordinary strategy for developing your business.

Fortunately, while enlisting somebody like Weiss can spare you or your workers from investing the energy to direct examine on your competitors, you can likewise utilize a few systems to take care of business for all intents and purposes for nothing. Here are 10 hints from business visionaries and entrepreneurs on how you can begin gathering data on your competitors.

1. Go past a Google search. There's no uncertainty that any exploration venture nowadays should start with a basic Google search or visiting your competitor's website page. However, there are likewise an assortment of apparatuses either provided by Google or identify with Google's list items and AdWords battles that may give you fascinating bits of knowledge into your opposition. For instance, Sheel Mohnot of FeeFighters, a correlation shopping site for Mastercard preparing, says he utilizes the accompanying devices to watch out for his opposition:

SpyFu: "An extraordinary asset to look into what catchphrases and Adwords our competitors are purchasing,"

Google Trends: it's useful when he needs "to remain over the most recent in [his] industry, contrasting [his company] with others, and seeing where individuals who come to [his] site go."

Google Alerts: "We keep alarms for ourselves yet in addition for the majority of our competitors to comprehend what they are doing,"

2. Do some announcing. There are incredible and cheap assets for determining the status of your competitors on the web and offline. "I suggest routinely following what the business expert firms like Gartner are detailing about your industry, just as exchange affiliations and promotion gatherings," "These associations are doing exploration and concentrates that assess the individuals who are and ought to be your

competitors. What are they enlightening you concerning where the business is slanting? Where are the neglected market needs that you can fill?"

Different assets you can use to uncover data on your competitors include: Alexa, Compete, Keyword Spy, Hoovers, and ReferenceUSA.

3. Tap the informal community. Obviously, given how organizations are progressively utilizing person to person communication locales like Facebook, LinkedIn, and Twitter as marketing outlets nowadays, you may have the option to get intriguing realities about your opposition - and perhaps your own organization - just by tuning in. "We find that checking tweets, Facebook posts, online journals, and other new media notices of our opposition is a simple, financially savvy approach to remain tuned in to and aware of everything about the open's assessment about our competitors," which is a week by week arrangements website that offers top of the line spa and excellence offers.

In a comparable vein, we track our opposition by keeping an exceptionally close eye on survey locales, for example, Yelp and Citysearch. We scour through audits to discover notices of our competitors' arrangements, and afterward focus on that specific Yelper or Citysearcher's other most loved businesses so we're constantly one stage in front of the challenge." Even if your opposition isn't web based, it's a decent guess that they produce pamphlets - either email or print assortments - that you can pursue to get the best in class news and updates on things like new items or administrations they are presenting and what occasions they may visit.

4. Ask your clients. When it comes to identifying wellsprings of data about your opposition, don't avoid the conspicuous ones - like your clients. "Addressing clients is truly outstanding (and least expensive) methods for social event genuine data on competitors," says Weiss. "Whenever you win another client, discover who they utilized previously, and why they changed to you (for example the reason they were disappointed with their past provider).

Do a similar thing when you lose a client - identify what they favored about your competitor. If you accumulate enough of these accounts, you'll get an exceptionally clear thought on what competitors are offering that clients see as best. You would then be able to change your own offering to beat that of the competitor."

5. Go to a gathering. Going to industry public exhibitions and gatherings - just as joining industry affiliations - can be an extraordinary method to find out about who your competitors are and what they're offering, says Amy Lewandowski, who heads up marketing at online retailer, PepWear. "We go to these shows at any rate, so we try to visit competitors' stalls while we are there and watch their communications with clients, get writing, and look at the nature of their items.

6. Check in with your providers. If you work in an industry where you share indistinguishable providers from your competitors, it could pay to present them with some basic inquiries. "Converse with your providers and invest energy becoming acquainted with them," "While they may not reveal to you what your opposition requested or their

volume, pose better inquiries." For instance, if you solicit from them the number of units from a specific item that have been pre-requested for the following month, you may discover what your opposition may have requested and what different items your provider may acquire.

7. Contract your opposition. Another strategy is to contract workers from contending firms - particularly sales reps - and collaborate with competitors' accomplices, "Nobody find out about within those associations than the workers. "Discover all that you can about how these organizations work, and all the more critically, what's not too far off for them? Where are they taking their business? What markets would they say they are wandering into? How are they utilizing development to cut expenses and advance profitability? Where is the most abnormal amount of disappointment with their items or administrations? Nobody has more and better insight when it comes to deals than displeased sales reps."

8. "Furthermore, watch who they're contracting. You can likewise get the hang of something by considering the sort of occupations/positions your competitors are hoping to fill," says David B. Wright, the head marketing official at W3 Group in Atlanta. "For instance, if an organization is enlisting a software engineer, they will incorporate data about precisely what advancements the up-and-comers need to know, which reveals to you what they use, likewise, see what positions they are procuring - if they're searching for a patent lawyer, they could be taking a shot at some enormous new innovations. If they're contracting for a few HR, they might plan to grow generally."

9. Lead a review. If you're keen on getting a thorough report of the considerable number of players in your industry, you should seriously mull over leading a review. "A year or so prior, I employed somebody to email a few of our competitors and ask them similar inquiries about their administrations," "We took a look at value, reaction time, how the business solicitation was taken care of, and so forth. By doing this, we figured out how to obviously differentiate our business procedure from that of our opposition." While we took in a ton from the procedure and plans on doing it once more, he has one admonition: "I am a major enthusiast of redistributing this. You would prefer not to keep running into somebody you were keeping an eye on at an industry gathering."

10. Call them up! When you have done what's necessary, research to identify who your competitors are and attempt an old school strategy to take it from that point: Just summon them up and inquire. "Probably the most ideal approaches to investigate rivalry is to call them and ask whatever you'd like, you'd be shocked how often organizations will let you know all that you'd like to learn via telephone, particularly if the inquiry is expressed in a setting that bodes well.

For instance, if you need to realize the number of individuals who work there, you can say: 'I'm searching for individualized consideration, and my dread is that your association is excessively enormous, and I'll lose all sense of direction in the mix. What number of mentors do you have on staff? Goodness, stunning, that is many. How much care staff do you requirement for a group that size?' This methodology has served me great."

Instagram is something beyond the web's #1 archive of latte craftsmanship.

It has an aggregate of one billion clients – truly, billion with a "b" – and 80% of those originate from outside the United States. Instagram additionally is presented as

youthful and hip, with the under-30 group making up about 60% of the platform, and young people being the main contributors to its developing numbers.

B2C brands can have a major impact with Instagram. Regardless of whether you're flaunting a delightful dinner, a beautiful vehicle, or an astounding office contraption, Instagram is the best approach to associate with customers who need to share direct, vivacious, outwardly captivating stories.

## All about Instagram campaigns and how to create your objectives

As the new home for brands, Instagram is the perfect spot to advance your business, arrive at new clients and connect with your group of spectators. Having a general strategy for Instagram is principal, however some of the time you need to put some additional exertion behind an especially significant objective.

That is the place an Instagram marketing effort comes in.

During an Instagram marketing effort, you're attempting to accomplish a specific goal over a fixed timeframe. The major elements of your battle is adjusted and centered around a solitary objective, which is specific and quantifiable.

If your Instagram strategy is a gradual, long distance race, crusades resemble runs. They utilize more vitality over a shorter timeframe, and yield results and bits of knowledge quick.

If you need to dispatch an item, associate with new clients or develop your image's notoriety, an Instagram crusade can enable you to accomplish your objective—as long as you set yourself up for progress. In this post, we'll familiarize you with different sorts of Instagram marketing efforts and offer tips for running a powerful crusade.

Reward: Download a free agenda that uncovers the definite stages a lifestyle picture taker used to develop from 0 to 600,000 adherents on Instagram with no spending limit and no costly gear.

Kinds of Instagram marketing efforts

There are a few general classifications of Instagram marketing efforts, each improved for different objectives and strategies. Here are the absolute most normal ways to give you a thought of where to begin arranging.

1. Mindfulness crusade

During a mindfulness crusade, you're pushing hard to build the perceivability of your organization, item, or administration. For developing brands or those attempting to associate with another crowd, this can be a crusade to exhibit what's particular, energizing and extraordinary about your image.

Because Instagram is where clients need to find and pursue brands (80 percent pursue in any event one organization), it's a characteristic stage for your mindfulness battle. Getting your elements/information together before Instagram clients are significant: 75 percent of clients make a move in the wake of seeing a brand's post, such as visiting their site

2. Cause battle

More youthful customers (like the ones who overwhelm Instagram) care about something other than what an organization sells. They care about the morals and social duty of the brands they support.

A reason crusade is an approach to support your image esteems. For example, you could advance an appreciation day or occasion or band together with magnanimous associations. Pigeon's #DoveWithoutCruelty campaign features the organization's pledge to evading creature testing in association with PETA and influencers who advance moral magnificence.

A reason campaign can fabricate trust and devotion from a group of people that offers your qualities and connects socially cognizant clients.

3. Deal or advancement

Running a deal with an Instagram-specific advancement is a successive strategy of brands. Its prizes drew in supporters and urged them to visit your deals and rebate codes. Since you can shop directly from Instagram, it's much simpler for clients to follow up on an exceptional deal.

Certain occasions and times of year are ideal for running a deal—all things considered, nobody truly becomes out of the school year kickoff fever. In any case, Instagram is likewise an extraordinary spot to run a blaze deal utilizing a promotion code that is material for a brief timeframe. It tends to be a ground-breaking approach to drive pre-deals before an item dispatch or move stock to clear a path for new things.

4. Instagram challenges

Challengers are passionate about Instagram, because they're hugely compelling at driving commitment. You can set guidelines for the section that helps your campaign's objectives. For instance, requesting that clients tag a companion to enter is a chance to arrive at new supporters. Requesting that they enter through a structure enables you to develop your email list.

Discover the numerous approaches to run Instagram challenges and the specific guidelines you have to know before running one.

5. Item dispatch

If you're propelling an energizing new item or administration, you may need a campaign to oblige it. This assembles expectation and fervor around your dispatch and offers you a chance to show off the different points of interest and characteristics of your new item.

For instance, Montreal-based retailer Frank and Oak built up an Instagram battle to advance their #StylePlan membership box.

Their campaign posts featured the worth and accommodation of the membership, shared looks from both their people's lines and proposed that clients can get it for themselves or as a gift.

6. Client produced substance battle

In client created content (UGC) campaigns, you're urging supporters and clients to share posts including your items, utilizing a specific hashtag to integrate the battle.

A UGC campaign not just advances attention to your image through the hashtag, it additionally furnishes you with content that you can use without any channels. A noteworthy motivator for interest by clients is the expectation that brands will repost their photographs.

These battles all have different objectives and techniques, however every one of them is centered around getting a client to make a specific move in a fixed timeframe.

Mindfulness or client produced content battles probably won't appear as though things you have to put a due date on, yet the information and strategies that you're utilizing will get stale if you keep them around excessively long. In the end, your group of spectators will quit reacting.

You can likewise consolidate components from these battles (for example, joining a challenge with a client created substance crusade). For example, wellness application Aaptiv joins a challenge with client created content with their #5KYourWay crusade:

Hints for Making Fruitful Instagram Marketing Efforts

Presently, you have a lot of thoughts, yet thought is just in the same class as the strategy behind it. We have tips to enable you to make an arrangement for progress and accomplish your campaign's objectives.

1. Set S.M.A.R.T objectives

When setting a goal for your campaign, you need to be specific, quantifiable, achievable, practical and time sensitive.

For example, state that you need to build your Instagram devotees. Separate that into:

Specific: Who would you like to reach? What do you need them to do? Be exact in your objectives. Ensure you have a solitary objective and that all your battle substance is unified to help it.

Quantifiable: How will you know if you're effective? Build up a standard for your present devotees and commitment so you can follow development.

Feasible: Is your objective practical? Could it precisely be estimated? Objectives should take diligent work to accomplish, yet they ought not to be distant.

Reasonable: This ought to be founded on your spending limit, the current pace of development and term of the battle. Do your examination and don't make a wild arrangement to go from 100 supporters to 10,000 of every two weeks (except if you promise every new devotee a free excursion to Hawaii).

Time sensitive: The span of your battle ought to be founded on your objective and the measure of time you think you'll have to accomplish it. Try to set realistic plans and deadlines for a week if your objectives are aggressive. However, ensure that you don't make it so long that you lose steam.

2. Plan your crusade content

When you've identified your objectives, you should plan out every one of your campaign posts. Make a guide schedule of the posts and stories you need to share every day. If you're contacting influencers, request that they post on a specific day that bodes well as indicated by your schedule.

Each post should bode well without anyone else while fortifying the general message of the campaign. If spectators see various posts, they should cooperate to assemble energy. If they just observe one, it ought to be sufficiently able to compel them to find out additional information.

The content schedule can incorporate posts that give an idea of your campaign (like if you need to declare a deal before you run it, or photographs of your item before you discharge it) to gather speed.

Battles are a ton of work, and you'll need to go after the Gatorade part route. Having a strong arrangement set up before you dispatch will make it simpler to keep up a reliable degree of value and innovativeness all through.

3. Utilize the Feed + Stories

If you're just running your promotions on the Instagram feed, you're passing up a major opportunity. Individuals watch 400 million stories every day but only 50 percent of businesses are utilizing them.

Stories can enhance your posts, or you can let Facebook Ads place your substance in either group. This Story from Girlfriend Collective, some portion of a free-delivery battle for their new line of bodysuits, is a case of an advancement that would work in the Feed as well:

Instagram crusade tips

Furthermore, it was enhanced by battle posts in their Feed:

Instagram battle tips

You can likewise tailor your substance for Stories and making Highlights, as Everlane accomplished for their ReNew crusade.

If you're threatened by the configuration, we have an introduction on beginning with Instagram Stories.

4. Utilize A/B tests

Need to take advantage of your crusade's lifespan? Utilize A/B testing to refine your strategy. Test numerous forms of your promotions at the same time, which will augment your spending limit via naturally choosing the best-performing adaptations.

You can A/B test pretty much every component of your advertisement: pictures, duplicate, arrangements, crowds, point of arrival. Furthermore, each test will give you more data about what works best, giving you a huge amount of information that will enable you to get much increasingly out of your next Instagram marketing effort.

5. Make a unifying stylish

Your campaign ought to line up with your image's general look and feel, yet you can, in any case, make it unmistakable. In contrast to a solitary promotion, which advantages from mixing great with the remainder of your content, a battle can stand apart without anyone else.

It ought to be essential and conspicuous, so each bit of the campaign signifies an aggregate, intelligible message. This will fortify your key invitation to take action and manufacture recognition each time somebody sees advancement

It additionally gives the crusade itself some character and a tone which will manage your content. Consider how you need individuals to feel when they see your crusade. Is it interesting? Quieting? Energizing?

Furniture organization Book made a shameless, amusing effort for a couch dispatch that establishes a connection:

Instagram crusade tips

6. Track the measurements that issue

If a challenge falls in the forested areas, and nobody is around to quantify how uproarious the sound is, did it truly have an effect?

Before you even dispatch your challenge, you ought to have identified the key measurements that you'll be utilizing to assess your prosperity (that is the M in your S.M.A.R.T objectives). For instance, in a mindfulness campaign, you'll need to focus on a group of spectators development, reach, and portion of voice.

These will change contingent upon the targets of your crusade. There are a huge amount of measurements you can follow via web-based networking media, and some investigation is one of a kind to Instagram. Contingent upon the kind of battle (like a deal or an item dispatch), you might need to follow measurements outside of the stage as well, through identifiable connections or the utilization of promotion codes.

Make a point to build up a pattern, so you can precisely gauge the effect of your crusade.

7. Cooperate with influencers

Influencers are clients who have an enormous, natural group of spectators on Instagram, and whose adherents trust their suppositions and suggestions. Therefore, influencers can be astonishing accomplices who interfaced you to a dependable and drew in crowd and add credibility and trust to your campaign.

Posts made by influencers for the benefit of your image need to submit to FTC rules and be obviously named as promotions, similar to these models from Danish watch organization Skagen's influencer marketing effort:

These associations possibly work if they bode well for your campaign and your image, so get your work done. Identify influencers who offer your qualities and look at their other marked presents to see how they present supported substance.

When it comes to spectators, focus on commitment and fit, not simply measure. Influencers with steadfast followings, can be an increasingly key (and prudent!) decision, particularly if they're a solid counterpart for your intended interest group. For more tips, look at this post from an influencer's viewpoint.

8. The spending limit for progress

Spending plans are the universally adored piece of a battle strategy, isn't that so? We as a whole need to do them, so we should do them right, when thinking of a battle spending plan, identify the strategies that bode well for your objectives, and make sure to incorporate those expenses.

You realize you'll have to cover advanced posts and Stories, however working with influencers and running challenges accompany extra costs. Accumulate your intel ahead of time and after that, incorporate those with your marketing spending plan.

Ideally, you'd have endless assets for every one of your campaigns, yet here on planet Earth, you may need to make acclimations to your strategies if your assets are constrained or run a shorter battle.

9. Consider the post-Instagram experience

Contingent upon the objectives of your Instagram marketing effort, you might send individuals off Instagram after they click on your posts or advancements. Remember about the post-click goal! A solid point of arrival will enable you to hit your battle tar

# CHAPTER TWO
# HOW TO CUSTOMIZE YOUR INSTAGRAM

---

Have you opened an Instagram account? You can immediately take care of a very simple thing, even before starting to post your first photos: customize your profile.

This is often one of the first elements that will see potential subscribers, so it plays a key role to make a good impression. But how to customize his Instagram? In this article, I will tell you about the five essential elements to inform for the first impression to be positive!

Overview of an Instagram Profile

If you look at an Instagram profile, you will find that it is composed as follows:

INSTAGRAM PROFILE: 5 IMPORTANT ELEMENTS

1. There is a username. It is thanks to this name that other members of Instagram will be able to mention you, it is also the name which will appear in the URL of your profile. For example, I am @salutbyebyeblog when I am mentioned and https://www.instagram.com/salutbyebyeblog/when I quote the URL of the profile.

2. There is also a profile picture, most of the time a logo, a picture of the person who manages the account or a photo symbolizing the

main theme of the account.

3. Then there is the name of the account (separate from the username): it is a name a little more marketing, which we see in particular in the search results Instagram.

4. The fourth important element is the Instagram bio, some lines of biography to put forward your account.

5. The last element is the link you include in your Instagram profile, which will be clickable.

These elements can be modified by clicking on the button "Modify the profile", which gives access to this screen on mobile:

EDIT INSTAGRAM PROFILE

1. Your username

This is one of the first things you have to choose to customize your Instagram.

If you have a website, be aware that the rules for choosing an Instagram username which amounts to also choosing a domain name.

A name that does not have spaces

A name which, ideally, does not contain characters too complex to memorize (points, underscores, useless numbers, doubled letters as in "elisabeeeeth" ...).

A name that takes your "brand" if you have a blog or you are present on several social networks, It makes memorizing easier.

A name that can be up to 30 characters while knowing that it is better not to fully exploit this limit and opt for a shorter name

And if the username is already taken

You can use a tool like Namechk to see at a glance if a name is available on Instagram as a domain name and on different social networks.

This is also the most common problem encountered: the Instagram username you would like is already taken. More frustrating still, it is sometimes used by an inactive account, which seems to be abandoned.

To date, Instagram does not offer a miracle solution: it simply advises you to choose a variant of the username you have in mind.

The alternative is to contact yourself the profile you want to retrieve the name: by private courier, by e-mail if the person provides a contact address in the bio of his profile, or by a third party site (search on Google the name of the Instagram profile, the person may have mentioned it on a blog or other site that it manages).

If it is an inactive account, chances are you will receive no response. It may also happen that you are asked for a sum of money in exchange for the release of the desired username: it is up to you to assess whether it is worth it, and to assess the risk of a scam ( nothing prevents the person from taking the money without releasing the account later).

Instagram

Even in the case of brands, Instagram remains quite protective vis-à-vis its users. If someone uses a name that is a registered trademark , you can not necessarily get it back. You have to prove that the person is using your brand in a misleading way that could mislead members of the social network.

If this is your case, go to this page , choose "I have a question about usernames" then "My request is for a business account" and then "This username is used by someone else and I can see its content when I access the web address "and finally" I wish to report an infringement of my trademark ".

Change or change the username

The username can be changed along the way, remember it is a pretty heavy decision: indeed, the username will change where it appears on the Instagram app itself (mentions, comments, etc.) but there will be no redirection of links posted to your profile outside the network (ex: websites that mention your account).

You can customize the Instagram username by clicking "Edit Profile" at the "User Name" line. The change is instantaneous.

Get a verified badge on Instagram

Some accounts have a small "Verified Account" blue badge next to their name. It is a badge attributed by Instagram to public figures, celebrities or well-known brands, which attests that this is their official account and not an impostor, as here in the official account of the Game Of Thrones series:

VERIFIED ACCOUNT WITH BLUE BADGE ON INSTAGRAM

A known personality or brand can make a verification request by going to the "Settings" menu of Instagram, then in "Account" and finally in " Request verification". All you will give is a proof of identity (official ID if you are a natural person, tax return or statute if you are a company).

INSTAGRAM VERIFICATION REQUEST

2. Customize your Instagram with a profile picture

The Instagram profile photo is an important part of your identity: it is displayed on your profile, in 110 × 110 pixels format in general. It is preferable, for a good quality display, to put it online in a higher resolution (at least 180 × 180 pixels).

You can choose a nice portrait of you, your logo or an image that perfectly embodies the theme of your account. If you are present on several social networks, it is often relevant to use the same visual everywhere to be more recognizable.

If your logo does not fit in a square, nothing prevents you from choosing only its graphic part, without text, if it is sufficiently recognizable ... Nespresso thus content with the "N" instead of the full brand name.

NESPRESSO ON INSTAGRAM

We can also opt for a more compact version of the logo, as do Galeries Lafayette, which transforms their complete logo into a sober "GL" on Instagram, while respecting their graphic identity.

GALERIES LAFAYETTE ON INSTAGRAM

It is often quite relevant to have a profile picture consistent with the general tone of the Instagram account (for example, applying the same type of settings if it's a photo).

3. The name of the Instagram account

As I told you at the beginning of the article, this is the name "marketing" of your account. It will appear on your profile, of course, but also in the Instagram search results if your account has the opportunity to appear there ... It must not exceed 30 characters.

INSTAGRAM SEARCH RESULTS

Initially, I made the mistake of repeating the name of my blog alone ... but in reality, it is advisable to use this space to include keywords relevant to your theme, much like you would on the homepage of a website, in the title tag , in a referencing perspective

We can either do it in addition to its brand name (which is repeated twice, in the username and in the account name), or completely get rid of the brand name and post only a name descriptive account.

This is the example of the Petit Bison children's decoration brand, with an explicit account name, "Children's Deco".

4. Customize your Instagram bio

The Instagram biography is just a few lines of text, which has the power to attract the attention of a passing visitor! 150 characters to exploit at best to convince!

The idea of the bio Instagram is above all to explain what you offer on your account. Who are you and why would you suddenly decide to follow you?

You can use hashtags (which will be clickable) and emojis . However, e-mail addresses and URLs will not be clickable even if you can add more. Feel free to skip lines to make your message clearer and readable.

A good bio Instagram shows your personality while explaining what you do. It can consist of a few sentences to deliver a complete message ... but also a few points in the form of a list if you share unrelated information.

The Instagram biography can or example include:

What you offer (type of content, products, theme, activity);

Where you are

One way to contact you

Practical information (e.g. for a shop, specify where you deliver);

Another account that is important to you (second Instagram account, YouTube profile, etc.);

A call to action (download an application, visit a blog, use a specific hashtag to share photos, etc.).

Emojis can be used wisely to save space in your biography: for example, use a flag to indicate your location instead of writing "Location: France"; use an envelope to highlight your contact information, etc.

Here is for example the bio Instagram account "A piece of cake" which offers high-end pastries. At a glance, you can find all the information you need to know: the activity; a contact address; a way to find out more; the places of delivery; the identity of the two pastry chefs who count.

Instagram account A piece of cake

INSTAGRAM ACCOUNT A PIECE OF CAKE

5. The Instagram profile link

At the bottom of the biography, Instagram allows you to add a URL . This is the only place on the social network as I write where the URL is clickable.

So you can use this space ... knowing that you do not have to include a link to your site's homepage at all. You can for example.

Put the URL of your last article (we can modify the URL as often as necessary, so many bloggers choose to add their most recent content).

Put the URL of your news of the moment (for example, a new collection in the case of a fashion brand).

Put a URL type Linktree : it is a URL that will refer to a dedicated page, with a menu to access all your important content. That's what Galeries Lafayette do, and here's their Linktree page:

Linktree for Instagram

LINKTREE FOR INSTAGRAM

Put a URL to a landing page dedicated to your Instagram followers on your blog.

Put a URL to creative content: your last YouTube video for example.

Put a URL to an action that is important to you: for example, a newsletter sign-up page, a donation page if you have an association or project to support, etc.

I advise you to use an "explicit" link rather than a non - personalized code link, like zoup.la/ezr439zea5. It makes you want to click when we know (roughly) where we will arrive! Also check that the page you are referring to appears on mobile ... because even if there is a desktop version of Instagram, the site is primarily used on smartphone.

Do not forget also an important element: your URL will be displayed just below your biography. It means that you can use the last line of the Instagram bio to encourage action on your link, put it in context.

And also for business accounts

To customize your Instagram when you have a business account, you have additional options, accessible by clicking on the button "Edit profile".

The Instagram category

It is visible only on the application, not on the desktop version of the site. It allows to indicate to which sector you belong, thus avoiding to repeat it in the bio Instagram itself.

Among these categories, there are either typologies of profiles (for example "Personal Blog", "Cruiser", "Local Company"), or themes

("Travel and Transportation", "Sports and Recreation" for example).

Communication options

As a professional, you can include contact information about your business: e-mail address, phone number, business address. This can also free space in your biography because these coordinates will be displayed directly on your profile as a call-to-action .

A CALL-TO-ACTION CONTACT ON INSTAGRAM

A call-to-action

Since we are talking about call-to-action, beyond the contact information, Instagram offers you, in the menu "Communication Options" after clicking on "Edit profile", to display an action button.

This time, it is a button related to different booking services (Appointments by Facebook, Eventbrite, OpenTable, TheFork, Yelp, etc.).

Customize your Instagram account to get started

When you come to customize your Instagram through these key elements, we already put all the chances on his side to deliver a clear message to people who will fall on the profile.

## Tips To Getting Followers On Instagram

Since Instagram has been acquired by Facebook, it is increasingly difficult to develop an account because the social network has implemented an algorithm that reduces the visibility of publications. But there are "safe standards" which I assume never will be negative!

Gain Subscribers at Instagram: Social Network Classic Guidelines First, there is a simple principle on Instagram as on other social networks: to win subscribers, you need to get interested in the network. Okay, really get involved. I note that often, because of lack of time (or because of laziness, it has to be admitted), I just like the images that fly before my eyes without actually making an effort to write a comment, to go in search of new accounts...

However, it is indeed when one is involved that one derives the most advantages in terms of visibility!

As a social network, Instagram receives the same types of advice as other networks: carefully complete your biography and choose a profile picture; do not flood subscribers with low value added photos; take advantage of the social functions of the network: be interested in others while respecting the ethical principles that we know well (sincerity, no advertising of the type' I follow' Some use the network just to share their daily lives with friends and family (and often have private accounts where they only accept those they know), others-this is my case-also use them to uncover talented artists, to imagine in front of stunning locations, to search decorative ideas...

Tips that work to get more followers on Instagram Original and insightful content Instagram remains a network of "beautiful images." It can be blamed for fostering a cult of excellence, but most of the accounts that grow rapidly and well are those that post quality content.

These are cool pictures, not usually shot with the last but still well framed SLR, not blurred...

A story to tell, I also think, after a few years spent on this network, that people appreciate hearing a unique and personal "voice" behind a (beautiful) image.

Share an anecdote, a life scene, some stories to feed his account, to get a little cold out of the "picture book." It's not easy to keep a certain discretion, but I'm sure it works.

Make your account known that Instagram is a network at the heart of your digital life. And in order to have more followers, you have to give it a place: promote your Instagram account on your blog (through an icon or by embedding any images in your articles), relay your Instagram photos on your Facebook page, build connections between the sites that you run so that we know the presence of your account, include your account in your newsletter...

Nothing also prevents you from pressing your account more explicitly, by posting a message on your blog or on another network to encourage people to join you on Instagram. This year, I did it 2 or 3 times and it helped me to win a couple of dozens of subscribers.

Exploit hashtags and geolocation According to a 2015 report by Dan Zarrella, analyzing nearly 1.5 million Instagram photos, adding hashtags on his pictures raises both the number of likes and the number of comments. Like Twitter, hashtags make it easy to find all the photos related to the same theme.

I discovered very recently that the practice I used was detrimental to my account: like many people, I don't want to "parasitize" the legend of my photo by posting 25 hashtags! And I decided to share in a comment my list of hashtags.

After several months of stagnating with the same number of followers, this helped my account to start winning again.

You can also allow the geolocation of your images. As a result, they will be more easily linked to a specific location when a person searches for information on the place in question (city, restaurant, trade, etc.), an additional way to gain visibility.

Use Instagram filters According to another Yahoo Labs / Georgia Tech study, filter-based photos are 21 percent more likely to be viewed and 45 percent more likely to receive comments than filter-free photos. According to the report, "the rise in contrast and brightness has a favorable effect on the number of views and comments." The same is true with retouching, which raises the temperature of the object by making it colder.

On the other hand, rising exposure appears to have a negative, though slight, effect on the opinions, even though it is positive for the comments. This goes back to Dan Zarrella's claim that low-saturation images earned 598 percent more than brightly colored pictures! In the same way, the bright photos collected 592 percent more like the dark photos.

At the end of the day, members of the social network choose filters or retouching that enhance the picture without distorting the filters that turn the image. We remain at this level in the search for authenticity.

For my part, I don't use the filters provided by Instagram anymore,

I prefer to manually adjust some settings (especially contrast / sharpness) to improve my picture rendering. But I'm avoiding the heavy editing that's too much of the original photo.

Chat with your subscribers

This is a point on which I still lack investment, recognize it :) If I think to like the comments that I receive or to answer with a small message when the commentary allows, there is one thing that I do little and works well on Instagram: work well your legends !

Photo captions provide a unique opportunity to share trivia, ask questions to your subscribers, tell stories. It creates a link and it's effective for engaging in a discussion.

As on a blog, we can test different things: short legends, long legends, ask a question, explicitly encourage subscribers to comment (according to Dan Zarrella, this explicit dimension would promote interactions).

Keep a coherence

Again, this is not always an easy point to respect ... but for the subscribers (or members of the network who discover you) find it there, it is better that your account releases a certain coherence , that it is in the contents that you post, in your interactions with your subscribers, in your publication frequency.

As on a blog, there is not necessarily an ideal publication frequency, but many studies suggest posting several times a week to increase its commitment.

Post at the right time

Instagram no longer displays photos chronologically, but highlights posts based on what you are likely to like. Nevertheless, the timing is important because the commitment you receive from the publication plays a lot on the visibility that the social network will give your photo (same on Facebook for me!).

Try to find out when your community is present: rather the evening after dinner, the morning before going to work, on the lunch break, during regular business hours? It can vary from one community to another, which is why I am always dubious when a study announces "ideal publication times"

## How To Create An Instagram Marketing Strategy For Your Business

Today, visuals have never been more numerous - be it a quick selfie of our lunch date or the latest video of our pet doing an amazing trick.

This increase in visual content flooding social networks is therefore even more pronounced on Instagram.

As a result, several brands are integrating Instagram into their strategy for growing their business. Videos, gifts and photos generate high engagement rates. If Instagram has become so important, it's because it creates a global social network by connecting people only through visuals, making it a powerful way to capture and hold people's attention.

In recent years, marketers and brands have been trying to capitalize on this monumental growth of Instagram. It has been proven that promoting your business on Instagram is a daunting tool if you learn the tricks to sell your brand on Instagram.

Instagram not only allows you to connect with people and gain visibility, but also paves the way for your brand to be recognized and trusted by Instagram users.

Here are some statistics that show that Instagram is a powerful platform for brand loyalty:

• In 2017, about 70.7% of all US businesses are on Instagram. That's almost twice as much as in 2016 (48.8%), and this was largely influenced by the inclusion of Instagram profiles in the business.

• 65% of all top performing Instagram posts involve products. Despite the fact that it's not good to promote yourself every time, Instagram users like to look at product photos from time to time. In fact, photos / videos of celebrities / influencers (29%) and lifestyle photos / videos (43%) are behind product images and videos.

• 7 out of 10 hashtags are tagged on Instagram. Hashtags not only help social media users to classify and organize content, but they have also played a key role in creating some of the most successful marketing campaigns.

You must now leverage this client source and use Instagram marketing to grow your business. To sponsor content on Instagram, you must have a Facebook page and use a corporate Instagram profile. Once these two preliminary operations are completed, you must configure your form, define its budget and finally publish it.

Here are the measures you need to use to develop your plan.

# 1: Start with a compelling Instagram Profile

Your Instagram professional profile should in no way resemble your personal Instagram account. And it is better that "you" rarely (if at all) appear on this Instagram page.

Here's how you can create a compelling Instagram profile that will help you improve your online presence to attract more customers:

biography screen instagram

A. Use an attractive bio

Experts also believe that an Instagram bio should prompt a customer to take action while highlighting the personality of the company.

Bio must be both interesting and informative. You should be able to hook your followers. You need to be convinced that adding Instagram users to Instagram will improve the content and value of your feed.

Provide details related to your business in a concise and relevant way. This should relate to your targeted Instagram audience, and should also represent the tone of your shared photos. Find out how you can share several ties in your Instagram bio too.

B. Only Instagram bios will put clickable links to your account so please enjoy. The space just below the definition indicates a connection to the web (at the top of the Instagram page).

It's critical for Instagram's marketing campaign to involve links to websites. Make sure the URL is legible, not a collection of random characters. Find a way to add several ties to your profile on Instagram too.

Develop a marketing campaign # 2 for Instagram: Creating an Instagram visual loop Product photos make a big contribution to online shopping. To multiply the strength, make Instagram your showcase.

Before making a buying decision, approximately 67 per cent of all customers depend on the product identity and giving them a higher priority than reviews or product details.

Feel free to aesthetically enhance your brand when showing off your goods.

Instagram 2 A mobile profile. Enhance the brand image You have to be willing to trust the company's brand name. Much of your Instagram feed's esthetics should be focused on your firm's brand. It's up to you to give the tone and the personality that you want to send back in the posted content.

B. Do not compromise. Focus on the target market

Respond to your target audience without compromising on your brand identity. Please note that the Instagram feed is aimed primarily at current and potential customers. Find out what in your product or brand is most appealing to your target audience. And reflect that in the posted Instagram content.

C. Stay consistent

Your business will only gain brand identity if you remain

recognizable. Make sure your Instagram profile image is consistent. Add the thumbnail of your profile picture to all your Instagram commitments and engagements

D. Find your competitors' strategies

Study the content of your competitors and get an idea of what they are promoting on Instagram and essential to get into your market. Do they use user-generated content for their products or services? What kind of content do they post to Instagram? How often? What is their hashtag strategy?

Get new information on what competitors are doing and new ways to improve your own marketing strategy.

# 3: Be creative with your Instagram captions

Creative Instagram legends are one of the keys to attracting new customers, but it's not easy to find the right description for your image.

A. Spend some time

Many users feel compelled to post images just after taking them. Instead of rushing, you need to take the time to properly define the caption of your image to captivate your audience. Your results will only be better.

B. Short but effective

Instead of unnecessarily stretching the legend, make it short but enjoyable. Remember, users will probably spend only a few seconds displaying your photo before moving on to the next one, make your text quality over quantity, through the description use your creativity to make the image more attractive. Do not be cold, but talk as you would outside the networks, it should boost your commitment. Instagram users hate formalities.

# 4: Use Strategic Hashtags

On Instagram Hashtags are used to encourage users to find the information they are searching for. Strategically you can use hashtags so that more people can identify your articles throughout the quest.

Here are few habits to help you get the best out of hashtags:

• Using in increasing post less than 15 hashtags.

• Pick certain hashtags which are commonly checked.

• Add hashtags that are only applicable for your target audience: less responses, but more contextual ones.

• Build hashtags which are labelled in the case of a brand unique hashtag.

• Use the location-based hashtags to guarantee the brand is in a particular region.

# 5: Create compelling stories on Instagram

Instagram has its most popular feature to be the Stories (400 million daily active users from June 2018). If you can relate stories to your brand identity, they will automatically connect you emotionally to your audience and add meaning to the content you post.

The stories you post contribute significantly to creating brand loyalty. Instagram offers you the best platform to post stories which gives credibility to the brand. Yet at the same time, the intent and identity of your company (and your brand) can be mirrored in your Instagram posts so long as they establish continuity. Random material can be misleading and detached. So pay attention to what you're going to write.

# 6: Build a Committed Group Because Instagram notifications shift rapidly, the content is likely to be lost in no time at all. The only way to improve this is by attaching hashtags to the Instagram posts.

In reality, hashtags have a significant role to play in putting your company on Instagram in various communities and are connected by a keyword that will help you to identify your posts as long as Instagram is online.

You may also recommend asking Instagram ambassadors to feature the brand / product on their streams. Having a network of ambassadors to distribute the brand's advantages to its members would enable you attract more consumers and retain them. Encouraging Instagram fans to share feedback and pictures also can enable you meet several other users on Instagram.

Nearly 78% of all consumers buy products / services based on a brand's social media. As a result, the more people you have to share and promote your brand, the more likely you are to convince potential customers to buy your product.

Another great way to create an engaged community on Instagram is to share the marked photos of your subscribers on your Instagram profile, adding the content of your users to your own Instagram feeds will create a good feeling, which will then be associated with the brand you promote - 65% of Instagram users believe that when a brand talks about them, they feel happy and honored.

Get off the beaten path! Feel free to try new things. The Instagram algorithm changes constantly every half hour. So, everything that worked for you last week may not work for you the next week.

Therefore, it is best to continue experimenting with new ideas all the time. If they work well keep them, otherwise, try something new. Be original.

However, you cannot avoid elements such as your brand content, high-quality images, user-generated content, engaging and engaging publications, and hot topics.

## How To Optimize Account and Sell

How to optimize and sell an Instagram account?

If you already downloaded the application to your smartphone and got your Facebook account as registration data, or if you generated new credentials to access your new profile, stop here and see how to optimize please.

Basics about Instagram accounts

What everyone doesn't know when they decide to follow a sales strategy with a presence on Instagram is that this social network was originally designed to share images, and text has a place.

This doesn't mean it's impossible to implement a sales strategy on Instagram, but in that case you need to know tricks and practices to attract traffic that not everyone knows.

For example, to attract traffic to a website or a specific URL, you must do the following:

See the highlighted links you have in bios in your publication so that your followers can visit it.

Be sure to use the Instagram links correctly because you use dedicated

use #hashtags mostly to indicate your brands to increase visibility and reach more people.

Share a mini video introducing news on the website.

Unleash your imagination and share a clickable Instagram story that hooks the community from the start.

Instagram offers many possibilities for optimization and content creation in various formats, but you should be aware of the following restrictions:

Characters: The career limit is 29-150, but you can write a maximum of 2,200 for comments and text accompanying a post.

Tags: You cannot tag more than 20 people per post.

Hashtag: Up to 30 per post (never from a third party).

Follow-up: 200 follow and unfollow per hour.

Comments: 60 per hour.

Like: I like 100 other posts per hour.

Automation: Until very recently, this was not possible with external tools. Well, you may schedule publications from some of the most famous tools such as Hootsuite and SocialFlow in a somewhat less restrictive way.

Need some tips for Triunfagramers who want to sell on Instagram? Then write down:

Tag people you don't know or comment and like using an automated application! Please respect the restrictions that may cause you to lose your Instagram account labeled as a spammer.

Do not abuse the hashtag of each publication. Also, do not combine this practice with including additional comments.

Never forcibly get followers in a short time, like buying followers or following / unfollowing.

## How Does The Instagram Algorithm Work

There is no doubt that with the passage of time and especially from the relevance that Instagram took in this 2018, the publications do not have the scope that was previously available.

This is nothing new, it happened with Facebook several times. Precisely because of the changes in its algorithm.

Therefore, it is important to learn how the Instagram System operates, to seek to do it right and thereby increasing the account's exposure.

The Instagram Algorithm is currently based on some key points that we will see later: • The community's participation.

• The contact of others you obey.

• Fast contact.

• The simulation duration;

• Accompanying hashtag.

• Do not behave robot-like.

• Another one.

Why is Learning the Instagram Algorithm important?

Knowing how the Instagram algorithm operates has a significant influence on the account's exposure.

That's easy, even if you do one or two items well, whether you want to expand your account or get stronger outcomes from your competition, it's probably because of that aspect.

If you have a company account or want your personal account enhanced, I always recommend that you evaluate the market.

In short, in order to develop and increase your popularity in this social network, you need to learn your competition and learn how to master the Instagram algorithm.

The Instagram feed versus the Instagram timeline

Something I want to remind you before you start talking about the Instagram algorithm, is that you have to understand the difference between a feed and a timeline.

What is an Instagram feed?

The Instagram feed is the list of posts that appear within your account. Basically your publications in chronological order

What is an Instagram timeline?

Instead the Instagram timeline, are the posts you see, when you enter the Instagram application.

You must learn to master the Instagram algorithm, in order to make your posts more visible on the timeline, beyond how beautiful, orderly or cool your feed is.

## How To Beat The Instagram Algorithm

Now, we are going to see recommendations based on the new Instagram algorithm, in order to overcome it and increase the visibility of your account.

# 1 - Increase engagement

The first thing you should know is that Instagram rewards publications that have a high dose of interaction (or engagement).

This means that Instagram takes into account the amount of likes, comments, views on videos, saved and others.

When you receive comments and I like in your posts that likes the algorithm of Instagram and therefore is a good sign for it

For example, a great way to increase engagement is that apart from uploading posts to your Instagram feed, take advantage of Instagram

Stories since the algorithm also takes into account the interactions in them.

# 2 - Interact with your followers

It doesn't matter if you have a comment or hundreds of them, you should interact with the people who interact with your posts.

This is another factor that the Instagram algorithm likes. There is not much to say here. You have to worry about interacting and generating as many conversations as possible. That means that publication is being a success.

# 3 - The frequency of your posts

Instagram growth algorithm

Following the tips to master the Instagram algorithm , there is the issue of how often you make posts. It's really about finding a balance. Neither exaggerate making dozens of publications a day, nor spend days or weeks without publishing anything.

Look at it this way, the less time you spend updating your Instagram feed, you will have less interactions and therefore, your visibility will begin to decrease.

# 4 - The speed of interactions

This is somewhat complicated to achieve and has to do with affinity. Imagine you have an accident, call 3 of your friends. One arrives in 5 minutes, another arrives in 6 hours and the other arrives in 3 days.

Which of your friends has more affinity with you? Exactly, the first.

This is how affinity works on the Instagram algorithm. The faster the interactions of your followers with you, the better, because it means there is greater affinity.

How to achieve this?

Ideally, maintain a good relationship with your followers, interact often with them and most important of all, publish in the hours you know that most of your Instagram audience is connected.

# 5 - The duration of the visualizations

Surely you did not imagine this, but the Instagram algorithm takes into account the time people spend viewing your post. Obviously here you will have to use all your creativity to make people, while reviewing their Instagram timeline, stop to see your posts in detail. So always think of having content that really makes people stop to look at it.

# 6 - Know your best times to post

My best schedules according to the Metricool planner, there is not much to say here. If you want to increase your interaction rate, increase affinity and thus dominate the Instagram algorithm, you should know the best times to publish.

Some important questions you should ask are:

- Who are my best followers?
- Who interacts more with me?
- What areas or countries are these people from?
- What time are they most active?

- What days of the week are they most active?

# 7 - The relevant hashtag

While the Instagram algorithm penalizes excess hashtags (Shadowban), it also favors those publications that use relevant hashtags. This means that before putting 15 or 20 hashtags to your posts, maybe with less than 5, but they are relevant, you can increase the visibility of your account. So remember to analyze well what Instagram hashtags work best and don't forget not to overdo it, but above all, they are relevant.

TIP: Save different groups of hashtags relevant for different occasions in your smartphone's notebook. For example 4 or 5 hashtags for “dinners” or maybe for “party” or for “holidays”

# 8 - Post Instagram Stories or use IGTV

This is simple.

If Instagram brings out a new functionality, then you should take advantage of it because it surely affects the algorithm. At the beginning Instagram was only for posting images. Then Instagram Stories joined and now there is Instagram TV (IGTV)

What does this mean?

What if you use Instagram Stories and also IGTV, Surely, you'll like the program, and you'll be compensated with greater visibility.

# 9 -Don't act like a robot

Did you ever notice weird comments in your posts? Comments that simply have an emoji or a phrase like "good image" and nothing else

It is very likely that they are Instagram bots. Usually these Instagram bots are configured to follow certain accounts, follow certain hashtags and even comment with phrases that are predefined and are always short, with some emoji and may even be irrelevant to the publication.

Well, don't do the same. For example, if all the comments of your followers, simply respond with a "Thank you" and a happy face, it is likely that over time the Instagram algorithm believes that you are a bot. Be original, answer the comments, vary the phrases, generate conversation. Don't be a meat and bone bot.

# 10 - Make Live Videos

Since 2017 Instagram allows you to make live videos, however, many of the accounts I follow do not usually use this feature. If you want to flourish on Instagram and defeat the algorithm note what I said earlier you can take advantage of this social network's features.

Use live videos every so often in your Instagram Plan. Apart from this is a perfect place to connect with your people.

# 11 – Taking advantage of Trends No, I don't mean you're joining some competition on the Internet, nor setting aside your plan to leverage a phenomenon that has nothing to do with your website, company or individual.

Yet patterns are still to be used. The patterns are typically filled with multiple web subjects, hashtags and other methods of communication. Take advantage of trends, are key to increase engagement and interactions at certain times.

# 12 - The use of Instagram features.

Finally, my last advice has to do with something I commented on several points.

If you want to master the Instagram algorithm, then it is key that you use all the functions that this social network has or leave.

It's easy, as Instagram introduces a new app, the algorithm is more likely to favor certain users who are early adopters, use them and even make them trendy.

Before I arrive late my recommendation is to arrive early and take advantage of this latest function to increase your exposure.

Monetizing Your Instagram Page How to make Instagram money: how to monetize your account

1. Marketing influencer

Most consumers dislike advertisements and this causes them to become more hesitant to take clear and cold marketing steps.

It is obvious that whoever has a good or service needs to offer.

"No one wants to be advertised, but everyone loves to shop!" If you have a forum, you'll realize that the advertisement banners render you lose reputation and that's why the influencer statistic has gotten greater and more conversive in recent years when it comes to selling a certain good or service.

If, due to Instagram, you want to become an influencer, you realize you don't need to be popular or have a model's measurements.

What is even more respected today is the degree of commitment, that is, followers 'loyalty.

One proof of this is Diana Miaus who began to work with companies when she only had 20,000 fans.

For eg, she is what controls a micro-influencer, because she has a smaller audience than many, yet at the same time she is really dedicated to her material

You might ask me at this point: Serena, how do I become a micro influencer?

Think about what you want, of your love, and when you waste too much time.

Build a special friendship with your fans, and do not become concerned with their total, as with your degree of dedication.

Simply placed, connect entirely with your followers and establish a good and trusting partnership.

Once you have obtained a small community, you can register with these platforms to close your first collaborations:

- Tapinfluence
- Influenz
- The Mobile Media Lab
- SocialPubli

- Coobis
- Twync
- BrandBacker
- The shelf

You have to register and some of them not only ask for your Instagram account but also your blog and other social networks.

How to find collaborations on your own

There are many companies that still do not understand the potential of Instagram and why they should use this social network.

There are others who don't even have an account and don't even know what Instagram is.

So, what to do?

To avoid wasting time and not falling apart, I recommend that you focus on companies that already understand the potential of Instagram.

To do this, you can see what your "competition" does and see who they close collaborations with.

What I do is enter an account similar to mine, look at the post and see if there are particular mentions.

If the account in question has a blog, this information is usually found in «Contact», Media Kit or in the «Collaborations» section.

Once the first companies have been identified, I recommend you create a document where you can name them or better, create some notes on your mobile to remember them. In this way, in a couple of weeks you can create your database with these potential accounts.

It will be much easier to start with companies with which they have already collaborated than to jump into the void.

2. Affiliate Marketing

If you have a blog, you'll know what I'm talking about.

If you do not have it, affiliate marketing means when you promote a product or service of another person and they pay you a percentage for each sale made.

On Instagram you can do it in two ways:

1. You can put the affiliate link in your BIO

2. Create a story, explain the product / service and add the link

There are many companies you can work with, such as:

Amazon Affiliates

Skyscanner

Airbnb

Tradedoubler

To shorten the link, customize it and track it, I recommend using bittly.com.

Also, if you want to better understand how this system works, I advise you to read this article by Frank de Lifestyle al Cuadrado: The mega guide of Affiliate Marketing.

3. Shout4shout

It is one of the methods that I have spoken to you in the Instagram guide and that many accounts use to grow quickly.

It consists of mentioning another account (for example in Instagram stories) and in turn, the other account does the same with yours.

This will make you known among his followers and the possibility of getting new followers in a very short time .

If it is done with a great account, you will have many followers, likes and click on the link of your BIO.

There are also accounts that, to grow rapidly, are willing to pay for this type of collaboration.

In fact, if you have a page with millions of followers, you could charge about $ 40 - $ 200 for s4s (shout4shout).

Now think.

If you manage to sell a shou4shout a day, you could earn interesting money by spending a few minutes of your day.

Interesting right?

That's how young American Tim de @gentlemensmafia got rich

His accounts have millions of followers and he created a network to exchange payment shout4shout.

But be careful, everything that glitters is not gold.

For a Shout4Shout to really work, you have to be careful:

a. Do not promote anything that is not typical of your niche

Do not forget that your followers follow you because they are interested in your page. If you propose something different, that does not fit with your niche, you could lose them.

b. Do not accept all kinds of offers

If the photo you are asked to promote does not convince you, do not do it.

4. Sell your photos

Although it is not as easy as it seems, there are people who earn money selling their photos.

As you can imagine, if you are a professional photographer, Instagram is the perfect showcase to publicize your works of art.

And these are some of the sites where the images can be sold: Foap Twenty20 5. Instagram as a traffic channel People who ask me how to get their account monetized still say the same question.

The most popular aspect if you decide to make real money with Instagram is that this social network is a traffic generator for your online company.

Creating a company that goes way beyond Instagram, is great.

How? How?

Create a blog or web page, compose a document, or build an email list, for example.

If you let your followers go to your sales page or site, you could get a lot of traffic.

But social networking experts and advertisers urge you to build an Instagram account as a referral driver for your blog and e-commerce.

Compared to other social networks such as Twitter, Instagram has significant promise.

Above everything, Instagram is free, and advertisements are cheaper if you'd like to spend capital.

Then, Instagram engagement is far higher than Facebook involvement.

Have you paused to glance at how much the previous FB user likes? And at IG?

6. Offer your Instagram account: You can build a huge network if you have multiple accounts.

And if you're getting sick of Instagram or ready to leave this planet one day, you can opt to sell your page, or everyone else can have it without beginning from scratch.

Where will I sell them?

Fameswap

Viralaccount

# CHAPTER THREE

## FINDING YOUR TARGET MARKET AND BEING AN EFFECTIVE MARKETER

---

Identifying and looking for your intended interest group on Instagram is the primary thing you ought to do when beginning to build up a strategy for advancing your items and administrations on this informal organization.

Have an independent mind:

To make an intriguing and helpful substance, you have to obviously comprehend what your supporters need to find in their feeds.

To think of awesome subtitles for your photographs, you have to comprehend what sort of correspondence appears to them the most reasonable.

At long last, so as to distribute your materials at the ideal time and accomplish most extreme inclusion, it is critical to recognize what time of day your potential clients like to be on the web.

At the end of the day, to utilize Instagram to its fullest, above all else, you should know the individuals to whom you will turn. Understanding the interests, inclinations, and practices of your group of spectators at last will make ready for you to a fruitful Instagram strategy. We will discuss it here.

1. Start with the purchaser persona

If you have been in business for over one year, you most likely as of now have a purchaser persona – the profile of a perfect purchaser to whom you seek to sell your item. There is no compelling reason to reinvent the wheel, so you can reuse this data when deciding the intended interest group on Instagram.

If you don't have this experience, request that your marketing division depict a regular customer of the organization. Afterward, when you drench yourself in the investigation of Instagram expository information, you will have the option to enhance this profile with countless subtleties.

In any case, first you have to address the accompanying four inquiries:

What item am I selling?

What sort of group of spectators would you like to pull in? (or on the other hand for whom was this item created?)

what is my group of spectators searching for?

How precisely am I going to draw the consideration of potential purchasers to my item?

In the wake of looking at all the data given, we can infer that the intended interest group should: a) have or plan youngsters/grandkids; b) have enough refined taste to welcome the first structure of items, c) love wood furniture, d) offer inclination to quality items, e) have the option to bear the cost of them.

This is a rundown of those qualities, the consistence with which will permit considering either individual a perfect purchaser, and it doesn't make a difference if he just visited the Instagram account, went to the site or go to the showroom.

Depending on the client profile is the ideal approach to begin building up your record. In any case, recall that the Instagram target group of spectators may differ somewhat from the common client visiting your physical stores. That is the reason it is imperative to focus on statistic qualities.

2. Inspect the statistic qualities of your Instagram supporters.

Knowing the statistic qualities of your Instagram group of spectators can be valuable. Go to Insights into the Instagram application and snap "Group of spectators." Here you will be given fundamental data about your supporters: their sex, age, and the district of home.

You will require this data later on when you need to utilize the advertising chances of the site because with this information you can just demonstrate your content to the group of spectators that you need.

View statistic qualities of your Instagram adherents

Here you can get profitable data about individuals who are as of now your supporters. If your optimal objective group of spectators is, state, moderately aged men, yet as per Instagram, most of your supporters are millennial ladies, at that point you are presumably distributing something incorrectly and your substance strategy should be totally modified.

If the attributes of your purchaser persona and Instagram markers correspond, at that point you must be praised.

Next, you should see precisely what your group of spectators is searching for on Instagram.

Along these lines, from the past investigation, it is realized that a normal customer of this organization is searching for unique answers for the structure of a kids' room and is prepared to pay a significant sum for a quality item. Be that as it may, your assignment is to comprehend what precisely the agents of this crowd who are keen on kids' wooden beds as houses, are searching for on Instagram.

As it were, what draws them in at this stage?

Do they search for motivation on Instagram?

Or on the other hand would they say they are searching for tips on kids' room plan?

Or on the other hand possibly they need to become familiar with every one of the insider facts of making wood items?

Taking a gander at socioeconomics, you will never think about it. In the meantime, a key part of a group of spectators research is discovering the interests and individual inclinations, propensities, and life theory of your potential clients. Measurements are not ready to give you that. How to be?

3. Start observing your endorsers.

Watch! Convey genuine observation. What you ought to never do, in actuality, will give you fundamental help with deciding the intended interest group on Instagram.

It is ideal to begin observing from those clients who are as of now bought in to your profile and get in touch with them.

Snap on the individuals who left remarks under your posts or who simply preferred your ongoing posts. You will be taken to the pages of their records. See what they post themselves, what hashtags are utilized and, most curiously, what language and how they sign their photographs. If things being what they are, your supporters have a soft spot for emoticon and youth slang, you ought to infrequently utilize these words and images in the marks of your productions with the goal that they look progressively applicable.

Start testing the endorsers

At that stage, take a gander in the membership section to see what is being bought into their image. This should show you an image about what they are on Instagram hunting for. They can be bought from your rivals or from certain similar documents about which you have no idea.

You will get familiar with a ton about what your supporters are as yet keen on. Notwithstanding the zone to which your organization has a place, they might be keen on design and hand made. Or then again, they will be fanatics of Scandinavian inside plan and bought in to the hashtag #scandinaviandesign.

How might you utilize this data?

Simple. Assume you find that your endorsers are intrigued in your productions as well as in records that distribute persuasive statements. Every now and then, sign your photographs with any moving truisms of extraordinary and acclaimed individuals and watch how these distributions resound with your group of spectators. Or then again, for instance, you figured out how to discover that the greater part of your adherents is bought in to a well-known kids' store. Get in touch with him and arrange a joint marketing effort.

4. A little immediate won't hurt anybody

There is nothing amiss with legitimately asking your supporter for what good reason he chose to buy in to your record and what distributions he hopes to discover on it. Particularly these inquiries should be posed to individuals who continually "like" your distributions and leave remarks.

So, go legitimately to the immediate segment and compose a straightforward message.

You can utilize the model underneath:

"Hi! We saw that of late, you have been giving a great deal of consideration to our profile, and we are thankful for that! Give me a chance to pose you one basic inquiry: what substance do you hope to see for us? We will probably furnish clients with the best understanding, so your criticism is imperative to us."

5. Study what your competitors are distributing.

Another approach to get your Instagram group of spectators together is to "take" it from your immediate competitors. Also, let this strategy sound not all that wonderful, let me clarify its embodiment.

To begin with, you have to figure out who, truth be told, is your competitor.

At that point go to their profiles and notice these two things:

what do they post?

What markers of contribution can flaunt their production?

Take, for instance, the German Indian record of the apparel store @jrotifairworks, which advances the way of thinking of the purported economical design. One of their roundabout competitors can be known as the @hemper_ profile, a Nepalese brand of carefully assembled knapsacks, the creation of which can properly be called ecologically cordial and hence of open enthusiasm for thinking about nature. If you see his record, you will discover, notwithstanding the pictures of the rucksacks themselves, data about making a trip to Nepal, which creates an abnormal state of inclusion. Truth be told, it is these productions that get the most grounded reaction from them:

Realize what your competitors are posting.

This implies the intended interest group of Hamper on Instagram is following the brand not just because of the items it sells – it is enlivened by this brand, individuals care about the network of similar individuals accumulated by this organization, and lastly, the helpful experience given by the brand on Instagram, because of the decent variety of distributed substance.

So if you are the proprietor of a German-Indian economic design store account, maybe distributing photographs of Indian subjects is certifiably not a poorly conceived notion. This can pull in those Instagram clients who are at present "hanging out" on your competitors' records!

You can likewise buy in to your competitors' devotees and start associating with their records. Don't hesitate to "like" their photographs and addition your "5 kopecks" in the exchanges under them. You will be astounded to perceive what number of individuals will buy in to you consequently!

What's more, you can straightforwardly discover who remarks on the productions of your competitors and puts them an approval – and furthermore "go to the surveys". If you don't hold fortitude, you can do it directly on the page of your competitor. Try not to be timid: transparently take part in self-advancement.

This tip is particularly powerful if you start without any preparation and you don't yet have supporters.

6. Ask straightforwardly in the feed.

The significance of directing reviews of the intended interest group regularly doesn't get due consideration in marketing. What a pity, because if you don't ask your supporters anything, you know nothing about them. Indeed, even Kim Kardashian isn't bashful about requesting criticism from her group of spectators. A year ago, she directly in a tape solicited her supporters asking what kind of style pulled in them, because she needed to build up a reliable Instagram subject.

Kim Kardashian

I WANT TO MAKE MY TAPE IN "INSTE" MORE CONSISTENT. Would it be a good idea for me to REDUCE ALL FILTERS TO ONE? It will be ideal if you HELP. I REALLY WANT TO IMPROVE MY INSTAGRAM PAGE

Spot a photograph and straightforwardly in the inscriptions ask your adherents what they need on your page. What sort of substance? What design? Are stories advantageous for them? With or without inscriptions?

Try not to be hesitant to inquire!

7. Use Instagram Surveys

Instagram surveys are another approach to discover what element your group of spectators wants to find in your feed. Maybe you as of now have a few estimates with respect to why individuals pursue your distributions, yet it would not be pointless to get some information about this and check if your suppositions are right.

National Geographic, whose group of spectators experiences voyaging, every now and then leads a study wherein it is keen on clients, which traveler goals they discover increasingly appealing, and what sort of content in their tape – all the more energizing.

Investigate these models:

Where might you want to go out traveling?

WHERE WOULD YOU LIKE TO GO ON A TRIP?

If in the subsequent study, the lion's share picks the "city", at that point, likely, photos of city locate and comparing visitor courses will get progressively open consideration. Unexpectedly, if the group of spectators didn't give a solitary decision in favor of the "area", this implies they are not in the slightest degree inspired by this subject. So, regardless of what number of such photographs you would distribute, this isn't justified, despite any potential benefits.

Use Instagram surveys to do custom research. Ask which themes they are keen on, which configuration they discover all the more energizing (short recordings, merry-go-rounds). What's more, as a matter of first importance, you ought to inquire as to why they bought in to your record and what is anticipated from it.

At the end of the day, request that your endorsers give you profitable data that will help improve the content strategy and make it increasingly alluring to the intended interest group.

8. Use hashtags

Utilizing the right hashtags can significantly expand the scope on the stage because they enable you to demonstrate a specific post to the correct group of spectators.

In any case, numerous individuals use hashtags preferably inactively over 100%: they pick the one they like and simply trust in the best. Then, this instrument can give substantially more. The intended interest group is focused on because it shares your interests, along these lines, if an individual uses the equivalent hashtags as you, it implies that you are fit to one another.

To begin with, identify the objective hashtags. At that point examine the substance that is put under these hashtags. When you find pertinent distributions, "similar to" them! At that point go to the client profile and put any semblance of a portion of his photographs. Seek not to waste a minute ... everything goes as it should! Leave one or even two significant remarks and if you believe like this company suits well into your community of spectators, you may also buy in.

It's consummately typical to buy in to other individuals, even as a brand, particularly at the earliest reference point of your Instagram account. You simply don't have to act boldly and buy in to everybody, withdrawing from them following they buy in to you. This is another incredible chance to interface with somebody who can be your ideal devotee. No compelling reason to ruin everything.

9. Decide viable activities and rehash them.

If you have officially distributed many photographs, it's an ideal opportunity to begin following the degree of association they create, to comprehend what substance your crowd discovers most intriguing, and to distribute just such materials later on. Many people who have a certifiable passion about what you're doing are the ideal party of spectators in Instagram. The goal is to draw specific consumers into consideration, like the agents of a perfect audience, which is, having identical desires and values, with the aid of the kind of materials that have delighted in achievement beforehand.

10. Distribute when necessary.

To focus on your community of spectators from Instagram, you need to publish content while the majority of it is on the site.

Distributing material as per Central Europe hour doesn't bode well if the expected target audience primarily resides in the Los Angeles time zone. To prevent that from happening, you ought to figure out which place the crowd resides in (you can do so by calling for a report on statistical markers).

# CHAPTER FOUR
# HOW TO SET EFFECTIVE ADVERTISING GOALS

---

Instagram advertising has developed since its commencement on account of incorporation with Facebook's incredible advertising stage. If you haven't tried Instagram advertising out, you're passing up a colossal chance.

Instagram is one of the world's biggest and most dynamic social stages with more than 500 million dynamic month to month clients. With an enormous network this way, it's nothing unexpected that businesses are progressively amped up for the advertising openings accessible.

Instagram is rapidly getting to be one of the top marketing channels for businesses because of the way that visual media is more powerful for connecting with spectators than other marketing channels on the web.

So by what method can a business like yours exploit Instagram's advertising abilities?

Here are seven hints for effective Instagram advertising to enable you to dispatch enthralling advertisement crusades on this prevalent social stage:

#1: Be Familiar with All Ad Types

If you're new to advertising on Instagram, you'll find there's as of now a wide scope of promotion positions accessible. The four noteworthy kinds of promotions are:

Photograph Ads – Photo promotions are what the vast majority are accustomed to seeing on their Instagram feed. These are single pictures with a little "Supported" symbol in the upper right corner.

Merry-go-round Ads – Carousel promotions let businesses incorporate various pictures inside an advertisement in a level looking over the arrangement. Merry-go-round advertisements were made because businesses needed to recount sequenced stories that lead to significant outcomes for their business.

Video Ads – Video promotions are an incredible method to contact Instagram's crowd and have appeared to give the most commitment. Individuals want to watch videos, however brief they can be. Video promotions are the prescribed advertisement type if you're searching for the best commitment.

Marquee Ads – Marquee promotions are single-day battles that offer ensured impressions and top advertisement places of Instagram's feed. With the Marquee position, businesses can demonstrate a promotion with shifting inventive to a similar client up to three times each day.

#2: Target Your Audience

Nothing could really compare to getting your advertisements before the ideal individuals. Perhaps the greatest bit of leeway of Instagram advertising is it's incorporation with Facebook Ads. That implies that you are entering the radical emphasis of Facebook on highlights such as Custom Audiences, Lookalike Audiences, Place, Age, Class, Language, Interests and that's just the tip of the iceberg.

Utilizing these focusing on highlights can build your active visitor clicking percentage since your group of spectators is exact and your promotions have appeared to individuals who are likely inspired by your business. Moreover, expanding your active visitor clicking percentage can likewise bring down your expense per click.

Simply try not to hurry through a group of spectators focusing on when making your promotions. Cautiously consider who your objective client is and make advertisement campaigns specifically for them.

#3: Team Up With Influencers

Collaborating with influencers is probably the ideal approach to expand brand mindfulness and become your Instagram following. There are numerous expert bloggers, web superstars, and online life phenoms who have enormous followings on Instagram that you can take advantage of.

Working with the privilege influencer, particularly one that your intended interest group identifies with, can give your business instant believability and trust.

#4: Make Your Ads Look Native

Probably the best performing Instagram Ads don't look like

advertisements by any means. Instagram works admirably making advertisements look local inside the client's feed without controlling the picture and inscription you use.

Rather than utilizing customary advertisement innovative for your picture, you should utilize inventive that mixes in with natural Instagram posts. Give simar encounter clients would get from natural substance. When clients are looking through their feed, you need your promotion to look simply like some other bit of substance they would see from their companions or individuals they pursue.

Something critical to remember is utilizing wonderful visual substance. Ensure you just utilize great pictures and video in your advertisements. Not at all like other social channels where the duplicate and call to activities are the central focuses, Instagram advertising is tied in with rousing visuals.

Test To Optimize Performance

Testing is one of the most significant parts of advertising. It causes you to build up your best performing promotions. Changing your picture, subtitle and CTA can totally modify your outcomes. Rather than constraining yourself to one advertisement imaginative, test a few varieties of it.

Instagram makes it easy to do A/B testing. You can copy your current promotions and change different components of your picture, inscription and CTA. A decent point to begin is with your CTA since Instagram gives an assortment to you. When you've caused changes for testing, to make sure to dissect your reports to see which variety conveyed the best outcomes.

DID YOU KNOW THAT YOU CAN DOWNLOAD THE AUDIOBOOK VERSION OF THIS BOOK FOR FREE?

CLICK HER FOR AUDIBLE US:

https://www.audible.com/pd/B08BPHLR92/?source_code=AUDFPWS0223189MWT-BK-ACX0-202801&ref=acx_bty_BK_ACX0_202801_rh_us

CLICK HERE FOR AUDIBLE UK:

https://www.audible.co.uk/pd/B08BPHQNNR/?source_code=AUKFrDlWS02231890H6-BK-ACX0-202801&ref=acx_bty_BK_ACX0_202801_rh_uk

# CHAPTER FIVE

# HOW TO MANAGE YOUR INSTAGRAM ADS

---

There's no exact science to Instagram and how to utilize it. Since I get posed a lot of inquiries on how I developed my record to more than 200,000 adherents, (and keep on developing more than 1000 devotees p/week), I thought I'd review a couple of tips I've learned in the eighteen months I've been a functioning Instagram client. It's essential to recollect that I've endeavored to fabricate my record, steadfastly posting each day since I joined, once in a while 4-6 times each day, to manufacture a solid association with my supporters. I didn't have a blog or site in those days. I simply cherished sharing photographs of my feed → which transformed into individuals requesting the formula → which THEN transformed into adherents mentioning I start a blog to keep my plans in a single spot. Plans that are simpler to discover and print. Furthermore, Cafe Delites was conceived.

Through that time, I've realized there's no set in a stone manner to 'Instagram'. It's tied in with timing. It's about what your supporters like, and not every person will like very similar things. Coming up next is just founded on what I've seen and realized in the time I've been on Instagram, and what I've discovered works best. It might be different for other people.

If you have some other inquiries or tips of your own, if it's not too much trouble don't hesitate to share them in the remarks beneath!

1. Your Instagram record resembles your portfolio. Make it great! If you need to direct people to your online journals, your Instagram should be set up that way. Some close to home shots, selfies or 'off camera shots work OK, yet if your adherents are there for your content, they don't generally think about 100 shots of your feline sitting on a window, or a fledgling in a tree (for instance). Instagram adherents are different to blog supporters. Odds are, they need good content!

2. Instagram Composition. Extraordinary photographs of food will bring adherents. Top shots and far away shots work OK, BUT close ups work better (not very close! Despite everything they have to perceive what it is). They should be clear and the food should be noticeable. Particularly cheddar shots; trickling syrup or overflowing chocolate. Make it about the sustenance, not the photo (except if your record is food photography based). If it looks 'yummy' to you and makes YOUR mouth water, at that point it will work. If it's just a 'decent photograph' all in all, it won't draw as much consideration. You need to think like your adherents. OK prefer to see that picture/food on your feed/landing page? Would that photograph make you need to tap on a connection for the formula?

3. Your profile ought to contain a short rundown about you or potentially your blog. Your blog site connection ought to be accommodated your adherents IN your profile, NOT in your subtitles. Make it simple for them to discover you and your plans, or they will erase you. Trust me. The vast majority don't care for tapping on

connections. They need the whole formula in that spot before them, so make it simple for them to get that formula.

4. Subtitles. Each nourishment photograph you post ought to have a decent subtitle with 'where to go for the formula' data. For instance: This formula is up on my blog cafedelites.com! Blog connection is in my profile @cafedelites !

Here, you've given the connection data to the formula in addition to a simple method to get to your Instagram bio by utilizing the @_______ connection to your Instagram page.

5. Pictures. You will begin to realize what your supporters like. Mine, for instance, have evil sweet teeth. So I know brownies and treats will work. I generally remember how to go for my Instagram supporters, not simply my blog. Liquefied chocolate chips; anything overflowing. Individuals go insane! So while your going for your blog, make sure to shoot 1 or 2 shots for your Instagram devotees.

6. Timing. When is your pinnacle hour? What day do you see more traffic to your posts? Where is a large portion of your adherents found? My adherents are principally U.S based. Being that I'm in a totally different time zone, through a great deal of experimentation, I worked out that my posts improve when I post first thing in my morning and extremely late in my night. The initial two hours of an Instagram post are the busiest. You'll see a decrease in association from that point.

7. Yell Outs. Discover pages like yours with an indistinguishable measure of devotees from you have (if your blog is vegetarian, discover veggie lover; if your blog is perfect eating, discover clean eating) and

inquire as to whether they'd like to do a shared holler. What's a whoop? A yell out is the place the two pages will consent to post a picture of a formula from every others blog with an inscription, for example, 'Wow these chocolate chip treats look crazy! For this formula and other clean eating plans, pursue @________ ! You will LOVE her/his page!' Something like that, in your very own expressions obviously so it sounds certifiable originating from you. Yell outs for the most part go for an hour or two hours, however you gain the most in the principal hour. You can generally repost a different picture in the subsequent hour to acquire devotees.

**It's critical to note, in any case, that if you do too much, they will pester your supporters. Not every person acknowledges shoutouts on their feed/landing page.

8. Greater pages won't do shared shoutouts with you. I've inquired. They are set up to profit with advertisements and post shoutouts for smaller pages, and so on. For instance: Pages with anyplace more than 100,000 devotees would prefer not to shared shouts with a page that has just 1000 adherents. Why? Because they won't increase any supporters in the shoutout. They will undoubtedly lose a larger number of devotees than they increase, and it's not worth their time. Keep in mind, a page with more than 100,000 devotees has endeavored to arrive. If you approach those greater pages for a shoutout, they may cite you $X sum every hour for a shoutout. It's the means by which they create income. Regard that.

9. Be cautious WHO you shout with. Ensure the page your shouting

out with is a decent nourishment page or a page like yours! Or then again you may lose devotees on your page. Individuals need to be sent to great pages. Individuals need to realize you care about them and your prescribing a decent place for them to go to. The shoutout isn't simply to your advantage, it's to theirs as well. Care for your supporters!

10. Breaking point Shouts. When you do a shoutout, it can wind up energizing and addictive watching your page blast and develop! Be that as it may! Keep them restricted and on the down low. When each couple of days is sufficient.

11. Use #hashtags. They DO work! I've tried without and I've tried with. Hashtag what the nourishment is, what it's about, magazines and sustenance highlight pages, brands, and so on. For instance, these are some I use, yet find what works for you: #weightwatchers #canon6D #foodgawker #foodphotography #foodblogger #feedfeed #instafood #foodideas. At that point if it's a chocolate formula, include #chocolate #chocolatecake #chocolaterecipes or whatever your food is about. Individuals do look for hashtags. Try not to utilize an excessive number however, or they won't be shown in the inquiry pages (I separate hashtag bunches into two separate remarks in a post).

12. Watermark your picture. Odds are if greater pages like your stuff, they will take your picture. Some don't understand they have to ask your authorization first before utilizing your picture; and some know precisely what they're doing and will take a picture straightforwardly from your Instagram page or blog; repost it with no credits given to you in an inscription, and overlook you when you call attention to it.

Watermarking your picture will enable your supporters to perceive your work, and they will consistently exhort you or tag you to tell you your picture is being utilized without your credits in the inscription should you wish to report them for Instagram copyright encroachment.

13. Collections. They work! If you have a formula with a couple of steps in it and it seems like a confounded formula, an arrangement can show individuals how simple it really is (if it's simple) and they will be progressively disposed to go to your blog with the beautiful connection you've given in your profile (stage 3). I utilize the Instagram arrangement application Layout or PicFrame, yet there are a lot of applications for your smartphone that work similarly as great.

14. Formula Features. Much like Fodgawker and Tastespotting, there are numerous Instagram pages with thousands (even millions) of supporters that are continually searching for an extraordinary substance to highlight. This is a success win for both you and the element page. THEY gain supporters from your work, and YOU gain followers from their span. Approach those greater pages that element blogger plans and inquire as to whether they'd like to include your formula. Give a connect to your blog and your Instagram page in your email so they can see your work. A large portion of them has email addresses shown in their profile, or Kik account data (an errand person application for telephones). You will see a spike in blog traffic if your blog connection is in your profile. New adherents will as a rule consistently proceed to look at you on your blog! Regardless of whether the formula that carried them to you is included on a greater page. They will see your

Instagram page loaded with food pornography and will need more!

*Keep as a main priority if your formula does truly well on their page and gets a huge amount of preferences, they will at that point utilize YOUR picture in THEIR whoops — without your credits in their subtitles — with different pages to enable THEIR page to develop. From the start, it's irritating to see, yet more often than not individuals will go to their page, see your picture and follow you. You will likewise observe a lift in blog traffic when that occurs.

15. Try not to dishonor Instagram. It's a decent spot to grow an after, direct people to your blog, get an individual with your adherents, and discover potential endorsers. I adore my devotees, and LOVE INTERACTING WITH THEM on Instagram. Kindly recollect, if they pose inquiries, answer them, regardless of how senseless YOU think it is. If they send you direct messages, answer to them, as you would with your online journals. They're IMPORTANT. Keep that in mind.

# CHAPTER SIX
# HOW TO USE HASHTAGS TO YOUR ADVANTAGE

Any individual who is a popular culture fan or an energetic devotee of looking through YouTube recordings has most likely observed Justin Timberlake's sketch on the Late Night with Jimmy Fallon show caricaturizing the abuse of hashtags.

Truthfully, hashtags, when utilized pointlessly can be a noteworthy irritation. Raise your hand if any of you have ever gone over an Instagram post that incorporated the accompanying:

#girl #boy #smile #yolo #sky #cool #yolohard #funny #sun #bored #love #likeme #BA #coolbeans #youonlylivelifeonce #forrealz #imcool #wehere #imaboss #ftw #awesomeness #hashtagforlikes #hashtagforfollowers #hashtagtillicanthashtagnomore

Irritated at this point?

Truly, when utilized the manner in which they are expected, hashtags are an unbelievably accommodating instrument to explore your way through the consistently changing, regularly developing universe of internet-based life particularly with your business. As indicated by Twitter, hashtags are "... used to stamp catchphrases or themes in a Tweet. It was made naturally by Twitter clients as an approach to sort messages."

From that point forward, hashtags have been actualized in different types of internet- based life and began a prospering pattern all without anyone else, being utilized by numerous both in their own and expert lives. Here are a couple of tips we've thought of on the best way to utilize them to further your potential benefit:

Need to 2.5x your Instagram likes and remarks? Flawless your hashtag strategy with this free direct. Get it now!

#1: Customize it!

On Instagram, hashtags can be utilized to sort out your pictures, much like a photograph collection. With this apparatus, you would then be able to transfer back to back photographs on Instagram and incorporate a reasonable, recognizable hashtag to arrange all your photographs to a comparing occasion. For instance, post photos of an ongoing office party on your official organization Instagram by utilizing the hashtag #tailwindofficeparty. All photos from the occasion will be sorted out in a perfect "collection" and prepared for your review with a simple hunt. Accommodating tip: ensure the hashtag you make hasn't just been utilized. You can look through it on the hashtag search bar to check whether it raises any outcome. If not, your hashtag is one of a kind and prepared for use.

#2: Search it!

Hashtags can be your likeness a Google Image search on Instagram. As of December 2013, Instagram has over 150 million clients. With a normal of 55 million pictures posted per day, you can make certain to locate any topic on Instagram. Model? Women, if you are feeling especially randy and completely need a token of the sheer amazing ness of Ryan Gosling's abs, you can look #ryangosling on the Instagram hashtag search bar and luxuriate in the entirety of his superbly etched build. Folks, searching for Kate Upton's Sports Illustrated spread? Simple. You can discover pictures of #kateupton's spread in a heap of channels utilizing the hashtag search bar. As a business, you can likewise utilize this alternative to investigate your competitors or research new thoughts in your specialized topic.

#3: Make it topical!

Need to fire a topical discussion or read up on another person's perspectives on a specific subject? Twitter and even Facebook can interface all posts/discourses/discuss utilizing hashtag. Search #politics on Twitter to perceive what is inclining in the realm of government undertakings. Type #fashion to see the most recent prevailing fashions. Most clients know at this point Facebook as of late included hashtags to "... transform subjects and expressions into interactive connections in your posts on your own Timeline or Page." This enables clients to look through posts about themes they're keen on.

This capacity is additionally useful to businesses, as experts often use Twitter as a gathering to talk about market patterns with others in their industry. By empowering exchange with different business clients, you not just expand your systems administration openings, you additionally get the chance to fabricate your image all the while.

#4: Instant audits!

A similar way clients find topical discussions through hashtags, you can likewise utilize them to get audits on eateries and administrations, just as motion picture or even music surveys. Disappointed clients often take to Twitter or even Facebook, cautioning others about their awful involvement in a tweet or an announcement. Moreover, clients will more than likely tweet about how one-dimensional and monotonous the new Jason Statham film is or chatter endlessly about how they can't get the new Miley track out of their heads.

From a business perspective, this capacity is an extraordinary method to get instant input from clients about your administrations. Thus, you get a real-life, down to business survey of what went well, things that should be improved and tips to change your methodology for your customer base. Note that when reacting to disappointed clients on any type of online networking utilizing an organization account, it is imperative to react in a quiet way to abstain from running over rankled or affronted. The manner in which you handle your communication with your faultfinders will vigorously impact the manner in which clients react to your business or brand, so abstain from being snide because you will lose them.

#5: Get Social!

If all else fizzles, hashtags are additionally an extraordinary method to interface with individuals. It's generally accepted that the best way to have more Twitter followers is by tailoring others. What better approach to get associated with somebody with indistinguishable interests from you than to tail somebody who tweets about the things you like? By perusing the slanting themes, you are opening yourself to a large number of individuals from everywhere throughout the world, all bound together in a worldwide system of social trades. This positively brings the world significantly closer!

So pre-users, would you be able to offer some other recommendations on the best way to utilize hashtags? We'd love to hear your ideas!

The snappiest method to inquire about hashtags.

We have gotten notification from a ton of advertisers that hashtag research was taking up a lot of their time and they weren't really finding the best labels for their posts. We tackled this issue with Tailwind for Instagram's Hashtag Finder and Hashtag Lists apparatuses which propose the best hashtags for your post dependent on the hashtags you're as of now utilizing. The instinctive shading coding makes picking between different hashtags simpler than any time in recent memory. When you've made a rundown of hashtags you like you can spare it as a hashtag list for sometime later.

Utilizing Instagram hashtags to develop your crowd

Instagram hashtags are all over the place yet does your image realize how to utilize hashtags on Instagram to get the most incentive out of them?

Hashtags probably won't appear quite a bit of a need superficially, yet they stay one of the most significant parts of advancing your Instagram.

When you start diving into utilizing hashtags on Instagram, you'll most likely keep running into a lot of questions: Do you know which hashtags are driving supporters to your page? What are the most well-known labels in your industry? What number of hashtags on Instagram do you attach a run of the mill post?

Without a sharp comprehension of Instagram hashtags and how they work, they can move toward becoming #overkill before long.

Luckily, we're here to help. This guide separates all that you have to think about how to utilize hashtags for Instagram to develop your group of spectators.

Rather than simply hurling many labels on a post and seeking after the best, you need a strategy for utilizing hashtags on Instagram. A few sorts of brands have it simpler on Instagram, while others need to get somewhat more inventive.

**Improve your Instagram presence with ViralPost by Sprout Social**

With ideal hashtags set up, ensure they're being seen during the best occasions on Instagram.

Let Sprout's protected Viralpost innovation take every necessary step for you.

Become familiar with how this element expands commitment by mentioning a customized demo or pursuing a free preliminary today.

For what reason do Instagram hashtags make a difference, in any case?

Great inquiry!

If you're absolutely new to Instagram, you may not "get" hashtags or see what the publicity is about.

There's a motivation behind why most of the businesses incorporate labels on their posts or make their own, however. The following are some key reasons why hashtags merit your full focus.

Hashtags make your substance simpler to discover

To put it plainly, hashtags are what make your Instagram content discoverable.

Consider the time and vitality that goes into any given Instagram post.

From catching the ideal preview to making a sharp inscription, you don't need the majority of that legwork to go to squander.

That is where hashtags come in. Clients can find content via looking for hashtags all alone or tapping through related posts for a specific tag. Here's a case of how hashtags can send you down a hare gap of applicable substance.

You can nearly consider hashtags like you may consider catchphrases for a web crawler, all bound to Instagram.

Disregarding Instagram hashtags means making your posts progressively difficult for potential adherents to spot, On the other side, taking a couple of moments to attach a few labels immediately makes your posts discoverable.

Hashtags empower a group of spectator's collaborations

Something to think about: as indicated by late Instagram measurements, posts including at any rate one hashtag score more commitment than those that contain none.

Adherents connect with hashtags, plain and straightforward. That is the reason such a significant number of brands advance their very own marked hashtags to energize collaborations with their clients.

For instance, look at how Punky advances its #punkycolour tag in its Instagram bio. Adherents who do so get an opportunity to be highlighted on the Punky feed by means of client produced content.

Your Instagram bio is maybe the most significant spot to advance your hashtag

Navigating labels, it's perfectly clear that Punky's devotees are glad to publicity up their most recent buys.

Instagram hashtags make it conceivable to urge your devotees to share client created content

Thus, Punky distributes adherent photographs to its own feed. They likewise figure out how to incorporate an assortment of excellence specific hashtags inside presents on further grow their span.

Brands oftentimes put Instagram hashtags in the body of their inscriptions notwithstanding the principal remark

Subsequently, devotees and influencers are enabled to consistently draw in with marked hashtags so they can in the long run be included themselves.

Perceive how that functions? Without marked hashtags for Instagram, these natural chances to secure brand promoters would be unthinkable.

Hashtags can educate you concerning industry patterns

If you're on the chase for what's hot in your industry, look no more distant than slanting hashtags.

Regardless of whether it's your intended interest group or individual brands, hashtags can educate you concerning what individuals are humming about.

Instagram hashtags can enable you to comprehend industry patterns and rising brands

Reliably following labels can enable you to watch out for competitors just as what individuals are stating about your very own image.

What's more, hello, that is the place apparatuses like Sprout Social can prove to be useful.

Grow's a suite of Instagram examination devices makes it simple to screen hashtags identified with you and your competitors. Furthermore, highlights, for example, social listening help guarantee that labels identified with your image depend on positive notices and communications versus negative ones.

Grow's pattern report can enlighten you concerning which hashtags on Instagram are picking up the most support.

Step by step instructions to pick hashtags for Instagram

Since we've featured why hashtags matter, it's an ideal opportunity to discuss thinking of a distributing strategy.

As such, which hashtags bode well for your business' posts?

There is no one size-fits-all answer here, however, here are a few plans to help fill in as a beginning stage.

Network and industry-specific hashtags

The best hashtags are the ones that communicate in your clients' language.

Basically, these are labels that are prominent enough that they'll really get utilized yet aren't mainstream to such an extent that your posts will become mixed up in the mix.

For instance, there are huge amounts of excellence related hashtags, for example, #unicornhair or #mermaidhair that address a more specific group of spectators than just #beauty.

Essentially, a wellness brand with an overwhelmingly female statistic may discover more accomplishment with labels identified with #femalefitness versus #fitness without anyone else.

You may be amazed at what sorts of specialty hashtags are out there. Past Instagram's very own suggestion motor, there are a couple of Instagram examination instruments that can enable you to find new labels.

Marked hashtags

As noted, making your very own hashtag ought to involve "when," not "if."

Ideal for advancing your Instagram and empowering client produced content, marked hashtags are absolutely significant. They don't really need to be advanced science, however. Here are a few thoughts for basic marked hashtag types and varieties you can conceptualize yourself.

Brand name hashtags (#Topshop)

Brand-specific mottos (#neverstopexploring)

Brand name varieties (#MyAnthropologie or #MySwatch)

General hashtags on Instagram

As noticed, any kind of label will right away improve your probability of commitment.

That is the reason general hashtags, for example, #love (noted to be the most mainstream tag starting at 2019) are a reasonable game, as well. You can sift through this rundown of the most-enjoyed hashtags for some extra thoughts.

Gracious, and remember about occasion hashtags including specialty social occasions. These kinds of tags are in vogue and time-sensitive, ideal for flaunting your character and acquainting yourself with new supporters.

Best practices of utilizing Instagram hashtags

With a superior thought of which hashtags, you should utilize, we should discuss how to put your hashtag strategy without hesitation.

Here are some accepted procedures of hashtags for Instagram to keep in the back of your brain.

Making sense of what number of hashtags on Instagram to utilize

Instagram enables you to incorporate 30 hashtags on some random post.

That doesn't mean you should, however. Truth be told, doing so commonly looks nasty and much the same as catchphrase stuffing.

As noted in our guide on the most proficient method to utilize hashtags on each interpersonal organization, brands can score commitment whether they're utilizing one tag or 15+.

There's a ton of discussion over what number of Instagram hashtags are viewed as ideal for commitment

Be that as it may, what's viewed as ideal? In light of research, top-performing presents show up on keeping the standard of "toning it down would be best."

Numerous brands take a "toning it down would be ideal" way to deal with Instagram hashtags

Taking a gander at the models sprinkled all through this guide, it's difficult to focus on an "ideal" number of Instagram hashtags to use on a post. Normally we see brands incorporate between two to five, plus or minus. This gives marks some squirm room dependent on their subtitles and what terms they're attempting to target.

For instance, Dyson figures out how to incorporate five tags on this post without feeling like needless excess.

Here's a three-label post from PopSockets for reference also.

The takeaway here? As opposed to fixate on the "right" number of hashtags, think "toning it down would be ideal" and be eager to explore. With the assistance of devices like Sprout, you can discover your image's sweet spot just as your top-performing tags.

Incorporate hashtags in your first remark

For focusing on more tags without swarming your inscriptions, it's normal for brands to incorporate their hashtags in the primary remark of their posts.

Look at how Fender does it beneath.

The principal remark of some random post is significant land for Instagram hashtags

Also, reward, the capacity to consequently distribute tags to your first remark is prepared into Sprout's Instagram planning suite. Decent!

Grow makes it a snap to distribute new hashtags to your first Instagram remark

Urge others to utilize your hashtags

If you need individuals to utilize your marked hashtag, you will need to inquire.

Notwithstanding your Instagram bio, make a point to advance your hashtag all through your marketing efforts. This incorporates nearby and by means of email, much the same as Barkshop does in this Instagram-specific bulletin.

Brands need to discover approaches to advance their Instagram hashtags, including by means of email and on location

Match your hashtags to the correct photograph

When you're focusing on as often as possible utilized hashtags, you need the photograph that goes with your Instagram inscription to stick out.

As we referenced before, the hashtags you use ought to be important to the photograph you're posting. This may appear to be an easy decision; however, it merits rehashing.

Keep in mind: despite the fact that including hashtags in your inscriptions can make your presents simpler on the find, the picture is the thing that will pull in clients.

# CHAPTER SEVEN

## ADVANCED TOOLS, FEATURES, AND TECHNIQUES TO WIN THE SOCIAL MEDIA WARFARE

---

What might happen to us computerized advertisers without our free marketing tools and techniques? They take a portion of the heaviness off our shoulders, help us to arrange ourselves, to do as well as can be expected with the brands we are overseeing and by and large make our lives much simpler. Here are some of the advanced tools and features Instagram has to offer.

Instagram Marketing Tools

Free marketing tools for Instagram

1) Crowdfire

Is it true that you are attempting to develop your devotee base on Instagram? If this is the situation, this free device for Instagram has all that you need. You can utilize its work area variant or the application for iOS or Android.

With Crowdfire, you can undoubtedly deal with your devotees and whom you pursue with the accompanying alternatives:

Consequently, unfollow clients who don't follow you.

Duplicate devotees from a different record.

See a rundown of your "fans" (clients whom you don't follow but they follow you).

View your new devotees and individuals who unfollowed you.

Crowdfire herramientas marketing instagram

2) Social Insight

A stunning instrument to gauge your Instagram advertising results. You can utilize it to control your commitment, supporter development, connections and substantially more. It is likewise valuable to choose when the best most are to distribute. As though this wasn't sufficient, it enables you to connect different records and effectively change from one to the next, making it flawless if you deal with a few records.

3) Latergram.me

This free Instagram advertising device gives you a chance to program posts for future dates. When the opportunity arrives, you will get a notification requesting your endorsement to distribute. It likewise enables you to look for and distribute content from the web and includes a few colleagues. It is the nearest you can get to mechanizing your Instagram account.

4) Repost

Do you not feel the absence of a "retweet" catch for Instagram content? This tool makes it nearly as simple to distribute another client's substance all alone account. You can spare photographs and recordings to "repost" them later, look for substance and repost with only a single tick. It even consequently cites the first creator.

5) Soldsie

Another incredible instrument for internet business accounts that are dynamic in Instagram advertising. Soldsie streamlines your profile content to the most extreme and connects your photographs to content your clients need to see. You can likewise pursue changes and make a "Shopping Basket" that consequently adjusts with your Instagram's item posts.

6) SocialRank

An instrument to truly become more acquainted with your clients through its three primary highlights:

Identify: with SocialRank you can get to every one of your adherents' profiles.

Sort out: when you have imported every one of your devotees, you can arrange them as indicated by different channels.

Oversee: make customized records and spare them on SocialRank, trade them to Twitter, or spare them in a CSV position.

7) Facebook Power Editor

Both Facebook and Instagram advertising utilize a similar interface to deal with their advertisements: Facebook Power Editor. Along these lines, if you need to get into advertising on Instagram, you should figure out how to utilize this instrument. Take advantage of the majority of its propelled division highlights to get straight to the group of spectators you need!

Facebook Power Editor Herramientas de marketing Instagram

8) IconoSquare

This free marketing device for Instagram isn't just incredibly valuable, it is likewise splendidly structured. With IconoSquare you can see a wide range of insights in regard to your record: absolute number of preferences, photographs with most likes, a normal number of preferences, all out number of remarks per photograph, adherent development and the sky is the limit from there, all appeared in alluring diagrams.

9) Canva

Set your inward creator free! Canva is an online plan application that gives you a chance to make a wide range of pictures with no particular experience or learning. For Instagrammers, Canva has embellishments, symbols, outlines, channels, stickers and that's only the tip of the iceberg, so you can make the best pictures as effectively as would be prudent.

Canva Herramientas marketing Instagram

10) Snapwidget

If you brand have an amazing Instagram account, don't abandon it, and show it all over! This tool is a sort of free Instagram gadget, intended to embed Instagram pictures and recordings in a sort of photograph exhibition on site pages and websites. It just takes insignificant design to be prepared to introduce, yet if you have any issues you can generally look at the instructional exercise that you can discover on their landing page.

11) PicFrame

A photograph altering stage loaded with highlights and choices to share your photographs. With PicFrame you can pick a casing with 73 different choices, including content and enhancements, pick hues and substantially more, and every last bit of it in HD. This tool is additionally perfect with Blackberry, Android, iOS and Mac. The best answer to giving that extra-proficient look to every single one of your photos.

12) Piqora

This apparatus is intended to make dealing with your Instagram people group as simple as could be allowed. Utilizing it, you can develop your locale, oversee content, break down pictures' and hashtags' outcomes and substantially more.

13) Tagboard

An instrument for you to securely, effectively and rapidly deal with your Instagram content. You can channel posts by watchword, hashtags and most prevalent posts, just as square posts and hostile remarks, and so forth. Its pursuit framework gives you a chance to discover content only seconds after it being distributed, making it perfect for keeping awake to-date.

14) Curalate

Another free instrument for Instagram advertising, with a few exceptionally fascinating highlights, particularly for brands in the web-based business area:

It improves your change rate, increments your adherent rundown and pull in more rush hour gridlock to your Instagram account.

Expository picture framework that estimates results as indicated by different criteria.

Screens the arrival on speculation.

Distributes posts.

15) ScheduGram

Another device concentrated on distributing posts, for you to have the option to truly make the most of your downtime, knowing it all is being dealt with. ScheduGram allows you to transfer and program pictures and recordings through a few Instagram account and different clients. It is unmistakably an incredible method to spare time and endeavors for you and your group.

## User-Generated Content for Creating Great Content For Instagram

It may shock you to hear that measurements state you're just about the last individual your group of spectators needs to get notification from.

As per Crowdtap, 20 to 30 years old are 50 percent more averse to confide in material from conventional sources (that is us), than client produced content.

Yet, don't think about it literally.

Incidentally, this reluctance with respect to 20 to 30 years old to trust and draw in with brand-driven substance can really be a wide open door for advertisers.

The main issue? Time.

Almost every substance marketing proficient stresses over how to stay aware of the unending number of requests on their time.

Luckily, there's an answer – Instagram.

Instagram probably won't appear the most difficult stage for substance creation, however, there's in every case progressively substance to make and apparently never sufficient opportunity (or cash) to do it.

Surprisingly more dreadful, the content we do deliver once in a while neglects to inspire any kind of substantial outcome at all. It's a genuine issue.

Consider things thusly, however …

Consider the possibility that recent college grads' doubt for brand-based substance is really – in a wiped out, turned kind of way – the appropriate response.

I trust it is.

Why? All things considered, while web clients are dismissing marketing messages everywhere, they're effectively creating, sharing and drawing in with substance delivered by different clients.

UGC infographic test for influence client produced content

A similar report from Crowdtap demonstrates that youngsters spend upwards of five hours consistently expending client created content (UGC).

They connect with it all the more unreservedly, trust it further and are more effectively moved to action by it than some other sort of substance.

Best of all, client created substance is simple for advertisers to saddle and profit by. Instagram, maybe more than some other stage, is the perfect spot to do it.

Regardless of whether this is your first time utilizing Instagram UGC or your hundredth, the accompanying eight hints will help improve your outcomes and forestall potential tangles:

1. Pick a ground-breaking hashtag for entries

One of the simplest and best approaches to get clients to supply you with substance is to urge them to tag photographs with an extraordinary hashtag. With a client's consent, you would then be able to snatch the best ones and post them on you own account.

Burberry, the popular English design brand, was worried that its image personality was becoming old and unimportant. They made an uncontrollably fruitful client created marketing effort worked around the hashtag #ArtOfTheTrench.

#ArtOfTheTrench hashtag for influence client produced content

Clients posted photographs of themselves wearing the famous Burberry channel coat to both a specific site and Instagram. Thousands took an interest and the brand's picture was revitalized.

Burberry scarcely created a solitary bit of substance.

A more fragile hashtag most likely wouldn't have yielded such sensational outcomes.

2. Make your item 'Instagrammable'

Keep in mind the Share a Coke crusade?

By just customizing their jugs, Coke transformed something that was pervasive in the public eye into something remarkable, individual and famously shareable.

We as a whole know how it turned out.

Instagram – and each online networking stage – was overwhelmed with pictures of Coke bottles for a considerable length of time.

If your item fits Instagram, you'll have no issue discovering client produced a substance to post. If your item or administration isn't normally attractive, discover a path for clients to increase the value of it.

That is to say, whose thought would it say it was to begin drawing on Starbuck's cups, at any rate?

If you're truly stayed with the majority of this UGC goodness, Instagram marketing offices like Kickstagram spend significant time in helping businesses make their items and administrations progressively internet-based life benevolent.

Whatever the case, recall – UGC is tied in with adding new voices to the discussion.

3. Make sharing commonly advantageous

This is kind of an easy decision, yet it merits your time.

If Instagrammers don't feel complimented or energized that you're keen on their posts, they presumably won't submit them to you. You should have the option to offer them some sort of impetus.

Instagram post from Buffer's Instagram represent influence client created content

Despite the fact that you positively would, I'm able to not suggest that you offer any sort of monetary or item based motivating forces like most client produced substance battles outside of Instagram.

I'm trying to say that you have to offer something in return for a client's endeavors.

Give them a whoop if you utilize their post. Pursue their record. Give them a coupon. When it's in a client's best enthusiasm to share high caliber, imaginative posts with you, you'll never need for content again.

4. Set the bar high, yet dispose of hindrances to passage

You can't share simply anything.

With the end goal for this to work, the client produced substance must be beautiful and significant, much the same as each other content type. Thus, be particular about the presents you pick on offer on your official feed.

If you can't see a post reverberating with your group of spectators and yielding high commitment rate, disregard it.

All things considered, it's significant that anybody could conceivably be highlighted.

Organizations that are effectively utilizing UGC on Instagram effectively energize photograph entries from anybody and everybody. If you limit your enthusiasm to proficient picture takers or influencers, the enchantment of UGC will be generally lost.

5. Get your site included

Instagram is an incredible marketing apparatus; however, it works far superior when matched with other media channels as a feature of an incorporated crusade.

Is it accurate to say that you are attempting to get clients amped up for submitting content? Make an extraordinary page on your site for entries and figure out how to make an advancement out of it.

Starbucks' authentic site for influence client created content

Both Burberry and Starbucks utilized their ubiquity on Instagram to venture into effective UGC marketing on the web. Burberry made an online style file made out of free clients wearing their channel coats.

Starbucks held a challenge to structure another cup, which brought about 1,800 sections – and some truly cool cups, to be completely forthright.

The two organizations extended their group of spectators and reached by associating Instagram with other marketing channels.

6. Claim a lifestyle

Brands like REI and GoPro have been massively fruitful on Instagram, utilizing only UGC. The key to their prosperity is owning a specific lifestyle.

REI is a solid open-air brand that highlights a ton of photographs from clients. When Instagrammers have cool climbing or outdoors photographs and need exposure, they submit them naturally.

GoPro does likewise with the way of life of outrageous games and experience travel.

Pause for a moment to ponder the lifestyle related to your image. Odds are you'll discover some socially pertinent point to underline and assemble your crusade around.

7. Try not to trust that content will come to you

Entrenched records don't for the most part experience any difficulty discovering client produced a content to distribute. Be that as it may, if this is your first endeavor at a UGC battle, it may take more time to get things ready for action.

If you've made a hashtag and requested entries, however, haven't gotten anything extraordinary, don't be hesitant to go searching for it.

It's consummately satisfactory to connect with Instagrammers by means of remark or direct message, requesting to utilize a post. Most clients will be complimented and accommodating.

When you have a couple of UGC posts up on your feed, others will be bound to present their very own as well.

8. Try not to end your own substance generation

UGC is moderate, straightforward and exceptionally successful.

Huge numbers of the best marked records on Instagram distribute only UGC. Be that as it may, it's great to once in a while post something from your very own camera.

Goody Silverstein's Instagram represent influence client produced content

By keeping an equalization, you'll be better ready to control your image account and keep your group of spectators educated as to any newsworthy happenings and up and coming occasions.

## Best User-Generated Content Campaigns on Instagram

When it comes time to settle on a buying choice, who are you bound to trust - a brand, or a kindred shopper who uses the item?

We're bound to take suggestions from loved ones than brands when it comes time to settle on purchasing choices - And this is the reasoning behind user-generated content via web-based social networking.

User-generated content, or UGC, comprises of any type of content that is made by users and customers about a brand or item. UGC isn't paid for, and its validness makes the user the brand advertiser also.

UGC is especially common on Instagram, where brands can without much of a stretch repost UGC from users' records. What's more, it's beneficial for brands to do this - 76% of people studied said they believed content mutual by "normal" individuals more than by brands, and about 100% of buyers trust proposals from others.

In this post, we'll talk about exactly how fruitful UGC on Instagram can be - just as audit 10 brands utilizing it effectively.

**Why User-Generated Content?**

In the current year's Internet Trends Report, Mary Meeker displayed some convincing information about the accomplishment of UGC for brands on Instagram.

UGC can generate greater commitment on Instagram - which means more remarks and likes on posts. What's more, commitment is fundamentally imperative to brands' prosperity on the stage - because the more users draw in with your stuff, the higher your posts are organized in the Instagram feed, and the more probable it is that new users will locate your content on the Explore tab.

A lot of worldwide brands is sharing Instagram content reposted, or "regrammed," from fans and users.

Since we comprehend the significance of UGC, how about we jump into how a portion of these brands are slaughtering the UGC game on Instagram?

**Examples of the Best User-Generated Content on Instagram**

1) The UPS Store

No, we don't mean UPS, where you may go to send care bundles or occasion gifts to your friends and family. We mean The UPS Store, which uses its Instagram to grandstand the clients you probably won't consider as promptly - entrepreneurs. Entrepreneurs on Instagram post content utilizing the hashtag #TheUPSStoreCustomer, which The UPS Store at that point offers to its own record, as so:

This is a cunning UGC battle other B2B brands should observe - particularly if the items and administrations themselves aren't particularly attractive. Instagram posts including pressing tape, shipping peanuts, and cardboard boxes probably won't be outwardly fascinating, yet off camera accounts of genuine individuals and brands The UPS Store is aiding are.

The takeaway for Marketers: Use UGC to exhibit a sudden or extraordinary part of your image. Regardless of whether it's content from your clients, your users, or individuals from your locale, request that different Instagrammers submit content that demonstrates "the opposite side" of what your image is about.

2) Aerie

Ladies' dress organization Aerie's #AerieReal battle is #UGCgoals. The battle is basic, however, ground-breaking.

There's been expansive discussion and clamor over the exorbitant utilization of photograph altering in marketing advertising - fixated around its effect on the young ladies devouring magazines and pictures via web-based networking media. There's been specific worry around the effect altered photographs can have on ladies' confidence and feeling of a sound self-perception.

So Aerie made a promise to quit modifying photographs of models in its swimsuits. Furthermore, for each Instagram user that posted an unedited photograph of themselves in a swimsuit (utilizing the hashtag #AerieReal, obviously), Aerie presently donates one dollar to (NEDA) the National Eating Disorders Association.

The takeaway for Marketers: Give individuals motivation to engage in your crusade that is greater than Instagram itself. Regardless of whether it's a mindfulness battle or a gift drive like Aerie, clients need to purchase from organizations that help significant causes. If you can, band together with a reason or magnanimous association your message resounds with to get Instagrammers amped up for your UGC battle. You'll do useful for the world, you'll drive commitment on the stage, and more individuals will find out about your image through verbal exchange if it gets on.

3) Buffer

Web based life booking device Buffer uses the #BufferCommunity to grandstand the photos and characters of its a wide range of users around the globe. These pictures aren't special - or even remotely brand-driven - and that is the thing that makes them so compelling (OK, the adorable pup presumably helps as well).

Support's tools are tied in with making it simpler to share and strategize via web-based networking media, and these photographs verifiably share the message that Buffer's people group individuals can work from anyplace, on a wide range of undertakings, much appreciated (to some degree) to its usability.

The takeaway for Marketers: Cultivate a brand character so solid that your users need to impart their life to you via web-based networking media. Make an incredible item, exceed expectations at helping clients succeed, and minister a nearness via web-based networking media your users need to continue connecting with. At that point, request that they share with you so you can keep adding character and decent variety to your content to demonstrate what your locale is about - helping individuals be better at web-based social networking, for Buffer's situation.

4) Wayfair

Online furniture store Wayfair has a fabulous time UGC crusade that lets clients exhibit the consequences of their web-based shopping binges. Utilizing the hashtag #WayfairAtHome, users can post their home arrangements highlighting Wayfair items:

At that point, Wayfair reposts UGC and gives a connection so users can search for the things included in a genuine client's home - a shrewd strategy for consolidating client tributes and plan motivation across the board.

Wayfair has another UGC battle that is not as well known, however, it's a charming compelling approach to demonstrate its items in real life with the assistance of the #WayfairPetSquad.

The takeaway for Marketers: Leverage UGC to help Instagram users find and shop for your items. Keep in mind, individuals trust client tributes, and if you show them being effectively utilized by genuine individuals, it's simpler to get them to your site to begin shopping.

5) IBM

Programming goliath IBM utilizes UGC on Instagram fundamentally from its clients and network individuals utilizing the hashtag #IBM. Its UGC strategy is more straightforward than some depicted already, yet it works admirably at giving an inside take a gander at one of the greatest innovation organizations on the planet.

It's cool to see genuine people working at IBM and utilizing its items and administrations to do things you and I do each day - like taking slyly presented photos and leading gathering conceptualizes.

The takeaway for Marketers: Showcase the human side of your image - particularly if your item or administration can't be effectively imagined, as on account of IBM. Source content from clients, representatives, and network individuals to indicate what your item resembles in real life so different Instagrammers can imagine themselves utilizing it as well.

6) Netflix

Well known video spilling administration Netflix utilizes UGC to advance fans' posts about specific shows and motion pictures - and hashtags the title Support share awareness about latest release.

Netflix is inclining toward making progressively unique

programming, so getting the word out about new discharges is a key piece of its online life strategy. UGC indicates other individuals are getting amped up for new demonstrates as well - and makes Instagrammers going over Netflix's Instagram charmed to perceive what the complaint is about.

Takeaway for Marketers: If you're making a declaration or discharging another item, use UGC to get the word out about your fans and clients giving it a shot just because. You'll help make an input circle to support an ever -increasing number of individuals on Instagram find out about you - and what new item they can engage with.

7) Hootsuite

Internet based life the executives programming organization Hootsuite utilizes the hashtag #HootsuiteLife to advance UGC about what it resembles to work at Hootsuite around the globe.

Hootsuite's way of life is something the organization is glad for - and it utilizes this fun method for living and attempting to draw in gifted individuals to join them. #HootsuiteLife is about representatives and network individuals exhibiting how much fun it is to function at Hootsuite all over internet-based life. It utilizes the hashtag to engage workers to impart their days to the remainder of the world via web-based networking media.

An auxiliary UGC crusade - #LifeofOwly - gives workers a chance to show off the organization's adorable mascot in real life, as well.

Takeaway for Marketers: Collaborate with your selecting and HR groups to check whether you can consolidate powers to drive online networking commitment and help procure new individuals at the same time. If your association has a ton to offer and you need to feature your way of life, occasions, and advantages, collaborate to make a worker UGC battle that enables representatives to share and draws in incredible new ability.

8) Starbucks

Each December, Starbucks dispatches the most recent #RedCupContest to advance its vacation themed regular refreshments and - you got it - red cups. It urges espresso consumers to submit shots of their espressos the opportunity to win an expensive Starbucks gift card - and consumers consistently convey (there are in excess of 40,000 posts of red cups and tallying).

The #RedCupContest is a brilliant UGC battle. It boosts fans to take part and connect online by offering a prize, it advances a regular crusade, and it generates deals - because you need to purchase a red cup to snap a photo first.

Takeaway for Marketers: Use a challenge to advance and generate buzz around a UGC battle. Offer a prize for investment (utilizing a marked hashtag, obviously) to get individuals amped up for remarking, posting, and sharing on Instagram.

9) Adobe

Innovative programming organization Adobe utilizes the hashtag #Adobe_Perspective to source and share content from specialists and content makers utilizing its product to carry out their responsibilities consistently.

It can at times be difficult to envision what you can do with a product without seeing it in real life, and this UGC crusade gives Adobe a chance to show off its abilities while connecting with its locale of users.

#Adobe_InColor is Adobe's Pride Month-themed UGC crusade that is as of now generated almost 300 posts in the initial couple of long stretches of June. This UGC battle lets Adobe exhibit the ability of its clients and the qualities and culture of its locale plainly and effectively via web-based networking media.

Takeaway for Marketers: Encourage clients and users to share their outcomes from effectively utilizing your item. These pictures will help give planned clients a thought of what they can expect, and incredible outcomes will represent themselves to advance your item. Also, if you're doing a social battle, open it up to your whole network, and not only workers, to generate mindfulness and buzz around a culture activity you're pleased with.

10) BMW

Vehicle organization BMW utilizes #BMWRepost to share Instagram posts of pleased BMW proprietors and their wheels:

BMW offers extravagance autos to proprietors who are without a doubt glad for their accomplishment, and this crusade offers proprietors the chance to show off - and lets BMW hotshot its pleased and faithful base of clients. If I were on the chase for a vehicle and saw these numerous cheerful BMW users, I should seriously mull over one of its autos for my buy. (I don't have a clue how to drive, yet you get my drift.)

Takeaway for Marketers: Give clients and users a stage from which they can gloat about their buy. You don't have to sell extravagant things - there are a lot of ordinary brands with religion followings who love to get connected via web-based networking media regarding why they cherish purchasing specific brands. Make a hashtag that gives clients a chance to share why they adore you, and they'll cherish you back.

# CHAPTER EIGHT

# HOW TO RUN SUCCESSFUL INSTAGRAM CONTESTS

With 400 million month to month dynamic users and in excess of 80 million posts every day, Instagram has built up itself as a conspicuous stage for brands hoping to extend their scope and connect with their crowd.

Making sense of how to dispatch a successful Instagram contest, be that as it may, is significantly more subtle. Indeed, it seems like a powerful strategy for working up discussion - it gains by user generated content (UGC) and commonly requires next to no dedication for members. In any case, where do you start? What's more, how might you make sure that you're considering every contingency?

The most effective method to Run an Instagram Contest: A 10-Step Guide

1) Plan destinations and objectives.

Before you plunge into an Instagram marketing contest, it's critical to design it in full first. The way to running a successful contest is to have a reason - one that lines up with the interests and practices of your intended interest group.

Regardless of whether you're hoping to develop your image likeness on Instagram or work out your rundown of adherents, it's significant that you set a specific objective with the goal that you're not left pondering whether you were successful at last.

To help tighten your center, consider the group of spectators you're attempting to reach: What sorts of posts do they like seeing from you? What sorts of posts do they appreciate posting individually? How would they behave on the platform? If you're hoping to scrounge up a great deal of commitment, you should mean to focus your objectives and reason around content that your group of spectators really needs to post and connect with.

Remember to set up a time period and spending plan for your contest, as deciding these strategic subtleties forthright will enable you to structure an increasingly viable contest.

2) Create a section strategy.

In spite of the fact that the best connections with Instagram contests are those that are really fast, ask your crowd to post their own photographs; there is a number of different ways brands can make contests on Instagram. Because of this, it's imperative to set up and underline the importance for your group of spectators to really participate in the contest.

Here are a few thoughts for how your crowd may participate in your contest:

Have your crowd post a photograph or a video to Instagram with a specific hashtag and a specific subject.

Have your group of spectators exclusively tail you or do as such notwithstanding making a post.

Have your group of spectators label your image in their post.

Have your group of spectators Like or remark on one of your posts.

Ensure you set up what the rules are to participate in the contest and make that unmistakable on your limited time materials. Possibly your contest is revolved around a hashtag that does exclude your image name. Regardless you need your image to be labeled to gain acknowledgment, you need to make that unmistakable in your standards.

3) Find the ideal hashtag.

A decent hashtag is a key to any captivating Instagram contest. Without it, there's no connection between the contest and the content being generated. As it were, hashtags help make brand as well as contest acknowledgment by filling in as an instrument for sharing and driving investment.

The issue is, making the ideal hashtag can be precarious. If your contest will have a time allotment (and it should), you need to create a hashtag that you're not going to need to use again and again. Also, there are huge amounts of hashtags being made every day, making it difficult to come up with something that is one of a kind and snappy.

To enable you to think of the best fit, consider these contest hashtag rules:

Short: Create a hashtag that sticks in individuals' psyches. The more meaningful and identifiable your hashtag is, the better it is for your contest.

Significant: Make sure you're making a hashtag that is unmistakably related back to your image name, item, or administrations. If you choose a conventional, swarmed hashtag, for example, #ThrowbackThursday, all things considered, you'll experience serious difficulties making sense of who your members really are.

Important: Users are probably going to see advancements for your contest preceding really posting the content. This implies your hashtag should be essential enough for users to consider it once and make sure to act at some point later. Attempt to make your hashtag appealing, simple to find, and simple to compose. Stay away from odd spellings and confusing word choices.

All inclusive: Think about your group of spectators. Does everybody communicate in a similar language or utilize comparative words? If you have a universal group of spectators, ensure you're cautious about utilizing slang words or locale specific terms that may befuddle individuals.

Uncommon: Make an inquiry before you pick a hashtag. Are there loads of users utilizing your optimal hashtag for some different purposes? If along these lines, you might need to make a beeline for the planning phase.

A case of a viable, drawing in a hashtag:

Prior this year, Mint.com, an online individual planning and monetary administration organization, facilitated their #MyMintMoment contest.

The contest was well-intended for various reasons, one of which is its hashtag. The hashtag - #MyMintMoment - is short, important, and straightforward. It remained on-brand and had an unmistakable subject.

The objective of the contest was to get users to post about the things they were putting something aside for. Members posted pictures of tattoos, excursions, weddings, kids, vehicles - and so on.

This is an incredible case of a viable hashtag, but on the other hand it's an extraordinary case of how UGC can be utilized to drive marketing choices. Consider it: Mint got some information about things they were putting something aside for. Sounds like a simple method to pick up understanding encompassing the remarkable thought processes and interests that fuel the use of their administration, isn't that right?

4) Clearly characterize a subject.

Because most Instagram contests are UGC-based, it's critical to pick a subject so your users comprehend what sorts of pictures and recordings to post.

In a perfect world, you need to pick a topic that lines up with your market, item, or administrations. In any case, you can likewise exploit seasons, and occasions that line up with your item or brand.

A case of a viable topic:

The previous summer, D Magazine, a city and lifestyle magazine situated in Dallas, utilized the Texas summer warmth to make a viable #StayCoolDallas contest. The contest urged members to submit photographs of approaches to remain cool in the Dallas heat. Entries included everything from drinks at most loved bars and cafés to fun summer exercises.

This contest and hashtag worked especially well because of the multifaceted nuance of "cool" - which at last left space for members to get imaginative with their elucidations. This is an incredible case of how to make a commitment too simple.

While the hashtag wasn't thoroughly marked specific, the subject was especially in accordance with their image and energy for everything Dallas. Furthermore, because of the contest, they were left with a huge amount of new material to get ideas for their next issue.

5) Decide how victors will be picked.

Some portion of a well-planned contest is illuminating your members regarding how the champ will be picked. Most contests are resolved dependent on one of two different ways: a vote or a jury. How about we investigate how every choice functions...

Casting a ballot:

An incredible method to help the virality of your contest is to have members vie for the most Likes. If the prize is profitable enough, your members will probably impart their presents on their companions crosswise over diverts so as to get however many Likes as could reasonably be expected.

This strategy augments your crowd's span. Simultaneously, it tends to be adverse to your contest, as you keep running into issues with people utilizing "Like bots" to increase artificial Likes. To keep away from any complexities here, you'll need to advance unmistakable principles that address the utilization of these kinds of workarounds.

Jury:

For quality and by and large decency, the jury technique is the unmistakable victor. With the jury technique, you select a gathering of specialists to settle on a victor, as opposed to depending on a democratic framework.

There are advantages and disadvantages to votes or juries, however, regardless of the manner in which you pick, make a point to obviously express your technique so your users realize what they're competing for. Numerous brands have a blended strategy approach and utilize a mix of democratic and jury to decide the victor.

6) Choose a fitting honor.

When figuring out what the honor for you contest ought to be, you have to think about your intended interest group, your budgetary limitations, and how forceful your objectives are.

Keep in mind that by requesting that your group of spectators take part in the contest, you're requesting that they make a move on something. Similarly, as with any exertion like this, you'll need the estimation of the prize to exceed the expense and vitality required to participate in the contest. While individuals may bypass a chance to win a free shirt, almost certainly, they'd be happy to go through the motions for something like a free trip.

While your prize should coordinate the passage activity, it ought to likewise line up with the interests of your intended target group. Ask yourself: What might my intended target group like to have? Your rundown of answers for this - spending plan not considered - may be enormous. Of course, everybody needs that free trip we referenced before, however that is not the point. The objective is to find a prize that is both significant and applicable to your image.

Gift cards, free benefits, coupons, giveaways, and item goodie packs are on the whole basic prizes that brands use for contests, however we're generally for getting inventive, as well.

Ideas of an innovative contest prize:

One of our preferred instances of contest prizes was Sperry's Photo Real Design Contest. Sperry urged users to post "epic photographs" that spoke to an "odyssey."

Members at that point submitted photographs of a wide range of things - nature shots, brilliant workmanship, genuine individuals, and so forth - to be made a decision about dependent on innovativeness and the number of Likes it got.

The victor that was picked got an extraordinary pair of Sperry shoes highlighting their photograph. Discussion about an innovative prize, isn't that so? Also, it filled in as an incredible case of how brands can utilize contests to rouse genuine item thoughts.

7) Create terms and conditions.

Remember that when you set a challenge with a prize, you should pursue lawful rules. The laws that will concern you rely upon where you're based and whom you permit to participate in your contest, so you ought to counsel your attorney for assistance drafting your terms and conditions. Making a terms and conditions page is an absolute necessity.

Here are some basic terms individuals include:

The name and contact subtleties of the advancing brand

The dates of the contest

The guidelines of who can enter, (for example, age and representative limitations)

The rules for how individuals enter

The rules for how a victor is picked

The date and way victors will be declared

The date and way the victor will be educated

The timespan the champ needs to react and guarantee their prize

The specific of the prize (counting number of prizes, the portrayal of prizes, and any provisos)

The subtleties of how the prize will be conveyed

Recognize that the advancement isn't supported, embraced or directed by, or related with Instagram or some other web-based life utilized all through the contest.

Note: Check out Instagram's Promotion rules and make a point to agree to their principles.

8) Promote like there's no tomorrow.

Since you have a strong arrangement set up, it's an ideal opportunity to advance the hell out of your contest.

Where's the best spot to begin getting the message out? The potential outcomes are apparently unfathomable, however, here are a couple of thoughts to move your advancement endeavors:

Your blog. Compose a post on your site specifying the contest and use it as a dispatch point for your contest's greeting page.

Internet based life. What better spot to dispatch an online life contest than via web-based networking media? Direct your current supporters to the contest by incorporating an abbreviated connection in your profile and referencing that connection in your special posts.

Email. Stretch out the welcome to partake to your email supporters by sending over a fast and agreeable email to report the offer.

9) Monitor entries.

Observing both your limited time endeavors and the degree of interest during your contest is fundamental for gathering your objectives and making an arrangement to catch up on your contest.

Try to figure out what measurements you'd like to utilize and how you'll monitor them. Here are a few measurements to think about utilizing:

A number of entries - Total number of posts submitted in consistence with your terms and conditions.

Preferences per accommodation - Helps you monitor potential victors if your contest is chosen by vote.

Number of members - If users can submit more than one entry, what number of extraordinary members added to your contest?

Top members - Who shared the most content during your campaign? Monitoring this encourages you to better draw in with your greatest fans.

All out Likes - Measures the complete number of Likes on all entries in your contest.

All outreach - Captures the number of adherents of your members at the hour of entry. Intended to demonstrate to you the potential reach of your battle.

Adherent development during the contest - Measure how much your following expanded during the contest's timespan.

If your present crowd is moderately little, and you don't anticipate that in excess of 30 entries to your contest, you may choose to screen your contest physically. To do this, allot somebody the errand of monitoring entries every day. Toward the part of the bargain, somebody should experience every entry and measure and record the outcomes from every entry.

If you're checking your contest physically, have a go at utilizing a device like Tagboard or Google Alerts to monitor when your hashtag is being referenced on the internet, making it simpler to follow entries. (HubSpot clients: You can set up a custom Stream in your Social Monitoring apparatus to watch a specific hashtag. Adapt progressively here.)

If you're expecting admirably more than 30 entries, in any case, you can envision how difficult observing your entries may be. If that is the situation, you might need to investigate an Instagram-specific apparatus, for example, Iconosquare.

10) Follow up in like manner.

When the contest is finished, you can't neglect to catch up on the principles you set in any case. Remember your terms and conditions when inspecting the entries to guarantee that you're 100% reasonable in your assessment.

Once more, this is the reason setting up your terms and conditions at an opportune time is so significant, as it will furnish you with an archived arrangement for choosing, reaching, and granting the champ.

When you've chosen and notified the victor, remember to make the declaration openly.

## The Best Tips And Tricks For Your Most Effective Advertising On The Social Media Platform Yet

It's important for businesses to advance themselves, regardless of whether through brand mindfulness, deals, content marketing or other compelling strategies. While numerous organizations comprehend that it's essential to advertise, they probably won't comprehend what this strategy completely involves, and perhaps miss taking significant strides in the process toward accomplishing their objectives.

As of now, numerous organizations are using internet-based life to assist their image. Yet, by not having a reasonable thought of what they are attempting to accomplish or how to go about it, time and cash are likely being squandered. Beneath, Active Web Group's Social Media, experts give profitable bits of knowledge to show the correct method to approach advertising on Social Media platforms.

Not exclusively will this learning set aside time and cash, yet powerful Social Media advertising will likewise achieve your business' essential objective to advance your image.

## WITHOUT A CLEAR GOAL

It is silly and a misuse of cash to advertise only for advertising. A viable advertisement consistently has a reasonable message, advancing mindfulness as well as influential activity. Without a quantifiable objective, the advertisement's quality will endure, as will the measurements, which are key components in successful long-haul battles (clarified beneath).

## OVERCOMPLICATING THE MESSAGE

An appreciation of the customer's point of view is important when advertising through web-based networking media. Like in most innovative communication strategies, internet networking offers people a stage to find and process data easily as it's all instantaneous. Many internet travelers would have limited attention capability and the message needs to be transmitted in five seconds or less, the period a visitor decides on whether to continue on or exit a website. It is necessary to pass on your message as quickly as as anticipated under the circumstances along these lines.

Web-based social networking consumers browse at their course of events in pursuit of material from the platforms they purchase through (companions, families, distraction, news, etc.) as such sources are what stimulate their desires. In any event, such consumers are not present to look for your ad(s) so make sure that your advertising attracts your attention, transmits a notification and either makes a lasting impact or induces an action (depending on the form of advertisement).

**NOT Checking**

No commercial is impeccable, so it is impossible to someone for all intents and purposes to render an extraordinarily good first run promotion. Regardless of how good or experienced web creators may be, checking multiple thoughts and renditions of a thinking for ideal outcomes is indispensable. It may sound like a lot of effort, but anything as simple as turning a single term may have the difference of performance and deceit.

**NOT ADAPTING TO DATA**

Past their underlying expectation, advertisements may offer optional advantage as they additionally give or gather significant data that can be utilized for your on-going marketing endeavors. In view of the outcomes, you can change your content for reliable improvement. This could have to do with basic factors, for example,

- Timing
- Structure
- Verbiage
- Suggestions to take action
- Among many, numerous others

**Insufficient Targeting**

Powerful focusing on might appear glaringly evident, yet numerous businesses disregard exactly how significant this progression is. Evaluating your intended interest group isn't sufficient, broad research is basic. If your advertisement misses its imprint, you will burn through important time and cash.

**Why Advertise on Social Media?**

There are dangers to think about when utilizing any news source. Online networking success requires an underlying comprehension of who is the advertisement's intended interest group. For some (counting experts), focusing on is the biggest obstacle to conquer when making a progression of advertisements. Web based life (Facebook specifically) can make this profoundly basic advance a lot simpler by enabling the advertiser to focus by statistic highlights such including:

Age

Sex

Area

Salary

Instruction

Occupation

Religion

Political Views

Restful Interests

With such specific fields and propelled calculations available to them, Facebook can use data and precisely present your advertisement to prospects well on the way to be keen on its content. Other than the specific fields of measures, Facebook likewise targets prospects all the more proficiently as you're ready to pick different promotions, in view of your objectives. Facebook additionally catches progressed and ultra-specific examination that help measure results with exact detail. This guarantees practically no advertisement spend is squandered simultaneously. Could boards or TV advertisements guarantee similar outcomes?

Kinds of Ads

Facebook

Mindfulness

These are extraordinary for picking up footing and presentation for your image, which is perfect for more up to date pages. Mindfulness promotions work best when arriving at a nearby open, instead of concentrating more on socioeconomics, which in the end winds up unavoidable. Mindfulness promotions comprise of:

Brand Awareness

Elevates your content to build your image's message, which is perfect for leaving an impact on potential clients

Reach

Amplifies impressions/presentation – the more extensive the message, the better outcomes you will get

Thought

Thought advertisements are normally utilized more for better-settled pages. Running advertisements of this gauge are most worthwhile when your image has a characterized Content Marketing Strategy and Buyer's Persona is built up. Thought advertisements comprise of:

Traffic

Amazing for heading to a non-Facebook goal, for example, your site

Commitment

Broad when talking about online networking as a rule, so Facebook ventured to stall this promotion type into three sub-classes

Post Engagement

Builds post likes/remarks/shares – incredible strategy for making viral content

Page Likes

Elevates your page to those probable intrigued – significant for starting your page

Occasion Responses

Advances an occasion – useful for focusing locally

Application Installs

Advances your application

Video Views

Advances video content

Lead Generation

Generate leads – ideal for businesses hoping to assemble data and empower information exchanges.

Facebook has additionally included an extraordinary new highlight that enables you to part test your promotions. Exploit by rolling out unpretentious improvements, for example, duplicate, hues, invitations to take action, and so on to decide the best promotion for your target.

Transformation

Transformation advertisements help accomplish the main concern, which for some, businesses are deals. Transformation promotions comprise of:

Changes

In the wake of introducing a following pixel, content is advanced and pursues users, giving more knowledge with respect to how they reacted to your promotion past just changes

Item Catalog Sales

Makes promotions including items from your inventory

Store Visits

Advances mindfulness for block and-mortars with store headings

Instagram

Since Facebook obtained Instagram, you can connect records and run comparable promotions on every stage at the same time. Just keen on Instagram advertising? You can expel Facebook from the situation segment of your promotion to run your advertisement on Instagram as it were.

Twitter

Site Clicks or Conversions

Advances tweets where advertiser pays per connection click – Ideal for driving site traffic and deals

Devotees

Builds supporters – extraordinary for new pages

Mindfulness

Builds mindfulness for your image's message – advertiser pays per impression

Tweet Engagement

Elevates content to users destined to draw in – perfect for expanding quality prospects

LinkedIn

Supported Content

Enables work to mark mindfulness; most appropriate for B2B or enlisting endeavors

InMail

Target prospects and sends customized messages

Content Ads

Directs people to your site for expanded changes

Promotions Aren't Enough!

While advertising via web-based networking media is without a doubt significant, we should incorporate that advertising is just one part of the puzzle. Related to a first rate marketing and content strategy, advertisements can increase reach, commitment and deals, however, just as previously mentioned that not where the work ends.

Natural Content

A relentless equalization of natural content keeps up the consideration of your group of spectators and shows your image is exceptional. Promotions are normally intended to help the impact of your natural content just as increment deals and site presentation. The bigger your natural reach is, the more remote your free day by day natural content will expand your image.

The 80/20 standard is an arrangement of rules to follow in which 80% of the content you post is instructive, for example, online journals, news about your organization, marked content, significant books, and so on while the other 20% is content identifying with leads and deals. If your limited time content is excessively substantial, your group of spectators may be killed to the possibility of your image, as they need to be instructed and engaged, as opposed to sold.

Audiences

One HUGE misguided judgment business have on adherent tallies happens inside the numbers. Individuals accept success has been accomplished when they see countless adherents or supporters but neglect to think about the estimation of every individual devotee. Not all supporters are made equivalent!

500 quality supporters who will draw in and in the long run buy is unquestionably more important than 5000 devotees who are following for a pursue back. If an adherent isn't focusing on your content or purchasing, at that point they aren't significant. When evaluating the significance of adherents, think about why you have an online life nearness in any case.

What You Can Do To Get The Most Out Of Your Instagram Advertising

Instagram has never been more well-known than it is presently. It was at that point on the road to success when it propelled in 2010, and it appears to have tied on a jetpack after Facebook's procurement of the site.

As per eMarketer, the quantity of organizations utilizing Instagram for advertising has consistently expanded year over year, and this number is probably going to outperform other social channels like Twitter by 2017.

Instagram is getting to be one of the top channels for advertisers, likely because of the way that visual media is undeniably more helpful for connecting with spectators than other conventional marketing channels on the web. Regardless of whether this prevalence is brought about by the development of portable innovation or the broad utilization of cell phone and tablet applications by Millennials is more diligently to decide.

A significant part of the success that advertisers have had the option to accomplish from the photograph sharing site originates from Instagram's advertising division utilizing Facebook's information packed advertising calculation. The blend of the two advertising stages takes into consideration the multi-layer group of spectators focusing on, including everything from essential statistic data to investigation on users' conduct and premiums.

Notwithstanding, utilizing this amazing stage won't really ensure successful result for each crusade. Crowds are as yet a flighty pack and your advertisements need to go a long ways past the customary "purchase this presently" approach so as to stand separated from the challenge and reel in new prospects and clients.

We should take a gander at how you can get progressively out of your Instagram advertisement crusades with these seven hints:

Reward: Looking to grow an Instagram following quick? Socially Rich gives a done-to you administration that gets you genuine, directed Instagram supporters on your own or business Instagram accounts. While never going through Instagram! Attempt it for nothing here.

1. Utilize Instagram's new zoom include

Instagram as of late propelled an update to the administration that enables you to somewhat shut everything down with your Instagram advertisements.

Instagram's new zoom highlight enables users to squeeze the screen to focus in on both photographs and recordings. The option was executed because of the high number of user demands Instagram was getting to have the component added to its foundation.

It didn't take long for brands to begin trying different things with the zoom include either. Some smart organizations even evaluated moderate movement impacts and new channels, notwithstanding advertising using narrating on their Instagram feeds.

Each new element offers open doors for brands to flex their inventiveness and find better approaches to make their promotions radiate through the ocean of unsatisfying, excessively salesy advertisements pushed out by their competitors.

The zoom highlight can enable you to amplify commitment on your Instagram advertisements, particularly if you incorporate a concealed diamond that users can find in your photographs.

Pulling at their interest with the idea that to some degree intelligent content could be sufficient to make them stop whenever they run over one of your photographs in their feed.

2. Advance your best content

The commonplace methodology organizations take to producing new content for promotions ordinarily includes them cautiously scripting advertisement duplicate and creating suggestions to take action that will have the best sway with their group of spectators. If you need to have more contact with your advertisements, don't pursue this methodology when advertising on Instagram.

You as of now have an abundance of content that you realize your fans appreciate.

Think back through your natural presents on discovering pictures that garnered the most commitment from your group of spectators. Repurpose those presents as promotions on getting gigantic lift accordingly from a more extensive group of spectators.

That is the thing that Paper Boat Drinks did. Look at this unique post on their Instagram page:

In the wake of seeing a not too bad commitment on the main post, the organization chose to reuse the photograph and its inscription to make an Instagram advertisement. Toward the part of the bargain week battle, the post saw more than 26,000 preferences, a surge of remarks, and a gigantic lift in their image's perceivability.

Only one out of every odd battle you make will be a crushing success, given every one of the factors that go into making and focusing on promotions. Be that as it may, you can improve the probability of success by beginning with something you realize your crowd as of now prefers.

3. Improve your focusing on

The way that Instagram draws on the broad user information accessible inside Facebook's advertisement stage implies you can truly focus in on your group of spectators inside Instagram.

However, you need to realize how to use different parts of the platform to truly make it work for you and your image. Beside the standard focusing on systems, there are some different highlights that can enable you to limit your core interest.

Custom and Lookalike Audiences: The carbon copy group of spectators highlight enables you to build a custom crowd for your promotion that duplicates your current supporters. This can enable you to acquire new individuals who have comparative interests, socioeconomics, practices, and work foundations to your present group of spectators.

Remarketing: Facebook has a pixel you can put on your site and track guest conduct. While its main role was proposed for checking and following transformations from social, it can likewise be utilized for advertising.

You would then be able to build a custom Instagram advertisement group of spectators comprising just of individuals who have visited your site. Different modifiers can be included too, for example, just focusing on the individuals who visited your site and either made a specific move or deserted their trucks.

Since the normal truck surrender rate is over 68%, remarketing through Instagram can be an incredible method to win back those lost clients.

Utilizing the progressed focusing on highlights will get your promotion before the most pertinent crowd portions, which ought to improve your navigation rates. When you specifically target individuals, who are bound to change over, and your navigate rates along these lines increase, you'll cut down your expense per snap rate also.

Invest additional resources exploring different avenues regarding Instagram's group of spectators focusing on highlights, as they can drastically affect your crusade's presentation.

4. Try not to make your advertisements look like promotions

If you need to help commitment and score more snap throughs with your Instagram promotions, at that point don't make your advertisements look like promotions.

Your group of spectators is unquestionably bound to react to posts that resemble normal content instead of unmitigated item advancement. Fusing real individuals into your pictures and recordings is basic; pictures that contain countenances get 38% a bigger number of preferences than different sorts of content.

Ensure your fans don't feel like you're always attempting to sell them something. While some wouldn't fret the marketing endeavors, you should in any case mean to make the most natural experience conceivable. Thus, plan your promotions cautiously. When you're preparing to dispatch another Instagram advertisement, start making natural, high-esteem posts with a similar topic as your promotion.

After your promotion goes live, make a couple of comparable natural posts. Making a subject for your advancement will prompt a smoother change that intertwines comparable advertisements of both the paid and natural assortment.

5. Utilize the invitation to take action catch

When you make an Instagram advertisement, you can incorporate a suggestion to take action catch close to the picture subtitle (base right of the picture). This CTA catch is in a similar spot for Facebook promotions. The catch offers you a few decisions in the informing of your suggestion to take action.

If you discover one that is pertinent to your campaign, use it.

Clover, a dating application, propelled an advertisement campaign on Instagram to advance their versatile application. The advertisement focused on 18-multi year-old singles. The objective of the crusade was to contact a more extensive group of spectators and increment the quantity of versatile downloads of the application.

Utilizing Instagram's promotion stage, Clover built up a progression of advertisements highlighting single people (see the above guidance on utilizing faces), alongside the "Introduce Now" catch on the advertisement.

Before the part of the arrangement, Clover saw a 30% expansion in new memberships and diminished their new user procurement costs by 64%.

"Pass on, Instagram has been the best stage for gaining superb application users," said Kris Armstrong, Director of Marketing for Clover. "We're acquainted with Facebook's advertisement the executives stage, which has truly helped us streamline our battles rapidly since Instagram utilizes a similar interface."

6. Advance with video

When the vast majority consider Instagram, particularly the individuals who don't utilize it often, they presumably envision an interminable stream of static pictures. They overlook that Instagram is likewise an extraordinary channel for advancing recordings.

Recordings quickly catch the consideration of users because they stand apart from the content around them. Individuals love watching recordings, regardless of whether they are short. When Instagram presented recordings, there were in excess of 5 million recordings shared inside the initial 24 hours. If you put item recordings before your clients, they are almost twice as liable to make a buy, particularly if you couple it with an invitation to take action catch.

If you're experiencing serious difficulties concocting material for a video, go to your group of spectators. User-generated content is a useful asset for structure trust with your locale. Minister their recordings or get video of your clients with your items on area or at occasions. Offer their excitement for your image and advance those recordings through advertisements.

7. Recount to a story with picture merry-go-rounds

You aren't left with a solitary picture for your Instagram advertisements. The stage depends on a merry-go-round, which means you can feature more pictures for your fans to peruse.

If you're attempting to sell an item or administration, mesh a story into the content.

# CONCLUSION

Regardless of how inventive your online life battles are, you can't anticipate that they should succeed if you continue focusing on an inappropriate audience. Rather, you have to do some explorations and figure out who the individuals that you have to connect with are. To do this, you have to make a purchaser persona for your items and administrations and contrast it and the statistic qualities of your Instagram devotees. You likewise need to examine your devotees' advantages and do your best to draw them into your Instagram posts.

It is additionally critical to effectively contact clients that you consider would be an incredible qualifier for your business. This can be particularly significant for exceptional brands, as it enables them to set up important associations at an early stage and bit by bit manufacture a dedicated client base.

Seeing how the Instagram target group of spectators can discover your record, what it is keen on and what it is searching for in this informal organization is a significant phase of your marketing work and is anything but a one-time occasion. Each round surrenders him to-date information for the last timeframe, after which they become old and require refreshing.

This is a vocation for what's to come. The additional time you spend on it, the more you will find out about your group of spectators and, eventually, the more modern and centered your strategy is in drawing in leads.

DID YOU KNOW THAT YOU CAN DOWNLOAD THE AUDIOBOOK VERSION OF THIS BOOK FOR FREE?

CLICK HER FOR AUDIBLE US:

https://www.audible.com/pd/B08BPHLR92/?source_code=AUDFPWS0223189MWT-BK-ACX0-202801&ref=acx_bty_BK_ACX0_202801_rh_us

CLICK HERE FOR AUDIBLE UK:

https://www.audible.co.uk/pd/B08BPHQNNR/?source_code=AUKFrDlWS02231890H6-BK-ACX0-202801&ref=acx_bty_BK_ACX0_202801_rh_uk

Publisher: Agnes Körmöczi

# YOUTUBE MARKETING

**Workbook to get customers and subscribers, create a brand, become an Influencer and make money online**

**By**

**Edward Keller**

This document is geared towards providing exact and reliable information with regards to the topic and issue covered. The publication is sold with the idea that the publisher is not required to render accounting, officially permitted, or otherwise, qualified services. If advice is necessary, legal or professional, a practiced individual in the profession should be ordered.

From a Declaration of Principles which was accepted and approved equally by a Committee of the American Bar Association and a Committee of Publishers and Associations.



The information provided herein is stated to be truthful and consistent, in that any liability, in terms of inattention or otherwise, by any usage or abuse of any policies, processes, or directions contained within is the sole and utter responsibility of the recipient reader.

Under no circumstances will any legal responsibility or blame be held against the publisher for any reparation, damages, or monetary loss due to the information herein, either directly

or indirectly. Respective authors own all copyrights not held by the

# DISCLAIMER

All Erudition contained in this book is given for informational and educational purposes only. The author is not in any way accountable for any results or outcomes that emanate from using this material. Constructive attempts have been made to provide information that is both accurate and effective, but the author is not bound for the accuracy or use/misuse of information.

# CHAPTER ONE
# INTRODUCTION

---

YouTube marketing, in short, means using YouTube videos as one marketing channel. Why YouTube? YouTube, which is the second most popular site on the Internet. And not just the site but also the second most popular search engine after Google. It is therefore clear that, as a platform, YouTube has sovereign control over the provision of video on the Internet. It's worth remembering that Google owns YouTube, which means that Youtube videos have at least some advantage over Google search.

Video marketing should be considered when planning your company's marketing package and marketing strategy. There is enough data on the profitability of video marketing, but one is raised: The viewer internalizes 95% of the video message. Of the same message in text format, the viewer internalizes only 10%.

One of the common misconceptions about (video marketing) is that video content only works in certain industries, such as sports, games, and cooking. While it's true that in some industries, producing video content is easier and more intuitive than in others, I argue that any company can produce content on YouTube if it so desires. There are several different approaches to producing a video. A law firm can explain your company's tax planning with your video, a hotel can make a demo and atmosphere videos of its premises, and a construction company can take you to the site for a day.

# WHAT IS YOUTUBE MARKETING?

YouTube promotes videos. The video can be placed at the beginning of the clicked video, in the search results, and the middle stages of the video. YouTube marketing is managed through Google AdWords. YouTube marketing is very effective due to precise targeting as well as underpriced visibility.

This blog treats YouTube as a marketing platform. In short, YouTube is a service that uploads videos. There are several ways to implement YouTube marketing.

The company can create its channel on YouTube to upload marketing videos. This blog focuses on how companies can market their own promotional or marketing videos on YouTube for a fee.

## Ad location

There are three main locations on YouTube, where a business can display their promotional videos.

### In-Stream

The marketing video will start rotating before, during, or at the end of the selected video. Viewers will always have the option to skip the ad after 5 seconds of viewing. If the viewer skips the ad, there is also no charge for showing it.

### Video Discovery ads

A preview image of the marketing video is displayed in the search activity above the results. As well as to the right of the video being watched. It is somewhat reminiscent of the way Google search results ads work.

### Bumper ads

The marketing video will be displayed before watching the selected video. This maximum 6-second video cannot be skipped and will be charged based on impressions.

Of these three locations, In-Stream is the most efficient. We will delve deeper into different locations and compare actual numbers between different locations.

### YouTube ad history

The effort to develop YouTube ads really started in August 2006, when the first advertising concepts were launched: participatory video ads and branded channels. One of the first big advertisers was Cingular with an underground music competition. In late 2007, YouTube launched InVideo Ads and the YouTube Partner program, followed by several developments in 2008: YouTube Insight (analysis tool), Click-To-Buy e-commerce platform, sponsored videos and pre-roll video. In 2009, the acquisition of DoubleClick was completed, allowing Google to take advantage of DoubleClick. In early 2009, Homepage Ads was extended from 1 to 7 formats. Also, YouTube launched individual video partnerships and targeting those same videos, as well as tests for deactivate pre-rolls. In March 2010, YouTube launched mobile ads. Since then, the video platform has really focused on integrating it with Google display activities, which allows advertisers to better control the distribution of ads and to design scalable campaigns covering both the Google content network and YouTube.

**YouTube ad platform statistics**

Here are some statistics that justify the value of the YouTube ad platform:

- YouTube's mobile revenue doubles from year to year.
- YouTube generates 6% of Google's advertising revenue.
- YouTube Partners revenue has increased 50% year over year in the past three years, with the highest-paid partner (PewDiePie) earning $ 12 million in annual revenue in 2015.
- The number of channels earning at least $ 1,000,000 a year on YouTube is up 50% year over year.
- The number of advertisers showing video ads on YouTube is up over 40% from the previous year. And for major YouTube advertisers, average spend has increased by over 60% year on year the other.
- Users who finished TrueView ads, viewed until the end or at least 30 seconds, were 23 times more likely to visit or subscribe to a brand channel, watch that brand more, or share the brand video.
- Users who are exposed to TrueView ads, but don't watch until the end are still ten times more likely to do any of these.
- When brands use TrueView, they see their views increase up to

500% after the publication of new videos.

Even if the advertising space becomes more and more competitive, the growth reflects the success of certain brands on the platform. If you think that using YouTube ads for your brand or business is of potential interest, we invite you to follow step by step the creation of an ad, so that you put all the chances on your side to succeed.

When advertising on YouTube, the minimum amount should not be used. The question well always remains, how much should you spend on a YouTube ad, and how much it will cost your business to display the ad.

First, it's important to note when you have to pay for your ad. If someone views your entire ad or clicks on your ad, you'll be charged for this action. Paying for impressions or clicks depends on the type of ad you create.

Also, what can you expect to pay when someone clicks on your ad?

YouTube video ads can cost between $ 0.10 and $ 0.30 per click.

It's not a regular price every time, but it's a typical price that companies experience when investing in YouTube ads. This price varies depending on the quality of the video, your target audience, and your campaign goals.

The amount you spend on a campaign depends on the daily budget you set for your campaign. Most companies invest at least $ 10 a day to launch an ad campaign on YouTube. The number grows as companies learn more about the effectiveness of their campaigns.

In most cases, you pay according to the cost scale. Every time someone views your ad, you pay for it. It's important to set the maximum amount you want to spend on impressions, so you don't exceed your campaign budget.

**What determines the cost of YouTube ads?**

The cost of YouTube ads is determined by a few factors, including:

- The type of your ad
- your offer
- The auctions you selected
- targeting

These factors usually affect your YouTube advertising rates in different ways. For example, your bid is likely to have a more direct impact on your YouTube advertising costs than your bid selection because you've set the final number for what you're willing to pay for a click or impression.

## Getting started and managing

An ad campaign is created and managed in Google AdWords. A daily budget is set for the promotional video, but you can adjust it up or down later if you feel like it.

Google is known for the tools found to measure an ad campaign, and the same tools are used in YouTube marketing. In addition to this, YouTube has its Analytics service where you can view performance. We will also discuss more measuring YouTube marketing in future blogs.

One of the biggest reasons for the effectiveness of YouTube marketing is its targeting capabilities. The marketing video can be targeted at, e.g., with the following criteria:

- Country of residence
- Living City
- Language
- Device to be used (mobile phone, tablet, computer, etc.)
- Sexual
- Age
- Input Level
- Interests

However, the targeting possibilities really don't stay here, but even this is such a broad thing that you can make your blog post here as well. Targeting can also be done strategically, even for people who have visited your website (remarketing).

## Promotional Video

In YouTube marketing, the content and quality of a video have a huge impact on its effectiveness. People come to the service to watch videos and expect to get something worth their time. For this reason, it's not advisable to invest marketing euros in a video shoot with a "little there" attitude on a mobile phone. Of course, if there is a style to your business, then there is nothing in it. It's good to stick to your style and brand.

## The cost of YouTube marketing

The price of YouTube marketing is divided into two parts. For video production and its distribution. The cost of video production is completely dependent on the scale of implementation. At its cheapest, video production can be outsourced for a few hundred euros. The average price of distribution in Finland is € 0.05-€ 0.10 per view. It is significantly cheaper than Google advertising. For a more detailed estimate or cost estimate, contact the company that implements comprehensive YouTube marketing.

YouTube marketing as a channel is a marketer's dream. Powerful, emotional, and measurable. However, it should be integrated into a comprehensive marketing strategy to achieve the desired outcome. The goal of modern marketing is to identify the same customer in different channels, but also to be self-identifiable to the same customer in different channels.

### YouTube advantage

From a business perspective, YouTube marketing has introduced new technologies that many companies are not taking advantage of it yet. The following YouTube guide will show you through

these marketing opportunities on YouTube -

- Evaluate different ways to use YouTube for marketing.
- Inform and educate the public via YouTube.
- Explore video content ideas

- Use YouTube to support the conversion.
- Leverage the YouTube community to promote your video.
- Branding of your YouTube channel.
- Increase your objective and your visibility.

**Important notes**

You can focus on the following points to become a YouTube star:

- You must arouse the curiosity of video consumers by creating unusual videos
- content.
- You must ensure that your video is detectable.
- Consider joining YouTube celebrities to get audiences already organized.
- Always make sure the video links to your website and includes a call to action.

Finally, be sure to follow the regular messages you send to your YouTube channel.

**Marketing your business online on YouTube**

A YouTube video made can add a viral component to a company's online marketing strategy. You see, when you upload a video to YouTube, that video gets life for itself. Thousands of YouTube users watch it, publish on many websites and blogs, and send email to the

Internet. Anyone watching your videos is now a potential customer, assuming you include your website address or other contact information in the video itself.

Not surprisingly, it seems that YouTube is replacing traditional TV viewing for many users. According to Google, the average YouTube viewer spends 164 minutes online every day; instead, viewers spend only 130 minutes a day watching traditional television. The number of videos and users on the site continues to grow, which is ideal for businesses looking to take advantage of the opportunity. Growth has been purely stratospheric; site traffic has doubled in just two years.

**How can YouTube be used to market a business?**

Given the large number of companies that accept YouTube videos, it's no surprise that there are many ways to use the site. Each business has its own unique goals in YouTube marketing. Some companies use YouTube to create brand awareness. Some people use YouTube to promote a particular product or generate sales in their store or website. Others integrate with YouTube as part of their product offering or customer support, use videos for product training, or even use YouTube for recruitment and employee communications. What you say in person or to a group of people can be said in the video and disseminated through YouTube.

**YouTube to increase brand awareness**

Large domestic companies and large advertisers often use YouTube to improve brand awareness. And Instead of focusing on individual products or services, these videos elevate a company's brand, often in the same way as traditional television advertising.

Online videos convey brand awareness better than traditional TV commercials. A study by Millward Brown found that online listening led to 82% brand awareness and 77% product recall, while only 54% brand awareness and 18% remembrance of advertising products were accounted for by televisions. Also, Experts believe this is because online viewers are more interested than viewers; The web is a more interactive tool than passive visualization of television. Brand awareness videos are usually entertaining and use a soft selling method to capture the brand and image in the minds of viewers. A good example is the video series produced by Old Spice, which takes advantage of the popularity value of its 2010 commercials "The Man your Man Could Feel."

**YouTube product advertising**

If you can use YouTube to promote a global brand, you can also use YouTube to distribute individual products. It requires a more direct approach, although it is always important to make video informative, educational, or entertaining. To promote a product, you want to show it in your ad, as Nike does with its Bootcamp Drill videos. You can display the product in action or use it as part of a demonstration or tutorial. Just make sure you add lots of close-up product images and a link to your website for more information about the product.

**YouTube for retail promotion**

You can also use YouTube to promote your company's retail stores. These videos can be general (which gives the videos a long lifespan) or focus more on short-term promotions ("check out this weekend's specials!"). But a video that is nothing more than an in-store ad is unlikely to attract a lot of viewers. A better way is to find a way to showcase the store without taking advantage of 20% discounts and "only this weekend" offers. For example, you can record a short visit to a store or highlight individual services or storage services. You can even produce educational videos that describe the products or services your store offers, such as Home Depot products.

**YouTube for employee communication**

You can use YouTube for all kinds of business communications. Instead of holding a big business meeting just so the big boss can give you the company's annual address, ask him or her to save the address and publish it on a private channel on YouTube. Employees can watch a presenter say their stuff from the comfort of their own office on the road or even at home. Many companies see YouTube as a quick and effective way to share information about all kinds of employees. Done right, it sends data in almost real-time with all the benefits of face-to-face communication, which is much better than sending impersonal memos via email.

**YouTube for recruitment**

Also, don't underestimate YouTube as a tool for recruiting new employees. If you have a welcome video from the company, upload it to YouTube and make it public. Think of it as a PR exercise that attracts new talent to a company, which means doing it right - it's as much a marketing project as something from the HR department. You can link to a video from any of your recruiting media, even your traditional ads. Don't be limited to just one long puff video: you bring separate videos for each department, as well as to describe the company's values, benefits, services, etc.

**What kind of promotional videos should a company produce?**

We pay particular attention to promotional videos - videos that are produced to market a company, its brands, or its products and services. What videos work best to get your message through? While there is a wide selection depending on the type of business or product being marketed, the most important thing is to provide a video that YouTube users want to watch. It means a video that has some form of entertainment, education, or informative value. In other words, the video needs to be entertained, educated, or informed - or no one is watching it.

**1. Informative videos**

One way to do this is to create a YouTube counterpart to the infomercial. That is a video that provides useful information to the viewer. This information can be anything from a guided tour of a new product to a company spokesperson talking about key trends in the industry. It's a recent approach that gives viewers more information than they were before viewing began.

For example, if you are a travel agent, you can produce an informative video that provides a guided tour of one of the featured destinations. You can also take a more meaningful approach and ask your agent to discuss travel trends for the coming season. Or maybe you've put together PowerPoint slides by comparing travel destinations to different destinations.

The key is to provide information that your current or potential customers find really useful. It will help establish your business as an authority in this matter; when the customer wants to pull the trigger, he will think of you because of the useful information you provide.

The key is to provide enough useful information to be of practical use to your viewers, and then allow them to easily click through to your site for more information or to buy what you need to sell. It cannot be a simple advertisement; it must be real information, presented as directly as possible.

**2. Entertaining videos**

Information and education are important, and you can attract a lot of YouTube viewers if you do these things right. But everyone loves entertainment, which is why pure entertainment video usually appears at the top of the most-watched YouTube video lists. What is entertaining? It is impossible to say. Maybe you will find a fun way to use your product or service. Maybe you put your president or CEO in a fun situation. Maybe you've developed a product or industry review that focuses on the lighter aspects of things. Or maybe you believe in creative work for professionals and hire a creative agency to produce your videos. Whatever you do, it has to be something that viewers find interesting and at least a little humorous. It has to withstand repeated viewing, and it should be something that people would like to share with their friends. Viral videos are the result of sharing links between people - and people want to share the videos they find most entertaining.

# BENEFITS OF BIG DATA FROM YOUTUBE

You may have read many articles on the benefits of big data for marketers, but sometimes the term big data is used without being very clear about what it means. Big data can mean several different things:

- **Amount of information:** a huge amount of information reveals and confirms the consumption habits of the public, for example. Think of YouTube as a giant poll where people vote for the content they love every day. It is a powerful tool for access!
- **Data Speed:** The speed of large data means that sufficient data for a given period, often for a short period, reveals when something is in fashion or emerging. For example, America Centers for Disease Control (CDC) uses data from Google's search engine to monitor influenza epidemics in the United States. The YouTube counterpart would be the trendy video pages that use data to float videos at the most viewing speed.
- **Data Diversity:** Big data can only mean different. If YouTube is a survey tool, it asks millions of questions about everything every day; what people want to watch, how and where they watch it, what makes it shared, what devices they use and more.

YouTube is so big that it contains some of the biggest big data. It has the Amount, speed, and diversity of data, and uses the lessons learned from its data to marketers.

YouTube's big data helps reduce marketers 'costs. You can choose to reach a specific audience that converts with a single click or buy the best one, which saves you money because you only buy the media that works best for you. It is no longer true that part of the performance of your marketing campaign is unknown.

You'll become more efficient in the time it takes to create and implement marketing campaigns, tools, and features that think about you, such as media location, how much money you need to spend on better performance and analysis of what creation works best and why. These features and options are the results of in-depth research based on YouTube's Big Data repository. For example, YouTube develops advanced audience targeting methods that are so sophisticated and yet easy to use, making your marketing budget more difficult and effective.

You also have access to constantly evolving tools that will help you find information about your audience and give you a deeper understanding than before. YouTube comes with incredibly sophisticated analytics, developed based on millions of experiences and many comments, to help you figure out what you can do to get more results. YouTube used its vast knowledge to create the simplest solutions for marketers to get the best results.

# CHAPTER TWO

# YOUTUBE ADVERTISING: A STEP-BY-STEP GUIDE TO ADVERTISING ON YOUTUBE

No matter how good your video advertising content is, without the right YouTube advertising strategy, it can be difficult to get good results from your video campaigns.

Unless you already have a large audience on social media, posting your video to Facebook or YouTube can earn you a few thousand impressions. Still, if you really want your video ad to appear, you need to put it on YouTube.

Although YouTube ad campaigns are set up and run through Google AdWords, YouTube advertising is very different from your regular paid search or even display the ad.

Well In addition to targeting the right audience and creating video content to succeed in YouTube advertising, you need to know what options to choose and what video requirements to meet.

The good news is that in this book we are going to cover everything. We'll teach you everything that you need to know to start advertising on YouTube today.

Let's start with!

# WHY YOUTUBE ADVERTISING?

Creating compelling video content is much more difficult than writing a text ad or creating an image ad. So why are marketers so enthusiastic about YouTube advertising?

The answer is simple: YouTube advertising offers marketers an affordable alternative to television advertising.

Television advertising has been the most effective form of media advertising for decades. However, while a typical 30-second time on a national television program can cost more than $ 100,000, all the benefits of television advertising are beyond the reach of most small and medium-sized businesses.

YouTube is changing all this.

YouTube is a new television in many ways. While television interest has declined in recent years, the YouTube audience has increased. The world actually watches 1 billion hours of YouTube videos every day. It's for 100,000 years. More than all human history - in one day!

In addition to YouTube's huge reach and Audience, YouTube advertising is also much more readily available than traditional TV ads. Instead of costing thousands of dollars to secure a 30-second TV, YouTube advertisers usually pay pennies per screen and only if the viewer watches the ad for more than 30 seconds (or the entire ad if it is shorter) for 30 seconds).

Well According to Google, people who watch YouTube ads to the end are 23 times more likely to visit or subscribe to a brand channel, share a branded video, or watch more by brand. Even those who don't follow are ten times more likely to do one of these things.

In other words, YouTube advertising works.

Add high-level targeting (including the ability to target people based on their recent Google searches), and you'll have one of the most effective advertising platforms in the world. With YouTube advertising, you can make sure your great video ads appear to the Right Audience at the right time, without breaking your bank.

**How YouTube Advertising Works**

Google offers a variety of video advertising options on YouTube: TrueView In-Stream Ads, TrueView Video Ads, and Buffer Ads.

Google also allows display ads, overlays, and sponsored maps to appear on YouTube:

These ads are actually displayed network extensions, not video ads. So we stick to the video advertising options in this book (click here for more information on YouTube advertising options).

Let's see how each type of YouTube video ad works:

**TrueView In-Stream Ads**

When most people think of YouTube advertising, they think of TrueView In-Stream ads. In-stream ads are ads that appear just before the video you want to watch.

In most cases, viewers will need to watch the ad for five seconds and then the opportunity to skip another ad or continue watching

If you assign them directly to your YouTube video, you can create end cards or screens that encourage viewers to do something special, such as click on your website. Alternatively, you can also set up a click-to-call (CTA) call that YouTube will show for the first 15 seconds of your video (more on configuration later).

For example, Shutterstock's clickable CTA is shown here:

These CTAs are simple and will give the public an easy way to act once you've seen your ad.

While these CTA cards seem much more professional than your classic YouTube card, they aren't very eye-catching as a terminal card or monitor, so it's often a good idea to install final cards and monitors for video on YouTube.

In addition to the classic 5-second skip TrueView InStream ads, you can also create a skip video ad that will play before your videos. These ads can also appear in the middle of videos that are 10 minutes or more in length.

The great thing about InStream TrueView ads is the wealth of information AdWords gives you about video performance. With AdWords, you can see how many people are watching your videos to the end, how fast they're dropping, your CTA, and more.

If you're smart during the video creation process and shoot additional content, you can use this information to optimize your video for maximum performance. Well For example, if you have a lot of drops in 5 seconds but few viewers for your final video, your hook (the first 5 seconds of your ad) may need work.

In this situation, you can try to modify your hook and run the new version to see if other people are staying otherwise, clicking, or changing them. Let television provide such information!

**TrueView video ads (formerly known as InDisplay ads)**

TrueView video ads are not as well known as InStream ads, but they are still quite common. well If you've ever searched for a video on YouTube, you've probably seen a video tag ad like this at the top of search results:

It wouldn't be Google if there were no ads at the top of the search results page, right?

Besides, video search ads will also appear in the video's right sidebar:

Video discovery ads are especially useful if you're trying to promote a video longer than 15 to 60 seconds. While they're interested in your content, most people wait up to five minutes for your InStream video ad to end before watching the video they tried to watch before pausing.

Well If they clicked on your ad after seeing it in search results or the right video bar, they want to see your video. Therefore, they are more likely to watch even a long video ad.

**buffer Advertisements**

Finally, at the opposite end of the spectrum of video research ads, there are buffer ads. Buffer ads are short (up to 6 seconds) ads that cannot be disabled and are primarily used to create and reinforce brand awareness.

Buffer ads are not used often. I have been searching for dozens of videos on YouTube To find you a screenshot of the ad bumper; I still have not seen a bumper ad.

It is partly due to the workings of YouTube. When you pay for each view, it makes sense that most advertisers want to stream a longer video that has a better chance of generating clicks and new business.

The bumper ads can be a great way to get to know your business or strengthen your video marketing campaign. For example, in Disruptive, we used buffer ads as part of a tracking campaign targeted at people watching the following video:

In this video, we compared the choice of an advertising agency to dating. The video is quite memorable, so we decided to launch a retargeting campaign that combined the romantic 5-second photos of the couple featured in our video with the words "It could be me.

Since anyone who saw the buffer ads saw the original video, it was a great way to reinforce the message in the original video without displaying the same content over and over again.

Buffer ads usually work best with this type of approach because the ads are so short that they don't allow a lot of messages or actual advertising. But if you have an audience you want to stay frustrated with, bumper ads can be a great way to do it!

# CREATE A YOUTUBE VIDEO AD CAMPAIGN

For purposes of this book, I assume you have already created a Dynamite video ad (if not, see this book and the book on how to do this). Here we focus on how to use this ad in your YouTube ad campaign.

**Upload the video to YouTube**

You must first upload a video to YouTube. I hope you already have a YouTube channel, but if not, click here for more information on setting up a YouTube channel.

Once you've connected to your YouTube channel, click the profile icon in the upper right corner and click "Creator Studio":

Then click the download icon in the upper right corner and upload the video to YouTube.

Once you have the video URL, you can go to your Google AdWords account and start creating a new video campaign.

**Create your campaign**

For this book, we say we plan to create a video campaign promoting the following video ad:

Log in to your AdWords account, click the 'Campaigns' tab, click the blue '+' button, and click 'New Campaign.' You can choose from several types of campaigns.

Select Video, then decide if you want to increase brand awareness or results. The right goal depends mainly on your video content, but since our video doesn't make a particularly difficult sales transaction, we move on to brand awareness and coverage.

**Campaign Settings**

The following page has many options, starting with your campaign settings:

Choose the right name for you, a budget that meets your needs (for more information on choosing a budget, see this book), a language that matches your content, and start/end dates that match your marketing strategy.

Then, unless your target audience is really all in the U.S. or the rest of the world, I recommend using the search bar under Items. Here you can actually enter specific locations and then select from a list of targeting options. AdWords allows you to target or exclude certain placements. If we wanted to target the whole of Florida, except for Sarasota, this is an option.

It is important because many businesses target everyone in a state, territory, or country without realizing that they don't really want to pay for clicks in that region. For example, if you're a dentist working in Tampa, Florida, you probably won't be able to convince someone in Sarasota to drive hours to your office no matter how good the ad is!

You may not even be able to arrange for a resident of St. Petersburg to drive to your office, so even showing ads in a larger area of Tampa-St. Petersburg may be a waste of money. So while your smart location setting may not be particularly exciting, it's well worth your time.

For now, we'll leave these settings alone, but if you want to change your bidding strategy or make sure your video only appears on YouTube, you can edit it under "Bidding Strategy" and "Networks." If you'd like to use time separation to ensure that your ads run only during certain times, you'll find this option in the Advanced section.

**Ad group settings**

Next, you'll need to define your ad group. Here you can choose your ad targeting options. Therefore, you should be careful through this section.

Choosing a name and maximum bid is pretty simple, but things get a little more complicated when you choose who you want to target with your ads. and The Audience you choose here will have a huge impact on the success or failure of your YouTube advertising, so let's take a closer look at each targeting option:

**demography**

While it sounds simple, many advertisers ignore the power of demographics in display advertising. For example, if your main target audience is women under the age of 25, and your video ad is shown primarily to men 65 and older, you may need to change something.

To see who your target audience should be, open Google Analytics, click the AudienAudiencend the Audience submenu, and then click Overview.

Then change your Converters segment:

With this report, you can easily see the age group and gender you need to target in your display ads.

If you like a customer in this GIF format, targeting people under 25 or over 44 is probably not a good idea. This customer is simply not getting results from Pentagen.

You can also use the AdWords Report Editor to learn more about your target audience:

In this case, this customer receives three times more clicks from men than from women. For this customer, targeting women exclusively, which would probably be a bad idea.

Once you have this information in hand, it's time to look at your demographics in advertising. Open AdWords, click the appropriate campaign and click Display Network. Click Demographics:

do you notice the similarities between the last two reports and this?

In this report, AdWords, which shows you the age, gender, and parenting status of the people who see, click, and convert your ads. In general, it's a good idea to match the demographic targeting of your YouTube ad groups to the demographics that visit your website and convert from your ads.

So while your demographic settings may seem to be part of defining and forgetting ad groups, fixing this can have a huge impact on your video ad results.

**public**

In this section, you will choose from three different audience types that Google generates based on their online behaviour:

it will allow you to put each of these classes at your service.

**affinity**

Let's look at Google, who knows a lot about us. In total, 67.5% of search queries occur on Google, and Google tracks the searches you do, the sites you visit, and even the actions you perform on those sites.

By using the information, Google puts us in "buckets" based on what it thinks our interests are. These "compartments" are called affinity audiences.

Say what you want about privacy, also but for online advertisers, this type of information can be incredibly practical.

While these kindness hearings can be very helpful, these "buckets" are not always as narrowly targeted as we might think. Therefore, targeting an affinity audience often meant that you ended up targeting a wide range of people who had relevant interests but who were more likely to become a client.

The modified relationship hearings changed everything.

With custom affinity audiences, you don't want to choose one of Google's predefined "buckets". Instead, you will choose who you want to reach by using topics and even URLs.

So if you have a competitor with a name for your industry. All you have to do is create a personalized relationship audience that targets the people who visit this site. And there is a very good chance that your display ads will appear to a relevant audience ready to buy.

**Life purpose and events**

The market audience targets users in a particular vertical area who display buying behaviour, such as conversion on landing pages, clicks on ads, etc. In other words, if I am looking for options for a new car that I am buying, you can use this market audience to target me with new car purchase ads. It actually gives you a much better picture of earning a click than a conventional display ad.

It is not only hypothetical. Also, Companies like Wayfair and Toll Brothers have seen a 20% improvement in ad response rates and a 50% drop in acquisition costs.

The target market audience has tripled the click-through rates of these companies!

Likewise, you can target based on life events. So if you are renting a wedding venue, you can target potential customers using the "Get married soon" event category. Google doesn't have tons of life event categories yet, but if you're meeting one of their groups, this can be a great option to try it out.

**remarketing audiences**

The last Audience favourite because it is designed for people who have visited your site. But haven't produced results. The timing may be incorrect. They can get their attention via email or social media. Someone at work or home could keep them away before they can convert. The possibilities are limitless.

Unfortunately, most of the time, try and it stops.

It is where remarketing comes in. By placing a cookie in the browser, you can ensure that your brand stays in front of "lost" visitors and reminds them of how great you are!

**Keywords**

As mentioned earlier, you can actually target potential customers on YouTube based on what they're actively looking for on Google. It allows you to use YouTube advertising as an extension of your paid search advertising strategy.

However, for this, you need to target the right keywords.

It may sound like a guessing game, but if you have paid search campaigns in addition to your display ad, you can easily find out which words and phrases people use when they are interested in your product or offer.

Well To see how people find your text ads, open AdWords, set the time window to 6 to 12 weeks, and then click the Keywords tab. Then click on "Search terms":

Here you can actually use impressions, clicks and/or results to identify the search queries that generate the best traffic.

If you like most businesses, you probably have one or more groups of similar and productive search terms that you can use to build your keyword lists.

Once you

**Get the most out of YouTube advertising.**

As soon as you start your video campaign, Google will review your ad. During the day, they should be approved, and you should start getting clicks and conversions.

However, YouTube advertising is not exactly "defined and forgotten". The main reason why most YouTube ad campaigns fail is to ignore.

Unfortunately, only around 10% of YouTube ad campaigns are optimized up to once a week. According to the accounts we reviewed here on Disruptive, 72% of accounts have not been in contact for more than a month!

How often should you optimize your account? It all depends on your traffic and your budget.

If your budgets exceed $ 10,000 per month, you should at least review your campaigns at least once a week. However, to get the most out of your account, you will likely need to review your campaign at least three times.

For a new video campaign, also you need to be more active. It is a good idea to check your account at least three times a day. Keep an eye on your views, impression times, clicks, conversions and display results: these are the most important indicators of the performance of your video ad!

Well If you don't spend thousands of dollars a month on AdWords, you're not producing enough information a day to ensure a daily audit, but it's always a good idea to keep track of things. Depending on the number of clicks you receive per month, about one review per week should be enough, especially if your campaigns have been running smoothly for some time.

Among them, the main rule is that the more time you spend working on your YouTube campaigns, the more they will perform. Of course, you don't have to make big changes three times a day or a week, but keeping a close eye on your account will give you the information you need to get really good performance.

**Campaign and network types**

Now let's move on to the different campaign and network types.

The settings for a YouTube campaign

There are three options for different types of YouTube advertising campaigns:

- Standard: This is for non-eCommerce advertisers, non-application installers.
- Mobile application installations: they are used to promote an application and to generate installations for it.
- Shopping: If you are in e-commerce and want to promote your products.

You also have a few network options:

These network settings determine where your ads appear.

- YouTube Search: it means when you want to show your ads in YouTube search results.
- YouTube Videos: This is useful if you want your ads to appear while the videos are playing.
- Video partners on the Display Network: To do this, you need to select the "YouTube Videos" option, which allows you to run your ads on YouTube videos outside of YouTube.com on the normal AdWords Display Network (like display ads).

To start, well, I recommend selecting both "YouTube Search" and "YouTube Videos" because we have found that their customer conversion target is higher than that of Video Partners on the Display Network. The reason is that you have less control over where your ads appear.

## Video ad formats

well There are six video ad formats to choose from on YouTube:

1- True View: these are the dominant advertisements on YouTube, and they come in two forms:

- In-Stream ads: these ads are broadcast before, during, or after the broadcasting of a YouTube video. They are played on YouTube.com or other sites/applications via Google Partners. In-stream ads are the type you can ignore after the first 5 seconds of playback. If they are ignored in the first 30 seconds without interaction, you don't pay a penny. So, hypothetically, you can continue to develop brand awareness for free. Note: The "ultimate goal" is to get people to engage enough to click on it and become a customer. Therefore, it is not even important to watch the ad until the end.

Here's a great example of Burger King using video pre-roll time to grab users' attention, even if the ad content is skippable.

- Discovcry video ads: These ads can appear in several places on YouTube and the Web via partner sites and mobile applications. They can be displayed as a clickable thumbnail in YouTube search results, alongside associated videos, on the YouTube home page, or partner sites and applications. Discovery video ads are associated with a small yellow "Announcement" area, as shown below:

Here's an example of a video discovery ad on the YouTube search results page

2- Bumper Ads: These ads are short 6-second video clips that viewers cannot ignore. You can always find this ad format in the options when you create a new ad group. Also, They are short and to the point.

3- Non-deactivate announcements: these types of announcements consist of 15 or 20-second videos and cannot be ignored. They are, therefore, always viewed in their entirety. Google is rumoured to end non-skippable ads by the end of the year, but they may still resurface at some point. The "catch" with these videos is that they require a minimum investment to operate. So you won't see the smaller brands/advertisers using them. Here is an example:

4- Display Ads: Now remember, we don't have to use video ads for advertising on YouTube. We can also use text ads and image ads (with dimensions 300 × 250 and 300 × 60 pixels). If you want to target any specific videos or channels in YouTube, you can use their URLs as placement targeting for this ad format because they will appear to the right of a video that your potential customer is watching. It is important to note two things:

- It's a cheaper ad format than a skippable InStream ad.
- These ads only appear on desktops/laptops (which means no mobile).

Here is an example of display advertising.

5- Overlay ads: This is another variant of the display ad, but their location appears directly on the video being viewed. Below are examples of horizontal ads above a video and the square display on the right. The dimensions for this type of ad are 468 × 60 or 728 × 90 and can also be a regular text ad.

Overlay ads work the same way as the display but appear on the video, not on the sidebar.

6- Sponsored cards: This ad variant is a boost for eCommerce advertisers who want to highlight the products that are seen in the video. Right next to the video itself. Here is an example :

Here's where the sponsored cards appear.

To create YouTube maps, go to Creator Studio> Video manager> Edit video drop-down list. Below you will see the options for creating maps:

## Add-ons to ad formats

There are two add-ons: synchronized banners and call-to-action overlays, which run alongside the ads.

1- Synchronized banners: these announcements are optional. These are not single ads, as they must follow alongside a video ad. Their advantage is that they increase the clickable area on the screen. If you select your medium, stay at 300 × 60 pixels and maximum file size of 150 KB. If you choose to use them, and you don't have your content, Google will automatically create one based on the visuals of your video ad.

2- Call to action overlay: Call to action overlays allow you to associate text and images (74 × 74) with your video ad. These are essential to get the most out of your YouTube ad.

CTA overlays are a great way to customize your offering based on the video content displayed.

Here's how to add a CTA overlay to your video ad:

Find the "Videos" tab for your YouTube campaign and follow these steps to add a call-to-action.

### Targeting video ads

Targeting YouTube ads works much like the Display Network, with a few key differences.

Demographics: You can choose the age, sex, household income or parental status of your audience. Be warned, however, just like search and display; many YouTube users are considered "unknown" for these segments.

Interests: These are essentially the same for YouTube as for the Display Network. Also, This is where you can target users based on the videos they watch and the websites they browse. In this segment, you have:

1. Audiences on the market: well According to Google, these are the users who are in the "research phase" of their purchasing cycle.
2. *Audiences on personalized centres of interest*: you can create your audience by superimposing different interests/domains.

Step 2: Refine your targeting by keyword, location, remarketing or topics.

Keywords: well This targeting allows you to choose your targeting according to expressions, specific keywords that you select. Also, Your YouTube ad will then be placed, with content, on the videos, channels, and websites associated with your selections.

Placements: Rather than targeting specific websites, target YouTube videos or channels of your choice. Keep in mind that these users/channels must be allowed to display ads with their content.

Remarketing: It works just like on the Display Network, but with YouTube ads instead. I recommend expanding your reach with a strategic video remarketing approach.

Topics: It is to target your audience on specific subjects (cooking, decoration, investment, etc.).

## Video ad creation

You will have to start by thinking about the type of content you want to create for your offer. I'll list a few examples below to get you started:

### Video testimonials

Do customers like your product? Of course. Are you making your customers happy? Obviously. Well, ask them to participate in a video interview on why your product makes them happy. How do you make them say "yes"? Plan the process, with a pre-written script, and of course, pay the bill to assure you're a happy customer that there is the minimal effort required on their side.

### Features and benefits

A very obvious approach for a video ad (or any other advertisement) is to target the different features/benefits that your product or service has to offer. For example, if your product is known for its durability, plan to show it in action so that viewers can "see it to believe it".

### How to make effective videos

Sometimes a simple explanation is all that is necessary to attract a consumer to the purchase. The practical videos are a great opportunity to capture those who have a strong intention of interacting with your offer. By offering useful information to an engaged audience, you will develop a positive reputation as well as the confidence of your network.

**Video content creation**

After thinking about some ideas for your video ad content. The next thing to do is to run the video itself. Also, It may sound daunting, but I'll help you get started with a few more or less expensive examples depending on your budget. But remember, it all depends on what you want to accomplish.

**Tell a story on mobile**

Telling a story can be as simple as a text conversation. An ingenious and profitable strategy uses text recording to tell the story of your product/service. Hooked.co is an application that tells short stories through fictional conversations. Also, They offer a paid subscription to access their content without a waiting period. They saw rapid marketing success on YouTube using cliffhangers like this:

**Animation**

If you haven't noticed, these videos have exploded in popularity in the past few years. They are popular because many business leaders wanted a nifty explanatory video like this:

**Stop motion**

Well, This type of video can be simple and inexpensive or extravagant and therefore, more expensive. It will vary depending on the type of visual content or material you use. Stop Motion videos are usually a combination of photographs, which are cut to create the illusion of smooth motion.

Like Wallace & Gromit.

### Video shooting

The last type of video (and probably the most expensive) would be real live video shooting. This strategy would be more focused on brands that also participate in traditional television advertising.

Here's some great Dollar Shave Club advertising that could be combined with TV advertising to provide a bigger boost.

### Tool and services

Now that we have a good idea of the content and style of our video, the next step is to make it happen. Here are tools and services to help you get the best value for money and the best return on investment.

- Shakr: Shakr.com is a video ad creation tool with over 1,000 models available in various industries. Using their drag-and-drop editor. It's quick and easy to group your media into a video ad; Especially useful for A / B test video ads, the process can be very fast compared to traditional video creators. Here is an example :
- Fiverr: Fiverr.com, which is the world's largest online freelance marketplace, especially for the creative space. You can certainly find affordable help to make your first video ad.

YouTube Director: The YouTube Director app is a mobile app created by Google, which also uses templates to help you create video ads.

YouTube Director Onsite: well, YouTube Director Onsite is a new initiative from Google for creating YouTube video ads. The process involves sending a filmmaker home or to your business to film, edit and deliver a video advertisement.

The service is currently only available in certain American cities but, if its success is growing, there is no doubt that it will come very quickly to Europe.

Animation/production studios: If you have a big budget and want a professional team to do all the work, you can always reach out to animation/production studios. Users will often see your video ads on the go, without any volume. You need to make sure your video ad has been properly captioned, so you don't miss these crucial views. It's easy to add yours to your YouTube account. Click on your profile picture (upper right corner)> Creator Studio> Video manager> Videos. Also Then go to the video of your choice, click on the drop-down menu and select "Subtitles / CC".

**Video auctions**

By default, you set up Google's CPV (cost per view) bids for your YouTube campaign. With this bidding strategy, you are billed for views/interactions with your video or related ads. Fortunately, a "view" is only counted once a viewer watches at least 30 seconds of your video (or the whole video, if your clip is less than 30 seconds).

Here is where you can configure the bids.

Also, note that it is possible to adjust the bids for "popular videos". It can be useful for advertisers who want to serve videos. They appear on the most popular YouTube ads and content.

To change and adjust the bids after the initial campaign is created, go to the "Ad group" tab and make your changes.

### Conversion tracking / Analytics

Fortunately, the conversion tracking setup for YouTube is the same as for AdWords ads. So, if you've already set up an account with your conversion tracking as well as Google Analytics, you're ready. If not, be sure to follow these Google instructions. YouTube also offers some cool features for analyzing statistics, as well as additional metrics.

## Examples of Successful YouTube Advertising

There is an important reason why most marketers do not take advantage of YouTube advertising. Indeed, video ads are one of the most expensive types of ads to create.

### Success Story # 1

Here is a great success of a YouTube advertisement by Lime-A-Rita thanks to hyper-relevant ads.

Here are three tips for creating hyper-relevant YouTube ads from Google.

Using this method, Lime-A-Rita has targeted a specific audience of women who love music. Lime-A-Rita has used targeted advertising for this audience, with specific placements on the latest Rihanna videos, as well as other pop hits.

### Success Story # 2

Next, we'll see how Duracell created one of the most successful YouTube "Bumper Ads".

A successful YouTube campaign can be divided into three points.

By breaking down their campaign on these three points of view, Duracell was able to formulate an advertising approach which was successful on several points. They used creative elements unique to their brand to build the trust and recognition that most consumers have with Duracell batteries. With just 6 seconds available in a bumper ad, also focusing on your product/offering is a must. Finally, Duracell quickly tested and optimized its campaign objectives. Using this bumper ad, they recruited viewers for a 30-second video ad. They did this to strengthen brand recognition with fast, punchy content to keep the Duracell brand on consumer speed cameras and increase purchase intent.

### Success Story # 3

Burger King made an awesome series of 64 pre-roll ads, all of which are similar. They used YouTube video placements to match a specific dialogue in their ad to 64 different popular videos to grab the user's attention. Rather than trying to advertise, Burger King has diversified by taking a fun and unique approach to their video ad content.

## Best practices for YouTube advertising

How did these brands manage to be successful on YouTube? Let's take a look at the most important elements regarding the content and media of your first YouTube ad. When it comes to content, and quality is king. Here's what to consider:

**1-** Emphasize the direct response, not brand awareness. Our goal with YouTube ads is to increase ROI through conversions, not to maximize brand awareness. For starters, you may not see many conversions from the bottom of the funnel unless you are remarketing or using a custom audience. I recommend that you develop two strategies, one to improve conversions at the top/middle of the funnel and the other to monetize your past visitors/viewers through remarketing.

Here, under the targeting options, select "Remarketing".

In this tab, you will have access to all remarketing lists.

Hopefully, you've organized your remarketing lists. Just select the one you want to target and add a video.

**2-** Your final goal is to make money, but think about the number of steps and actions to take before a potential customer takes his credit card. Consider simplifying the purchasing process for your potential customers as much as possible. Use your video ads to try to answer customer questions. Most of the time, you don't win over a customer or make a sale at first glance, so develop a strategy to feed users with the funnel.

**3-** Make the magic work in the first 5 seconds. Keep in mind that our goal is for people to be interested enough to buy into our offers. If you find that many people are ignoring your ad or that the reading time is short, consider changing the start of your ad. To be honest, the length of the videos doesn't really matter. It's your content that makes the difference.

# CHAPTER THREE

# A BEGINNER'S GUIDE TO YOUTUBE MARKETING FOR SMALL BUSINESS

---

Are you looking for other ways to promote your business online? Then look no further: YouTube is one of the largest and most popular websites in the world, making it an incredibly powerful marketing tool.

In this guide to get started with YouTube marketing, you will learn:

- Is YouTube actually the Right Solution for Your Business and Advertising Strategy
- Step by step instructions to Create a YouTube Video Marketing Strategy
- Step by step instructions to begin a system with video tips and thoughts
- Deal with your YouTube channel
- Instructions to streamline your recordings for the search engine for YouTube

**So Is YouTube Marketing the Right Solution for Your Business?**

As I mentioned, also YouTube is one of the largest websites - specifically, it is currently the second most popular website in the world. And while most people don't view YouTube primarily as a search engine, that's what attracts most visitors to your site. YouTube isn't just the second most popular website; it is also the second most popular search engine - only on Google. It means that the platform offers huge opportunities to reach your business.

The fact that YouTube is such a popular platform also means a lot of competition. According to statistics, as of July 2015, 400 hours of video will be uploaded to YouTube every minute. Also, if you want to be successful on YouTube, also you need to make sure that you have the time and resources to publish quality content consistently. In other words, you need a good YouTube marketing plan.

Well, another big reason why YouTube is such an attractive alternative for marketing purposes is that it's about video - and video marketing is now raging. Video has always proven to be one of the most effective forms of content in terms of Engagement. Just because you create them for YouTube doesn't mean you can't replay videos. Also, These videos would be great for your other social profiles, email marketing campaigns, website and landing pages, and any other platform or channel you use.

When it comes to video production, it's not as difficult to create marketing videos as it sounds. You don't need a huge budget, and so you don't even have to make a substantial investment in equipment - but we'll discuss video production and all that it adds in this guide.

In short: is YouTube the right solution for your business? In most cases, yes. If you sell products, so it's a great way to showcase and promote them and all of their uses. If you are a B2B company, this is a great platform to extend your reach and generate more leads.

**Develop a strategy for YouTube marketing**

as we all know that Marketing on YouTube is like marketing on other social platforms: the first step is to create a strategy. To create your YouTube marketing strategy, you need to start by defining your goals.

Write down the specific goals you want to achieve, such as:

- Clicks / Traffic
- commitment
- Range / Subscriber Numbers

Use the SMART model to help you define good goals: specific, measurable, achievable, relevant and time-bound. It will help you ensure that your goals are concrete, that they have a deadline and that they are capable of.

Well, Of course, you also need to be able to accurately measure your progress. In this strategic step, find out which KPIs (Key Performance Indicators) will help you measure results.

**Commit to the calendar**

Consistency is important on YouTube if you want to continue developing your channel. When you blog, the more content you post, the better your chances of reaching a wider audience.

The most successful YouTubers publishers have a very tight release schedule - and they stick to it. These YouTubes also promote new videos to their audiences on other social media platforms so that even those who are not subscribed to their channel can always know when a new video is coming. When defining a YouTube marketing strategy for your business, consider how often you can realistically commit to submitting new content and make sure you stick to it.

Once you have determined how often you can publish, you should also take this into account when publishing your videos. Also according to Oberlo, most viewers watch YouTube videos in the evenings and on weekends. Also, the best time to post your content is early in the afternoon during the week, or on Saturday and Sunday morning to index your Video based on the time that potential viewers are looking for.

Also, at this point, write down any upcoming vacations and events that are relevant to your audience so that you know in advance the possibilities for creating specific content.

# TYPES OF MARKETING VIDEOS

So now that you know your goals and want to publish, the question is, what types of videos can you create?

It is important to keep things varied so that your audience is entertained and returns more. Also, it's a good idea to try different types of videos from the start to figure out which ones work best and which don't.

well, this is some ideas to get you started:

**Listicles:** Listicles are a very popular form of content, both as blog posts and as media (videos, images, infographics, etc.). You can create lists that showcase your products or services - like the "10 innovative ways to use your products" - or they can be educational, informative, or entertaining. Remember that lists should always be tailored to the interests of your audience and the narrowness of your business.

**Help Videos:** Help videos generally work very well, as they offer a lot of value to the viewer. For example, if you sell social media software, you can create instructional videos that show your viewers how to start Twitter marketing or how to increase your Facebook follow-up. You can research the best performing blog posts on these videos or develop a plan for a recurring series. The JetBlue series offers a series of "Flight Etiquette" videos that show how you are not travelling:

**Backstage videos:** YouTube is a social network - the keyword here is "social". One way to humanize your brand and show that you are more than just a product or service is to share certain videos behind the scenes. For example, Sprout Social has a collection of videos with members of its group:

**Product Videos:** so Video is a great way to showcase your products or services. These product videos can help viewers use certain features, highlight new product updates, or announce new offers for your business. Mailchimp often posts videos about their products:

**Case Studies:** Another way to promote your business and your products or services is to create video case studies of your customers. These case studies don't have to deal exclusively with your products: they can focus on the customer's original stories, recent achievements or future projects.

**Interviews:** Interviewing well-known experts and influencers in your niche is another great way to attract new viewers. These experts have their followers, so if they also promote the Video, they can help drive traffic to your YouTube channel.

**Manage your YouTube channel**

so Now that you have a YouTube marketing strategy and a few video ideas to get started, Also you want to focus on managing your channel. Also, Engagement is a big part of YouTube, so it's very important to take the time to respond to comments you receive and get involved in other ways as well.

Some good way to manage your account is to use a tool to automate the process. Agorapulse allows you to pre-monitor your comments, review and respond to comments in the social inbox of your dashboard (which you can do as a team member + you can assign tasks), and follow YouTube to mention characters in videos and comments. Other useful management features include recorded responses (to respond to comments with a few clicks) and a social CRM tool to help keep track of subscribers and connections.

Another great option for channel management is VidIQ, which lets you track comments and respond as needed, collaborate with your team members, and find useful keywords and tags to optimize your videos.

Here are some other YouTube tips for increasing Engagement and prospects:

- Check your comments daily so you can respond quickly
- Use tracking to find other brand mentions and identify engagement opportunities
- Ask your viewers in your videos and video clips to encourage them to leave a comment
- Use the "Community" tab (located on the main page of your channel) to download images, GIFs and video previews, and to subscribe to subscribers. For example, Evan Carmichael regularly publishes polls asking his subscribers what they want to see in the next videos:

# CONTENT BASICS

In addition to the video content you make, taking into account certain creative considerations can give your content the best chance of showing up. These creative criteria were at the heart of the advice YouTube provides to advertisers and creators, and are based on observations on which YouTube videos work well.

You can see many of these principles in YouTube videos which, through creation, experimentation and collaboration, have figured out how to create a loyal audience of interested viewers. These YouTubers have partially broken down the code for YouTube video success while creating many rules on how best to use the platform. Some of these principles apply specifically to YouTube, certain videos, certain content, certain social media and marketing in general.

1. **Make your videos shareable**

Sharing is probably the highest form of thanks for making a video something really good because people only share things directly with their friends when they know they like it. Sharing is the holy grail of all marketers because it means you can use less paid media to spread the word.

Making shared videos can be very difficult, so I warn all marketers that they don't want to create a video that someone can magically watch one, split in half, then four, and then grow very fast until to go around the world. Unfortunately, divisibility really doesn't work that way.

Marketers should consider sharing their videos before making them. When thinking of a video idea, start by taking a step back and ask yourself if viewers are sharing your content. A good example is Rhett and Link from the Good Mythical Morning channel.

"When people share this, what ten words do they describe to their friends?"

You can see that the concept is played out in Figure 10-1. The video title from Rhett and Link, "The Most Amazing Optical Illusions on the Internet", is an example of a title of fewer than ten words that someone can use to describe a video when sharing a video with other people.

Check your YouTube video history to see the videos you've recently watched. Which ones have you shared with friends? Why did you share these videos? I bet you will find that some of the videos you have shared.

Are entertaining. It sounds obvious, but you liked the video, and you knew a friend would enjoy it too.

You are speaking of common interest. You knew your friend with whom you shared it, also interested in this type of content.

Confirm something about yourself. For example, it can support your beliefs or opinions.

For example, I was watching my story right now, and the last time I shared the video was my favourite car, Youugub, Doug DeMuro, titled "Here's why the 2018 Lincoln Navigator is worth $ 100,000". I shared this video with my friend Andy with the words "I want one". The video was entertaining, linked to a common interest and confirmed something I believe - the Lincoln Navigator is a cool car.

**Videos to share**

- Tell a good story. When you meet with friends, you tell stories, and the principle applies to share videos. People want to share videos that tell a good story.
- Are often funny or positive. You're probably sharing a video to enhance your Valentine's Day. Videos can, therefore, be more shareable if they are fun, uplifting, cheerful or optimistic.
- Are short and easy to watch. Very few people share an entire documentary (of course, you can recommend watching it), so the videos you share are often short. It is the kind of video you will be happy to stop watching.
- Say something about sharing. If you look back at the videos you shared, you may find that they say something about you. They may represent your sense of humour or belief, or that you share something that you thought was smart because you are also smart.

Ask people to share videos. You'll see more people sharing your video if you add a reminder to share your video. If you don't ask, you won't!

**2. Have a conversation**

YouTube, like other social media channels, but unlike traditional media, offers a unique opportunity to chat directly with your audience. As a marketer, you can use YouTube to ask your audience what they like and dislike, what they want more, and what they like about you the most.

The conversation is an important part of every most successful YouTube video and use. One of the things you notice when you watch almost all of the popular YouTube videos is that they talk to you directly in a chat-style and ask viewers to comment and discuss the content of their videos.

This debate developed in part because of many YouTubers started years ago sitting in his bedroom with his webcam in front of his laptop, looking directly at the camera and looking at them directly, creating content in a vlog style. The installation looked like a video call with a friend, so YouTubers used a chat.

Interestingly, at the time, this approach was so different from other television content. Instead of being a passive TV viewer, viewers felt like a friend and celebrity spoke to them. This personal feeling is one of the main reasons why YouTube and your YouTube membership really took off.

When you make your videos, you can take a creative approach to speak directly to your audience in chat mode. Talk Videos

- **Show your audience face to face.** You can show the person in front of the camera and speak directly to the audience in a casual style and voice. A forward-facing face is better than any other angle, or they don't use someone's face. Studies have shown that videos with a human face to face are likely to be better and remember. People love to see people's faces!

- **Encourage dialogue.** The video should especially encourage people to use comments to ask questions and answer questions. The right questions are instructive and concrete - not too open, broad or vague. Be sure to read these comments and respond to them in the comments themselves or the following videos, like or like the video is simple but effective recognition from the commentator.
- **Use a light script**. If you've ever been to a party and been chatting with someone you describe as a good conversationalist, it's because they're telling a fascinating story. It's almost as if they have a clear story in their head - because they have it! For example, using a lightweight script that tracks the few key points you want to cover and in what order will help provide a good discussion experience for viewers.

Watch some videos of the best YouTubers events and find out how they use chat focus to engage their viewers. Can you think of ways to take a similar approach to your marketing videos?

Challenge yourself to find new ways to make your videos conversational. While only vlog-style copying can work, there is a danger that you will not feel authentic.

3. **Engage your audience interactively.**

Adding interactivity to your videos is a great way to attract your audience and create a viewer level. Interactivity refers to whenever you ask your audience to be in direct contact with you and the content.

For example, if you are making recipe videos, ask viewers what they would like to see next, for example, what recipe they would like you to make. Do your viewers want to see beef prepared according to a Mexican-style recipe, or do they prefer to see beef prepared for cooking? (Me too - tacos every time!)

If you can create interactive ways to engage your audience, you will quickly know what people want to see from you. (See the nearby box "Epic Rap Battles of History" for a good example of how a YouTube channel implements this concept.) Interactive videos

- Create interactivity in them. The best examples of interactive videos are more than just questions to the audience, and they have a creative concept in which interactivity is embedded.
- Give strength to the audience. With your interactive videos, viewers can control the videos you make next. Sure, that gives you some control, but you show your audience that you're there for them, which increases loyalty.
- 

**4. Always be consistent**

Maybe my favorite creative principle is consistency because I think it's the key to success on YouTube. Many customers with good intentions are making videos and running certain campaigns. Still, they have finally lost interest and have not continued to work to create a successful YouTube presence that meets their marketing needs.

YouTube may require more effort than other social platforms, especially when developing your content strategy. Still, there is a chance of winning for inclusion if you are willing to commit to constantly creating quality content. Every successful YouTube channel produces consistently in a certain way.

You can be consistent.

- According to the normal release schedule: Your audience wants to know that you want to regularly post videos they want to see - for example, you download videos every day on the same day and at the same time.
- Make sure your videos are creative and consistent with your brand, tone and quality level. A YouTube friend recently made a video with his voice a bit muted, and people told it in a comment! They were not happy, even if it didn't bring much change. Your YouTube audience wants to see your videos follow the approach they like, and they want their quality to be always better (or better) every time.
- Find the shape that people like the most and stick to it. When you develop an audience in the desired format, deviations from it can be unpopular. You'll see this with a bunch of YouTubers who are popular thanks to continuous downloads in a human-like format, then try a different approach when their viewers don't like the new format. Regular experimentation is important, of course, but don't forget to keep your audience happy by constantly submitting videos

they love so much.

Consistency is important because viewers want to know that you are there when they want more content and that they know what they are getting before they start watching.

I love my favourite car driver, Doug DeMuro (find it on YouTube - it's worth it), so for several reasons:

- He has a regular schedule for submitting videos. I know when I visit her YouTube channel or homepage, I see something new from her.
- His personality is this impressive combination of being a deep expert confined to a nerd, cars and his somewhat absurd and joyful experience of a car. He makes jokes about the weight of the car using animals like giraffes, and almost every time he is accelerated in a powerful car, his smile is so wide that he can't help but laugh. His brand and personality are consistent and convincing.
- The format is always the same. This reason is perhaps the most important for me. I receive a 20-minute presentation, an exterior review, an interior and a driving experience, and all of this was consistent with interesting observations and jokes. I love watching Doug's videos right before bed because I usually want about 20 minutes of content before I go to bed.

**5. Target your public interests**

In other words, you want to create videos that target your target audience by tapping into their passions and interests. Your videos should be based on what you know about your audience and what they want to see.

The BuzzFeed team is at the head of the content machine.

The goal of which is to understand the content that its audience wants. And to target it with content that it knows how to like.

Now go to BuzzFeed (www.buzzfeed.com), the YouTube app and channels (www.youtube.com/user/BuzzFeedVideo), and see how smart they offer something that targets you. (See nearby sidebar for more information on BuzzFeed.)

Videos that keep targeting in mind »Always keep your audience's passions and interests in mind» Find new and interesting ways to capture their needs and wants »Listen to and respond to their comments in the comments» Try to constantly refine

6. **Make sure it is durable**

Although you can create a great video that starts by checking the boxes of several of the content criteria that I explain in this chapter, the effort will be wasted if you can't add more videos. The best videos you make are durable, which means you can make them easier. Don't break

just make one because it needed all the time or money!

The Fine Brothers offer (https://youtube.com/user/TheFineBros)

perfectly describes the endurance point:

"If we can't film at least three episodes in a day, we'll move on to the next idea."

I asked for a conversation with Joey Helms

(www.youtube.com/user/Joey2Rob), who makes great videos that take him at least a month to shoot and edit together. She decided that she wanted to create these videos that will work despite the time and effort required to create a beautiful result.

He has found a sustainable way to deliver several videos in the period he wants, and it's a different approach from The Fine Bros, which wants to shoot several videos a day and needs formats that they can change quickly.

I think this thing is, "If I made this video, can I do it more easily?" Do you have the time, the money, the will, the resources to do more? If the answer is no, you are making the wrong videos.

If your video content strategy is sustainable, you can do it.

- **Post your popular videos regularly and regularly.** A sustainable content strategy means that you can post a regular video call without a long idle time.
- **Respect your budget and the resources available**. It is a terrible situation when budgets are exceeded, or resources are exhausted. A sustainable content strategy is one that knows and plays within the limits of your budget and resources.
- **Provide the desired quantity and quality of the video.** It is a perfectly qualified strategy to want to make a high-quality video a month, but just as qualified is to find a format that you can submit every day. A sustainable approach ensures that you reach the number

of videos you publish while maintaining their quality.

**7. Maximize your chances of finding**

YouTube is a search engine. Of course, sometimes people visit YouTube and immediately find something on its home page that starts a viewing session. At other times, people start their YouTube session with a search. There are many ways people can meet your video, such as embedding it in a blog or sharing it via email with a friend. The question becomes how to ensure the accuracy of the video can be found no matter how someone uses YouTube or browses the Internet.

Findability is important, but it can be a real challenge considering the number of videos you download each day. Besides, discoverability is made more complex because it consists of a few different dimensions that are evaluated by the algorithm.

When you upload a video, the algorithm immediately begins to evaluate it. We examine the video to make sure it respects copyright and political rules. If the video passes these tests and goes online, the algorithm examines the performance of the video and decides how to send it to potential viewers.

The algorithm is very complex, but basically, its purpose is to see how many people are watching your videos if they like it, if they are watching everything,

how many other videos they watch after you, etc. All of these performance variables dictate where a video finds billions of hours of video content in a directory.

To ensure discoverability, you can do three things:

- Send certain information to your video that clearly and completely captures the video
- Use paid media to launch a video by earning views
- Create trendy or evergreen videos.

**8. Make your videos available**

The most effective videos on YouTube are videos that you can watch separately, which means you don't have to see other videos before or after to make sense.

Take the example of the 1990s TV series "Friends." The program was a success because you can watch any episode at any time, in any order, and you will always enjoy it. This accessibility makes the program perfect for endless syndication renewals, as well as individual episodes or Netflix binging.

When you create videos on YouTube, make them so that viewers can enjoy them without seeing other videos.

It's not that an alternative approach may not work because it's entirely possible, but if someone wants to watch your videos, you might lose it when they realize they need to watch one first. Other.

Ask yourself, "Can each episode enjoy a whole new audience?"

**9. Look for authenticity**

Authenticity can be an abstract concept and can be used on social media to such an extent that it becomes irrelevant. Despite overuse, however, authenticity consists of loyalty to one's personality, spirit, or character. People can instantly identify someone or something when it's not genuine.

Every video you make must remain authentic. If you're true to your values and stay true to your brand, your videos are authentic. You know as soon as you send something genuine - subscribers will call you without hesitation.

Authenticity in video content can mean

- **Always stay true to your brand and true to your values.** The best marketers know that everything that is produced must remain the brand of the company, which means that they create their choices in tone, look and feel, and more, they feel like they are representatives of the brand. And its values.
- **Make videos you can only make.** Don't make videos that have nothing to do with your brand, products or services. Sometimes people can create videos designed just to get views, but they won't help you reach your marketing goals. Prospects are never a goal, just a proxy for your business goals!
- **The search of original content**. If you're really good at it, you'll find ways to make your videos original and fresh instead of copying other videos yourself. Viewers will only watch these videos instead.
- **Listen to constructive comments in the comments**. While comments can sometimes be useless and false, find the gems of

constructive comments and use them to keep authenticity on track.

## How to optimize your videos to improve your SEO

Once your channel is created, you can optimize it for searches. As mentioned above, YouTube is the second-largest search engine in the world. Creating engaging content is essential, but it's not the only success factor. There are different optimization methods to get high SEO on YouTube and in Google's search results.

YouTube marketing experts rely on the creation and optimization of their videos' metadata. This metadata contains information intended for the spectators, like the title of the video, its description, its category, its thumbnail, tags and subtitles. Relevant information allows a video to be properly referenced by YouTube and to appear in search results. The metadata should be concise and clear. Your content may be deleted if you try to promote it with keywords that do not match it. You can check out the video and tips below to learn more about optimizing a video for search.

1. **Headline**

Like on-page SEO, it is important to optimize the title and description of a video. Titles are the first thing viewers see when scrolling through a list of videos. They must, therefore, be concise and attractive, to arouse the curiosity of spectators or to indicate to them that a video will help them to solve a specific problem. Perform keyword research to better understand the research carried out by the spectators. Include the most important information and also keywords at the start of your title. Besides, a title should consist of approximately 60 characters to be displayed in its entirety on the results pages.

**2. Description**

YouTube only displays the first two or three lines (approximately 100 characters) of the video descriptions. Viewers should click More to view the rest of the text. You should, therefore, include important links or CTAs at the start of your description, and write the text that will increase the number of views and interactions. Below, you can insert a transcript of your video. Transcripts can increase SEO significantly because videos are usually full of keywords. Also, You can also add a default channel description that will include links to your social networks, video credits and their breakdown. Finally, it is possible to include, in moderation, some #hashtags in the titles and descriptions of videos.

**3. Tags**

The title and description of your videos with keywords, highlight the most important of them in your tags. Tags allow you to associate your videos with similar videos, thereby increasing their reach. First, insert your most important keywords, then try to get a balanced mix between generic keywords and long-tail keywords.

**4. Category**

YouTube allows you to choose the category of your videos in the Advanced Settings, helping them to be associated with similar content on the platform. The following categories are available: movies and animations, auto/motorcycle, music, animals, sport, travel and events, video games, people and blogs, humour, entertainment, news and politics, practical life and style, education, science and technology and non-profit organizations.

### 5. Miniature

The thumbnail of your video is the main image that viewers see when scrolling through a list of results. It can actually have a very big impact on the number of clicks and the number of views of a video. YouTube automatically generates a few thumbnail suggestions for each video, but it's a good idea to upload a custom image. A YouTube report says "90% of the best performing videos use a custom thumbnail". When you shoot, take high-quality images that accurately represent your video. Also, YouTube recommends using a 1280 x 720 px image so that the thumbnail will appear perfectly on all screen sizes.

Your YouTube account must be verified before you can upload a custom thumbnail. To do this, go to youtube.com/verify and enter the verification code sent by YouTube.

### 6. .Srt files (subtitles)

Whether it's a transcription of the original text or a translation, the subtitles help viewers, but also allow you to optimize your video for research by giving you another opportunity to highlight words. - important keys. You can add subtitles by loading a transcript in an accepted format or a file containing synchronized subtitles. You can also import a full transcript of your video, which YouTube will automatically sync, type in the subtitles or your translation as the video plays, or hire a professional to translate or transcribe.

To add subtitles, open the Video Manager, then click Videos. Find the video you want, then click the down arrow next to the Edit button. Then select Subtitles. You can then save them.

### 7. End sheets and screens (notes)

Since May 2017, YouTube no longer allows its users to add notes to their videos. However, the platform encourages them to incorporate end cards and screens to collect the viewers' opinion, direct them to other videos or offer a link to an external site. End cards and screens are as easy to add as notes. The cards are small rectangular notifications that appear in the upper right corner of YouTube on desktop and mobile. Each video can include up to five cards. However, if you insert several cards, make sure to space them out so that the spectators can take the desired action.

To add a card, open the Video Manager, click on the Edit drop-down menu and select Cards.

Then click on Add file. You can choose to create a Video or playlist, Channel, Poll and Link record.

Once you've created your card, drag it when you want from the video. The changes will be saved automatically.

End screens allow you to extend a video by 5-20 seconds to direct viewers to other videos or YouTube channels, encourage them to subscribe to your channel or promote external links, such as those that direct to your site. They encourage viewers to continue interacting with your brand or content.

To add an end screen, open the Video Manager, click the Edit drop-down menu and select End Screen.

Then choose the items you want to add to your end screen. You can add them by importing the end screen used in another video, use a template or create them manually. It's important to note that YouTube requires users to promote another YouTube video or playlist on an end screen.

8. **Playlists**

Playlists are ideal tools if you create videos around specific themes. They allow you to manage a series of videos from your channel and other channels, to structure your channel and to encourage users to watch similar content at the end of a video while appearing separately in the results. Of research. The visibility of your content is thus reinforced when you create playlists.

To create a new playlist, open the page of a video you want to add and click the icon under the video. Then click Create playlist. Type the name of your new playlist, then click Create.

## Understanding YouTube analytics

You've spent a lot of time and effort on your YouTube channel. You have created interesting content, you have optimized it for SEO, and you have shared it on different platforms. Now is the time to measure its success.

Some teams may understand the review of YouTube analytics,

multiple data and different graphics. However, the task is simpler than it seems.

## 1. Define your goal

It is important to note that you cannot measure your success if you have not determined your goal. If you've filmed, edited, loaded, optimized, and shared a video without knowing what goal it would achieve, you're facing a problem. A specific objective must direct your video strategy, from its beginnings to its conclusions.

You must target a goal by video. The most common objectives are to increase brand awareness or the number of views, clicks, inbound links or even shares on social networks depending on the use of your video in your marketing strategy.

The objective could also be to increase the rate of opening of a series of emails To improve the conversion rate of a page of destination. YouTube is an ideal platform to develop brand awareness.

Indeed, the second largest search engine in the world allows videos to be found through natural searches or paid advertisements. By relying on videos, you have the opportunity to humanize your brand by presenting your employees, customers or partners. You can also establish your credibility by posting educational content that helps your target customers. The type of video to be created can be affected by the promotion, which will be carried out via advertisements or natural research. If you plan to develop brand awareness naturally, you may want to consider filming your company's history, customer reviews, or tutorials on using your products.

## 2. Main indicators to monitor

Once you have determined your goal, you need to measure success effectively. YouTube analytics can seem confusing at first. Additionally, it can be disappointing to find that a video isn't getting as many views or engagements as you'd expect. YouTube tells you how viewers found your content, how long they watched it, and how extensive their interactions were.

To find out what you can measure and where to find these indicators, go to youtube.com/analytics. The analytics dashboard shows an overview of the performance of your videos over the past 28 days. You can adjust the period of the analyzes by clicking on the drop-down menu in the upper right corner of the screen. This overview includes essential performance indicators, engagement indicators, demographics, traffic sources and popular content.

Several filters are available: content, device types, region and geographic location, all videos or playlists, subscriber status, reading contexts, traffic based on different YouTube products and translations. YouTube also allows you to display the results in the form of different graphics or even an interactive map.

There is no universal method for reporting and measuring the success of a campaign, but a few key indicators are essential.

### *3.* Duration of viewing and loyalty of the audience

Watch time indicates the total number of minutes your audience spent watching your content on your channel as a whole and for each video. So you can see which videos are actually engaging viewers, and which are just getting quick clicks before being closed. This viewing time is important because it is one of the SEO factors of YouTube. A video with a high viewing time is more likely to get better referencing in search results. YouTube provides a report on viewing time, several views, average view time, average view percentage for each video, location, publication date, and more. The average video view percentage, or retention rate, indicates what average video percentage your audience is watching with each view. A higher percentage indicates a higher likelihood of full viewing by your audience. You can try to integrate cards and end screens in videos offering a high percentage to increase the number of views received by your call-to-action.

*4.* **Traffic sources**

The traffic sources report shows how viewers find your content online. It is valuable information on where to best promote your YouTube content. You could discover that your audience finds your content through a search on YouTube or Twitter. For a more detailed traffic report, click on the Traffic Sources category. This data will help you refine your marketing strategy on YouTube and optimize your metadata.

*5.* **Demographic data**

With the demographics report, you can better understand your audience by finding out information about their age and gender. You can refine this data with other criteria, such as geographic location. This report allows you to better promote your content to your YouTube audience and to determine if your content is appreciated by your buyer personas.

*6.* **Interactions report**

The Interactions Report lets you find out what content is appreciated by your audience. You can thus know which videos receive clicks, shares, comments and promotion actions, but also determine the performance of your files and your end screens and therefore optimize the call-to-action of your future videos.

**YouTube video SEO**

well, As I mentioned earlier, YouTube is one of the most popular search engines in the world, which is one of the reasons why it is such an attractive advertising tool for businesses. Imagine the full potential with almost two billion monthly users!

It just means that if you take the time to optimize your videos and produce quality video content regularly, you can greatly increase your chances of reaching a large and targeted audience.

**So how do you optimize your YouTube videos?**

There are several important factors in the placement of research results. Some are entirely under your control - like the keywords you use and how you use them - while with others, you don't have as much power over them (like the number of people who subscribe right after watching a video).

well Here are some of the most important video locations you should know about:

Keywords in your channel: use the right tags to make sure YouTube knows what your channel is about.

Video titles and descriptions: Search for keywords to find out what your audience is looking for, and use those keywords in video titles and descriptions.

- **Video tags:** well in addition to keywords, you need to add tags to your videos - search for tags to find out which ones work best.
- **Video duplication:** the integration of a video copy is a great way to make your Video more scratchy for search engines. It is also good for viewers: if they have to check the spelling of a word or if they can't increase the volume of a video, they can still use the content.
- **Viewing time:** the total viewing time of the videos (how many minutes/hours / etc. people have watched your videos) is also taken into account in your ranking. The longer the viewing time, the better!
- **Thumbnail:** The thumbnail is displayed each time the Video is indexed, so it must be compelling and relevant.
- **Engagement:** YouTube also reviews your channel's Engagement, including the number of likes/failures you get and the number of comments and shares.
- **Subscriber numbers:** it doesn't just mean how many YouTube subscribers you have. As I mentioned earlier, it also matters how many subscribers after watching a video. These subscribers show that the Video was relevant and brought value to the viewer.

So In terms of useful SEO tools, Tube Buddy is one of the best options because it has many video SEO features, including:

- YouTube keyword research tools which help you find the right long-tail keywords to target
- Tag Explorer to find popular tags for your channel and videos
- Keyword ranking tracking so you can easily track the ranking and success of your videos
- A / B test for videos
- View and copy video tags

The last feature that allows you to preview videos and see what tags they have used. It is very useful because you can check out very popular videos that rank very well (and are related to your niche/videos) and see which tags have helped them reach this point.

When using your YouTube content on your other channels or website, make sure the Video is a page feature for the best investment opportunities. Crawlers do not retrieve hidden Video from a page, and Google usually only indexes the first Video.

Optimizing video content is important in determining your YouTube marketing strategy, and it can also help you get started with the content. Keyword research is a great tool for finding video ideas. Before creating new videos, it's a good idea to research your keywords and create videos based on the keywords you want to target.

**Next step: YouTube marketing success**

Used properly, YouTube can be a great way to increase brand awareness and reach more potential customers. To make sure your YouTube marketing strategy is doomed to success, start with the following key points:

- Set up your YouTube presence in advance and plan your videos to make sure you post new content regularly
- always Create different types of videos to appeal to a wider audience
- Take the time to chat with subscribers and viewers and try to catch every Video
- Optimize your channels and videos for the YouTube search engine to increase your goal

# CHAPTER FOUR
# YOUTUBE'S DIGITAL MARKETING GUIDE FOR SMES

---

If the value of a picture is a thousand words, what is the value of a movie? With well-created videos, your business can communicate with current and potential customers in a way that was never possible a few years ago. Plus, you don't need specialized knowledge or a huge budget to succeed on YouTube, as affordable tools and techniques have reduced barriers.

YouTube has grown in popularity since its inception in 2005 and has become the world's second most popular search engine. Google, which now owns YouTube, prominently places video content in its organic search ranking.

If you've ignored YouTube as a marketing option for your business so far, you're not alone. "Many companies that can succeed on YouTube don't use it," said social media consultant Krishna De. "But there are good opportunities to create valuable content for your customers or your target market inexpensively and effectively. The key is to determine what content would interest your audience, implement it correctly, and make sure it's visible. "

**Ways to use YouTube**

One of the most sought-after elements on YouTube is explanatory videos. "Creating useful and informative videos is a great way to get a trusted audience," De says. It can be sometimes as easy as answering a common question.

"The hostel in Dublin, called Avalon House, kept getting calls from the airport - often from customers with poor English language skills," De recalls. "So they filmed one employee making a trip dressed in bananas. In addition to helping customers, it saves hours spent in the field. Recommended videos are an effective way to build your brand." If your customers are ready for an interview, it's great, "De says." quotes and photos in videos. YouTube Creator Studio (in the YouTube Dashboard) is a great resource for this. "Product demos and explanatory videos are useful ways to showcase your expertise, but you can go further and create 'inspiring' videos with ideas your customers may not have had." I didn't think to join your product. Bold videos that show your mission, like this Dollar Shave Club video, can also be very popular and get the word out. It's also a great way to give personality to your business, as the high-end independent chalet company Alikats showed in the end-of-season movie.

# HOW TO INTEGRATE SOCIAL MEDIA INTO YOUR BUSINESS PLAN

The online social media for business owners, seems to be moving from "doing" to "how do I do"? I've been working on this over the last few days as part of the design of my job, and I have developed this special process for social media plan for small businesses:

**Start with a strategy**

Determine how social media serves your business. Usually, this is done through branding and awareness-related corporate marketing at the top of the marketing channel, but it can also focus on other business activities. For example, airlines use Twitter for customer service, food cars transport it for delivery through tweet sites, and consultants use a tracking counter and the like to reinforce their expertise.

The strategy is first, so you need to figure out the different options for social media. Megan Berry, a New York-based Lift Five community management expert, said: "Facebook is usually more personal, so if the product is fun and consumer-oriented, then Facebook is really good. Twitter has the benefits of public and commercial searches, so you can see how important the topic is. Google+ is made up mostly of technicians, photographers, and people who work for Google. "I think LinkedIn has more careers than certain companies, and Pinterest is great for photo collections. You can't do everything, and the fastest way to fail is to please everyone or do nothing.

To illustrate, the examples in my other example, focus on Twitter and use Twitter terminology. It just makes the story easier to follow.

**More special tactics**

Strategy means nothing without special tactics. On social media, this means making practical decisions. For example, imagine an ecologically better building materials manufacturer selling in a local market by looking at Twitter. Here are some tactics to use:

- **Which accounts follow:** Of course, in our example, we follow people tweeting about homes, green building, building materials, architecture, and the construction industry. Maybe also small businesses, small business management and local businesses. Gardening, landscape architecture? We also need to follow people who represent old-fashioned methods that the green building replaces, and yes, all of our competitors. And we want to follow industry leaders, the best blogs in the industry, and media professionals.
- **What content tweets and Retweets:** In the example, we tweet about building, building, architecture, and greenhouses to create a content stream that attracts like-minded people. We also probably want tweets about local events, local businesses and local people to attract local connections. However, we never provide content that promotes old-fashioned methods of our competitors. We install scheduled searches for hashtags such as #green and #greenbuilding, #homes and #greenhomes. (Hashtag badges are a Twitter feature that people use to make it

easier to find topics. People who post content include them in their tweets so those looking can find them.)

- **What to look out for:** We need to set up a study to get all the mentions of us, of course. Besides, an indication of our competitors, substitute products or competing products and (where possible) local construction problems.
- **When to reach:** We want to follow media professionals and topics that can create media opportunities for us, such as interviews with the founder or reviews in blogs or trade journals. Reaching on Twitter means either tweet that mentions certain handles or a direct message to specific people.
- **How to reach:** We want to reach correctly and respectfully, only in certain cases and for certain people. Instant messaging should always show, feel, or act as spam.

**Add specific variables, milestones, and tracking**

Your strategy and tactics are useless without specific concrete steps, measures and follow-up.

In our example of eco-building-oriented Twitter, we want to define the objective and traceable digital goals for how much:

- monitored accounts
- new follow-ups that are added every month
- tweets per day, week and month
- retweets to send

- retweets we want to receive
- subscribers we plan to add per month
- the lead we should get
- we track website visits from tweets, retweets and Twitter profile

And for review meetings, we want to start with the actual numbers of each measure. We then review these results and discuss changes in statistics, tactics, and strategy.

**YouTube Marketing: A Guide for Small Businesses**

When my series on using social media marketing platforms to market a small business ends (see previous posts on Facebook, Twitter, Instagram, Pinterest, and LinkedIn), we come to what is likely to be the narrowest content from the start: Youtube.

Well, if you want to use YouTube to market your small business, you're going to create videos that are simple and straightforward. While this sounds obvious, it should be noted that while social platforms like Facebook create, post and share different types of content. (videos, images, long text messages, short bets), etc.), creating content on YouTube means you invest your time only for video production and video production.

This note is not intended to stifle you, but to emphasize that a strong interest in creating video content is essential before posting on YouTube. Don't just set up a YouTube channel to take advantage of all possible forms of social media marketing if you're not really interested in creating videos. The process of creating a video is time-consuming and has a bit of a learning curve, so make sure this platform is one where you really have the time and interest.

Aside from that, let's get started.

**Set up your YouTube channel**

Setting up a chain couldn't be simpler, if you already have a Google Account, you already technically have a YouTube channel, even if you don't know it.

However, here is a YouTube guide that describes the basic steps for setting up your YouTube account.

Warning: well Even if you already have a YouTube channel linked to your Gmail account, it may be wise to create a new account specifically for your business to differentiate between your personal and professional activities on Google and YouTube.

Now you want to choose a name for your new YouTube channel. As with all your other social profiles, it's best to choose the one that comes closest to your business name (or what best describes the type of content you create).

Should you change the name of your channel? Today, you're in luck: Before 2015, you were permanently locked into your channel name, but you can now change it if you need to later. It only takes a while to choose a fixed chain name that represents your business and brand, because the more you can build brand continuity and reputation around the name, the better (and confusing) it will be. Customers and followers if you keep changing). Product photo!).

**Add a banner and create a trailer.**

Before you start focusing on regular video content distribution, it's important to make your YouTube site visual.

There are several ways to create a YouTube banner. If you are actually working with a graphic designer, it would be a good idea for a small project to turn to them. If you're using a DIY brand strategy, as always, I recommend Canva, which has a template specifically designed for your YouTube banner (use it called YouTube Channel Art).

The YouTube trailer is the first auto play video that visitors will see when they arrive at the YouTube page. It is their first review of your brand and what your YouTube channel contains.

Now, your channel is likely to attract visitors in two ways: they end up on your channel because of a link from some other social site, blog, or website, or they go to your channel themselves.

Here is a YouTube guide to creating a channel trailer. Find out what makes a good YouTube channel trailer? Fullscreen Media provides a solid and concise overview of the elements required.

**Create videos that reflect your brand**

Is your brand serious and formal? Prank or joke videos are probably poorly suited. On the other hand, if you've built your brand tone around a light conversational style, don't create video content that looks boring or too professional.

While that sounds obvious, it may be a good idea to check the tone of your brand before proceeding. Your videos should always be a clear continuation of the current tone you have created for your brand. Otherwise, you may have to build a subscriber base that has no connection to your actual product or service (and who never uses it!), And your current customers may feel marginalized or cheated.

In short: spend time making sure the content you produce matches the brand and sound you hope to convey.

**Focus on data videos, style, video series, or vlog content**

If you have a product or service, show videos of your product, likewise, if you offer a service, show how your service benefits customers. Information videos can be a great place to showcase your products or services in the "real world," giving customers an idea of what to expect if they buy from you.

YouTube videos can also be a great place to offer something "extra" to your fans for free for them. Don't just show how customers can use your products. What can you show them how to do it?

For example, if you run a landscaping and maintenance business, consider filming short videos with instructions on how customers can handle certain lawn care jobs. It will help build trust and set you up as a trusted point of contact for the information you sell with a simple product or service.

Likewise, creating vlog-style videos can help your brand create a more personal connection with your audience and allow you to create lifestyle-oriented content. It will help make your brand authentic and can also help build trust and loyalty to the brand.

**Present customer experiences or other customer comments**

When you think about what types of content you can showcase on your new YouTube channel, you can reach out to your satisfied customers. What can they say about your business that would add valuable value to your video content?

It can sound like a referral, an interview with specific customers who have managed to collaborate with your business, a series that shows how different customers use a particular product or service - the list goes on and depends (of course) on what you run.

However, as with all content marketing, avoid an overly "salty" approach. The goal is to show subscribers a wide range of experiences about real and real people who use your products or services; authenticity is the key.

**Pay attention to the keywords in the title.**

Much of your organic traffic is based on research. That is if someone searches for a "braided update guide" and you only have these keywords in the title of your YouTube video, it's more likely that researchers will find your video.

YouTube headlines follow the same rules as elsewhere on the Internet. So it's a good idea to familiarize yourself with the basics of SEO before creating videos. I usually refer people to Moz beginners for an SEO guide that is what it looks like, and a great starting point.

**Subscribe and interact with similar channels**

Well, one of the great ways to get your YouTube channel out to a potential new audience is to leave a thoughtful comment on other YouTube videos (preferably a YouTube channel that produces content like you). Hopefully, other viewers will vote on your comment, which will increase its visibility and thus potential clicks on your channel.

It's important to comment as early as possible and get something unique, relevant, or fun to add to the conversation. So, it doesn't just mean "Great video!" and waiting for subscribers to arrive is accompanied by a strategy.

For example, suppose you have a hair salon. Your strategy may include subscribing to several similar Youtube channels focusing on hair, makeup, and other beauty considerations. When one of your favourites posts a new video, comment and tell them how much you liked what you liked and why.

Adding a unique addition to the comments discussion section puts you as another potentially valuable channel for viewers to watch. (You can also follow the mention of your channel on the path in your comment but try to avoid over-marketing yourself.)

**Interact with your viewers**

When you start committing to your videos, make sure you do the same! Respond to your YouTube comments thoughtfully, which clearly shows that you tailor your response to each commenter. Avoid answers that seem preserved or vague.

Now, your YouTube channel may have reached a level of popularity that you just can't respond to in every comment. However, if that happens, it will certainly be far away. Responding to each comment from the beginning helps viewers display their comments and comments and welcomes commitment to your brand.

**Include a call to action and track your success**

**What is your goal in creating YouTube videos?**

Does it mean increasing brand awareness, having a complete presence on social networks, returning viewers to your site? You can define many different goals, and you need to be clear from the start. Including a call-to-action in your YouTube videos is a great way to get people to take action when they want to, at the same time as the goal you choose.

For example, if your goal is just to increase the number of subscribers, be sure to tell viewers that you like and subscribe at the end of each video. If your goal is to generate clicks to your site, encourage people to click, add the URL to your video and your description field below, etc. Like all goals, be sure to track your short- and long-term success to make sure you meet the necessary criteria. There is good internal analytics on YouTube that you can refer to (they are Google after all) and check out this book to learn more about measuring the success of YouTube content.

**Examples of small businesses that use YouTube well**

The singing dentist recorded nearly 200,000 views of a funny video shot on a mobile phone. Print, The Republic's candid video on the marketing strategy of small businesses, has proven to be very good

popular. At the same time, the enthusiasm of the pure food brand Hemsley & Hemsley really shows in their recipe videos.

# YOUTUBE MARKETING TIPS AND INFORMATION

1. **Start researching**

Before you start creating content, check what already exists. What are your competitors doing, and what do you think of your views and commitment to YouTube? Find inspiration for doing small business in different industries.

2. **keyword Research**

The easiest way to find out what's out there is to just do a YouTube search in the search box.

As with Google, completing a proactive sentence shows what the popular terms are. You can then deepen with a Google Adword search tool or a paid tool like Tubebuddy, De

advises. "If you do a search and the relevant video doesn't appear, that's a chance."

3. **Think about the name of the video**

In terms of SEO, the title of your video is especially important on YouTube, so use specific and interesting descriptive titles whenever possible. Choosing the right categories and tags will also help

your content reaches the right audience. In addition to the tags suggested by YouTube, you can add your own.

4. **Don't worry about perfection**

"The good news is that you already have what you need to shoot, edit, and share smooth video in your pocket - on your phone - and anyone can learn to do it," said Alex Pell, founder of Dashboard Media. which helps train small businesses to create video content. "In today's widespread videoblog, people also don't expect perfection. They just want to be aware and ideally entertained. Getting a clear message and space is more important than using the equipment.

5. **Create and Customize**

Aim for the target time of your videos by cutting the sequences that do nothing to create some effect. "Short videos tend to work better," says Adam Gray, author of Brilliant Social Media. "Check analytics to see how long people watch your videos." Before sending a video to a draft, ask your friends to see what you can improve or remove and make sure your movie sends the right message.

6. **Create content - but not for fun**

Popular YouTube channels usually have constantly updated video content. But choose quality over quantity; focus better on fewer high-quality videos that truly inform and inspire your audience than setting lower standards for your business with a weak or irrelevant video stream.

7. **Edit your channel**

YouTube lets you customize your channel, which helps you differentiate it from other YouTube pages. Mark your brand identity with a logo, colour tone and messages or slogans

that you want viewers to associate with your business. "YouTube doesn't have to fight on its own - you can create a link to your website and Twitter, for example," De says. "Video footage may refer to

channel viewers and how to contact them. "Encourage viewers to subscribe, so they are notified each time you upload a new video.

8. **Edit each video**

"The good news is that you already have what you need to shoot, edit, and share smooth video in your pocket - on your phone - and anyone can learn to do it," said Alex Pell, founder of Dashboard Media. which

helps train small businesses to create video content. "In today's widespread videoblog, people also don't expect perfection. They just want to be aware and entertain ideally.

A clear message and starting point are more important than the equipment you use.

7. **Descriptions play an important role**

Don't make the general mistake of not having a description of your video. In addition to describing the information that is useful to your audience, your description is important to SEO. Keep videos are short but informative and include your important keywords, links, and call-to-action.

8. **Include calls to action and encourage interactivity**

First, think about how you want your audience to react to the video. Include call-to-action in the video itself, such as asking viewers to contact you for more information, subscribing to your YouTube channel, and sharing the video on their social networks. Encourage interaction and feedback and respond to any feedback quickly or regularly if you can.

9. **Use subtitles, no annotations**

Enabling captions in your YouTube video is pretty simple - just turn on auto-captions and adjust the output to increase resolution. There are hundreds of millions of hearing-impaired users on YouTube

appreciate legends. You can keep the default captions, so they don't bother unwanted viewers. YouTube can automatically create subtitles for free, and you can go online per line and then correct them. Oppose adding comment pop-ups to your videos - add links and comments to the description instead.

## DISTRIBUTION AND PROMOTION

In general, the better the videos, the more views you get. However, when it comes to growing your audience, getting the word out is just as important as creating a great video. Unless a video is shared wildly, and it goes "viral," which is rare, Views are always proportional to how you spread the word.

1. **Create playlists**

Playlists help your audience find videos and make it easier for other people to include relevant videos, by setting your channel as a curator and not just a content producer. 'Playlists

appears in search results, "De says." You may not be authorized for a particular topic, so creating playlists with other people's videos is a good opportunity to give access to that information, especially if it's a useful complementary area related to your business. "

2. **Post links to playlist videos**

When you send links to your video, such as by email to a customer or newsletter, you can provide a link to the video yourself in the playlist. "This saves more 'viewing time' because the video is on your channel's list of other people, De says. "YouTube rewards this behaviour because it believes it does a good job of promoting relevant content - which

are! "

3. **Consider cooperation**

Collaborative videos are popular on YouTube. Viewers usually like them, and they create an opportunity for further exposure. Find popular YouTube channels with deals that compliment (don't compete) with your business. Suggest a collaboration to create content for someone else's channel or invite other experts to talk to you.

4. **Expand your channel**

Of course, the video you create for YouTube doesn't have to stay on YouTube alone. "It may be worth uploading the video to other channels like Facebook and Twitter to get it more mileage and reach different audiences on multiple platforms. "

**5. Add your Google+ account**

The YouTube comment system is linked to Google+ profiles, which are important for a referral to Google's organic rankings. Make sure your business profile is ready and ready for visitors

YouTube.

**6. outcrossing**

It's not because you're creating a YouTube channel that people are looking for, so spread the word to other social media platforms. When you post a new video, you want people to be to see and share, write a blog about it, tweet a link and post it on Facebook. Also, you can also embed videos on your website, especially guides and product demos.

**7 Advertising on YouTube**

YouTube advertising is affordable, well-targeted, and, when done correctly, effective.

**DIGITAL MARKETING**

YouTube offers several cost-effective solutions for a variety of digital advertising needs. In this book, I'll look at the potential of video advertising and the suitability of YouTube for effective advertising.

## Video advertising in a nutshell

YouTube is the second most popular search engine in the world. You read that right, think about it for a moment.

YouTube's search volumes and user numbers are so large that it's hard to understand common sense about the amount of moving video that the entire service contains. Hundreds of millions of hours of YouTube videos are watched every day.

It's also worth noting that the number of videos is still growing at an explosive rate. And there are already over a billion users on the service.

So from an advertiser's perspective, YouTube's popularity is a real goldmine. Namely, the advertising solutions used by the video service enable a very precisely targeted and inexpensive form of advertising. So, in a word, YouTube advertising is cost-effective.

## Video ad formats supported by YouTube.

YouTube's advertising formats fall into three main ad types. Available ad formats are TrueView In-Stream, TrueView Video Discovery, and Buffer Ad. If you have used YouTube, at least sometimes, you are likely to distinguish between these formats based on the following description.

TrueView In-Stream video ads refer to a promotional video that appears before a user-selected video. In practice, this means that when a user clicks on the desired video, the desired video is played back before the promotional video embedded by the advertiser. These video ads, displayed in front of the actual video, can be skipped after 5 seconds of viewing.

With a TrueView In-Stream video ad, an advertiser only pays for an ad impression if the video is viewed for more than 30 seconds or when the viewer of the video interacts with the video. For showing a video ad less than 30 seconds long, the advertiser only pays when the video ad is fully viewed.

There is also a non-skippable In-Stream video ad for this ad format. The non-skip In-Stream is 15 to 20 seconds long and repeats like the skip In-Stream before the actual video. While a non-skippable In-Stream promotional video can generate more revenue, blocking an ad skip will usually significantly increase the video bounce rate.

TrueView Video Discovery ads, well, on the other hand, appear in YouTube search results. In addition to the actual search results page. Ads are displayed on the video watch page as well as on the YouTube homepage.

This ad type consists of a static image and ad text. The combination of the image also text thus appears listed next to the actual videos at the top of the search results. By its nature, Video Discovery works well, for example, when you want to promote a specific product or service in videos related to the same topic.

The idea behind TrueView ad types is that the advertiser only pays for ad impressions that allow the user to show that they noticed the ad. Therefore, as an advertiser, you don't have to pay for unnecessary or occasional ad impressions. In addition to In-Stream ads, this same rule applies to Video Discovery ads. In Video Discovery, you only pay when a user clicks on your ad.

Buffer ads do not belong to the TrueView ad family, so their behaviour and billing logic are quite different from the ad types mentioned earlier.

A Buffer Ad is a 6-second video ad that appears like a TrueView In-Stream ad before the video. However, unlike the In-Stream ad, the buffer ad cannot be skipped.

Of course, because a buffered ad impression does not require user interaction (due to its non-skipping nature), this type of ad cannot naturally be associated with a click. For this reason, buffer ads are paid for a CPM bid.

## Targeting video advertising

One of the biggest factors in the cost-effectiveness of YouTube advertising is an efficient and accurate targeting system.

Video advertising can be targeted in many different ways, such as based on the user's age, gender, physical location, or even the topic of the video associated with the video ad. Video ads can also be targeted to, for example, a YouTube channel or even an individual video.

## The measurability of YouTube advertising

Video advertising can be built, optimized, and reported like search and display advertising from the AdWords interface. The familiar interface shows advertisers the same columns and metrics, regardless of ad format. AdWords is a rather deficient platform for reviewing and reporting key metrics for video advertising. YouTube Analytics, developed specifically for video advertisers, responds to this call.

YouTube Analytics is a free tool for all video advertisers to view up-to-date data, metrics, and reports. YouTube Analytics should also not be confused with the free Google Analytics for all advertisers. Which, despite its versatility, does not provide tax tracking data for the former to the video advertiser. YouTube Analytics includes, e.g., invaluable viewing time and engagement reports. Let's take an actually close look at the above and many other important features of YouTube Analytics in my next blog post.

# FIFTY EXPERT TIPS ON AUDIENCE TARGETING AND YOUTUBE VIDEO STRATEGY

YouTube, like marketing, is evolving. Previously, the platform for amateur videos is now more than a billion active users. Marketers learn that YouTube is a powerful tool; In fact, the 2017 Inbound Status report shows that 48% of all marketers plan to add YouTube as a content delivery channel over the next 12 months. Video, too, isn't just a fleeting trend: nearly 87% of marketers use video for content marketing campaigns, and Cisco predicts that 80% of all Internet traffic will stream videos by 2020. The really need for marketers to use video to reach an audience is more critical than ever.

So Using YouTube should be an important part of your content marketing campaign. If you have just started your business, creating a reliable and professional brand is essential to stay relevant. You need to come up with good content ideas, and of course, you need to design a great logo. Need to actually learn how to create a logo for your YouTube channel? Logaster has created an excellent logo design guide to help you get started.

Also, whether you're new to YouTube video marketing or looking for ways to improve your efforts, you'll get tips for engaging your audience, improving your strategy, and also using the platform as effectively as possible. And We've collected 50 YouTube video marketing tips from marketers, video experts, social media enthusiasts. And others in the industry to help you in your quest to create engaging videos and increase traffic, earn subscribers to your YouTube channel, and ultimately increase your revenue. To help you find the advice you need most, we've listed it in alphabetical order and then the advice in each category; Therefore, the 50 experts YouTube marketing tips are in no way categorized or rated.

**Audience targeting tips for YouTube video marketing**

**1. Adopt a mobile-oriented mindset.** Generation Z teenagers had smartphones before thousands of years ago, and every marketer who wants to target this population must take a mobile approach. By creating and posting short, fun videos with a strong propensity for a viral disease, marketers can take advantage of YouTube to target smartphones, previews related to the content you are looking for or viewing.

**2. Always Be as relevant as possible to your audience.** As internal marketing strengthens, more and more companies finally realize the importance of relevance. The consumer is in the possession and can easily ignore you, which is why you need to create content that is discoverable and relevant to them.

Fortunately, video allows you to show your audience what your product or service can do for them ... share useful content that solves a problem your customer is looking for.

**3. Select your chain image carefully.** There are two images to choose from. The first is a photo in your account that works in the same way as your Facebook profile photos. The second is a photo of your channel that appears at the top of your channel, As well as a Facebook cover photo. You should choose these photos wisely because they are one of the first things which users notice about your brand.

I recommend that the image in your account (which you set up through your Google Account) be some kind of brand logo. If you're a one-person business, this could be a professional portrait of you. Ideally, it should match your profile photos to other social media accounts for immediate brand recognition. On both sides, if some subscribers to another site encounter YouTube, you want them to recognize you, so they are more likely to appear, and vice versa, if a viewer searches for you on Google, you want them to be sure that the Facebook profile they click on is you. only when you edit your profile.

**4. Always Connect with your audience by telling a story.** Video content is an effective way to tell your story. Consumers not only develop emotional connections to videos through sound, movement, and visuals but are also more likely to engage in the video to the end (and see and hear any message) than reading content. When done right, video content marketing has a significant impact on your audience and provides you with the ideal platform to test your advertising campaign and content efforts.

**5. Consider the customer journey.** If you're a new YouTube user and haven't yet created subscribers, your first viewers are likely to find you through search. So, before you start recording or start creating a video story, think about how you want your customers or viewers to find you.

Who are you trying to attract? About YouTube and How You Can Help Them Find out what keywords your brand should rank for and create interesting and entertaining video content around those keywords. The most important thing is to think of the ideal path for your customer. Let's say your business is photo printing. Your brand might be of interest to people looking for things like "engagement photos ", "scrapbooks ", etc. If you want to capture those interested, it's best to create content for what they're already looking for.

**6. Create a new audience using downloaded mailing lists**. People on your customer list may not read your newsletters, but that doesn't mean they don't pay attention to the videos. Just as you've selected a comment list in the Library / Audiences section of the share," you can create a new audience using imported mailing lists.

Well, If you are really lucky enough to have a very large email list, consider uploading segments. (instead of uploading the entire list to a single audience), especially if you want to send a message to each segment or a slightly different call to action.

**7. Focus on increasing audience loyalty.** If people close your video while watching it for only 15 seconds, you need to think about how to make the video more interesting to viewers. If people leave the video halfway through, it might mean you've focused on a particular topic for too long.

**8. Help your audience find your videos.** Remember that YouTube is considered the second largest search engine after Google, so it's best to start spending time understanding how SEO works on this platform ...

Another tip to improve your video ranking is to integrate it directly into your blog, hopefully, a book that follows the best SEO practices and is related to the topic. Integrating books into your business blog will give them more flesh and value.

**9. Know your audience.** Your audience needs, and no two audiences are alike. This group of people who started following the content are people who are interested in what you are saying. You should be able to give them what they are looking for while staying true to your brand. Finding this healthy balance between brand needs and audience expectations is essential to maximize the way you market your content. Also, by using YouTube as a social media marketing tool, you connect with the people who support you in building your brand.

**10. Make the video a follow-up to the link.** Most people who watch your videos go through some kind of referral. It could be a link you shared via email or social media, an ad you posted, or maybe another video. That's why the content people expect to see is very specific.

When creating videos, you need to keep this in mind. What ad attracts people to the video? If you are going to attract people with an information offer, the video should immediately use that information. For example, if a link to a video says, 'Weekly Market Report', the video should start.

**11. Understand your target customer.** While this may seem agile, you need to have a deep understanding of your target consumers, including their tastes, product features, available revenue, spending behaviour, the sites you visit, and the type of content they use.

It should be noted that millennia tend to be more entrepreneurial: according to published data, 72% of high school students said they want to own their own business, and 76% said they want to turn their hobby into full-time work. They were written by Mashable.

**12. Use an unusual video to capture curiosity.** People aren't going to click on your videos to see a boring infomercial. Also, they may be willing to tolerate a dry tutorial if it offers unique tips, they won't find anywhere else. But the most successful YouTube videos tell the story originally and interestingly.

Finding good content ideas can be easier if you don't limit yourself to videos that are directly related to your product or business. It is especially important if you work in an industry where it's hard to get excited (like contracts) asphalt).

Don't go over this type of content. You've probably seen ads and had no idea from the end of the message that confused you about your business. Make sure your videos evoke the feelings you want customers to feel about your business, even if there is no link between the video content no direct contact.

**YouTube video strategy tips**

**13. Generate traffic to your site.** Add links to your social media profiles and websites in your videotape area. It will help people find you no matter how many times a video is viewed. Tell them how they can see videos that are interesting to you.

**14. Collaborate to get more reach and prospects.** Collaborate in a niche. If you're a fashion brand, look for the best chains in related fields like travel or hospitality, showcase them on your channel and see if you can perform on your own. This collaboration gives your brand a broader reach and a target audience that matches your audience profile. Also, you can even collaborate with influencers on Youtube or Vloggers and ask them to add videos around the theme/playlist. It works great if you are hosting an event or want to make a series of reviews/demos of your products.

**15. Create an interesting video.** Most of us never create a viral video because of millions of views because we don't have a cat playing the piano or a sneezing baby collar, but luckily, they aren't essential to success. Well, most of us couldn't handle a million new customers at a time.

Instead, you need to create content that meets the needs of your audience. Your goal should be to create useful, valuable, and compelling videos for your potential customers.

**16. Create useful and useful content.** First, a YouTube video should serve a purpose and also give consumers a reason to visit your channel. And Instead of trying to create the next viral video, focus on what types of information your customers use to explore and provide that information in an engaging and valuable way. A great example of creating the video content their audience is looking for. Your business channel is full of do-it-yourself videos. Remember that your YouTube channel is a great educational tool that can provide your target customers with valuable information and build a lasting relationship with your organization.

**17. Do not extend the length of the video to increase the viewing time.** When YouTube decided to put a screen measurement on hold, it changed it to" viewing time "or how long the viewer watches the video. Not only are individual videos categorized by viewing time, but also by your channel, YouTube: Channels and videos with longer viewing times are likely to appear higher in search results and recommendations.

Well don't be fooled into thinking that improving viewing time is as easy as creating longer videos. A 30-second video that people watch from start to finish ranks better than a '10-minute video that only takes a few minutes to watch.' The best way to increase viewing time is ultimately to produce videos that your audience wants to watch.

**18. Find the right influencers.** This is the era of digital celebrities; or as they are called - Influencers. These are the people who make people not only think about your brand but also buy from you! Unlike traditional celebrities, these digital stars continue to do their usual work and do regular things that subscribers can join. They have a good dedicated audience, unlike movie stars or celebrities who have a big but detached fan. Besides, brand mentions seem to be naturally appropriate for the content, as the sole purpose of their online presence is to share life with their fans. Measuring the return on investment for such impact campaigns is also easier than accepting fame.

**19. Focus on entertainment and not advertising.** If you want to advertise on YouTube, and it's best to pay through AdWords and advertise your ad on the platform based on relevant demographics. However, when you upload videos to your YouTube channel, keep entertainment instead of advertising. Remember the importance of the video in the purchase period.

Fun and informative content is shared above traditional advertising. As you plan to attract people to your page, make sure the content on your page is light and informative. It increases their chances of interacting (comments, likes) and sharing your videos.

**20. Focus on the quality of your content.** Don't worry about the quality of your video production, especially when you start creating video content. Content quality is more important than the quality of your video production. Your priority should be to create videos that are both useful and entertaining to your target audience.

So, I really believe it's not the quality of your camera or your equipment. It's about the value of the content you create and how much you answer people's questions or solve people's problems. And that's true for so many YouTube videos. Some videos have millions of views taken from the iPhone.

**21. Focus on stories instead of selling.** Before the rise of social media, if you wanted someone to see the ad, you have to rent a space from a popular media channel like television or print media. On social platforms, brands can directly reach the same audience. It means that branded products (advertising) compete with entertainment rather than interrupting it.

If you want to watch a video, it has to create value for the viewer. Videos that focus only on the brand or increase sales are likely to be skipped. The best video content tells stories that connect with the viewer. The better you tell stories about yourself; the more likely viewers will be to understand what your business offers and what it can do for them.

**22. Follow the creators concerned.** This YouTube tip is a bit of a ready-made strategy. Think creatively. Do miracles. Everyone sees all the options available on the platform and gets different results everywhere. One reason for the difference is that people who work harder and think they are ready will get better results. What we are talking about, this "relevant creator tracking strategy" will help you to engage your relevant audience and possibly meet some of their audience. C is how people develop their YouTube channels. YouTube collaboration is a vital growth trend that YouTubers accepts, but it happens when you have subscribers and others (you collaborate) also have an audience. start creating relevant content producers on YouTube, they will notice you, and maybe the communication process will start from there.

**23. Connect non-subscribers to the channel's demonstration video.** Your channel home page is different from subscribers and subscribers. Have you adjusted your channel pages accordingly? For example, on my channel, non-subscribers will see a demo video of the channel, but subscribers see something different. The trailer is hidden, and they will see my recommended video instead.

The introductory video for your channel is a primary property - and one of the most important ways to attract non-subscribers. It's important to remember that your channel's trailer is ONLY visible to new users in your channel. In other words, you need to speak directly to new visitors.

**24. Take advantage of YouTube SEO.** YouTube is actually the second largest search engine in the world, receiving more than 30 million visitors every day.

And with 72% of buyers turning to Google search to search at the top of the funnel, businesses have huge potential to take advantage of YouTube SEO after being ranked on Google and YouTube.

The first step to producing a video that fits your niche is to find the right keywords. You should find keywords that have YouTube video results on the first page of Google so that your video is also ranked at the top of the page with relevant search terms.

**25. Market your videos.** It's a song that most people forget! Remember what I always say - You can't just build it, and they will come. You must also market it, whatever it is. Create social media posts to send people to videos. Talk to people - here's how you can create those perspectives! These are NOT missed roles in the marketing of these videos.

People don't always find them simply - you may need to direct them to videos. The more people who watch your videos until the end (because you've done your homework), the more your content is high when people search on YouTube, and you will also get more views! And of course, if people like your content, they'll probably share it with their friends too. More marketing for you!!! And by other people!

**26. Market your YouTube channel and also videos on your website and blog.** So, market your YouTube channel and videos on your website and blog. First, add a YouTube tracking icon to your website and blog so your audience can easily find your channel. Second, embed videos relevant to your website or blog. Consider creating a YouTube video after a particular blog or sharing customer video reviews or case studies on your website.

**27. Maximize engagement.** Did you know that the more comments a video has, the more likely it is to rank on YouTube? BackLinko Brian Dean found that the number of comments correlated closely with placement when analyzing 1.3 million YouTube videos to better understand how the platform's search engine works. The more comments on a video are, the higher it ranks. Because YouTube focuses on user engagement, it's not surprising that's why it's very important to encourage people to interact with your videos. Close your video by encouraging viewers to like "comment" and "comment below".

Another very good idea is to include an opinion in the text. And highlight the part of the video that supports that opinion. Follow the comments you receive as soon as possible. Continue the discussion by asking open-ended questions, linking to relevant content, and thanking users for watching.

**28. Optimize titles, tags, and also descriptions with keywords.** Well, if your content strategy also includes written content; you probably know how important keywords are. Placing them in titles, tags, and descriptions can make it easier to find content on the video platform and for search engines.

A good step is to research the keywords and phrases your target audience would use. To make sure you're using the right people, you need to identify the most desirable long-tail keywords related to the content. Once you've found them, include them in all relevant places for your audience and search engines.

**29. Always prioritize the visual appeal of your YouTube channel.** Next, work with the visual appeal of your channel. Describe your channel content and add links to relevant content you've shared on websites and other platforms. It will make it easier for visitors who want to" double-check your login information or find out what your brand is all about. Don't forget the left and right margins of your channel. Use them to display photos and other content related to your brand.

**30. Promote your videos on social media.** As social media becomes more usable and popular, it is becoming increasingly important for companies to have their profiles online. If you don't have your profiles yet, setting up profiles now will be of great benefit to you. Also, you can find out how to set up your Facebook and Twitter pages here and here with our easy step-by-step guides. Facebook, Twitter, Google+,

Instagram, and Pinterest are the main social media channels that can help make your video a success.

**31. Trust relevant trends and keywords.** First, you need to start with thorough research on the keywords that people usually use when searching for content like you.

"Google Keyword Planner or some other keyword research tools can help you find relevant keywords and phrases based on broader keywords and evaluate each one's competitiveness along the way. A newer channel would make sense to start with easier and less competitive keywords or more specific long-tails, and once you're successful on more competitive terms.

"Using YouTube's autocomplete suggestions, you can also get good target phrases to consider, as well as gather new ideas for future videos. Also, Google Trends for YouTube Search can also help you measure the dynamics of popularity. Current keywords and phrases.

**32. Restore your thinking about YouTube channels and YouTube pages.** It's important that you restore the way YouTube channels are viewed relative to YouTube pages when you start thinking about YouTube strategically. Also, you need to think of YouTube as a different kind of website. Your channel is the home that anchors your YouTube website. Your videos are websites.

Every video on your channel strengthens the website because every video links to your channel page. The more authoritative your channel/home page is, the easier it will be to rank your site.

**33. Think of YouTube as a content site.** Don't be too aggressive about YouTube marketing. If you're uploading a sales video and wondering why it didn't go viral, it's time to understand that YouTube is a content site. Provide a good site to ask people to visit your website.

**34. Treat videos like blog posts.** Don't miss the opportunity to drive traffic to your YouTube channel through other social media platforms. Think of it like you would post a blog. The more rewarding it is for all your social activities, the more it gets. through newsletters.

**35. Use YouTube influencers as brand advocates.** The benefit of working with influencers is to have a unique relationship with their followers. If you use influencers like your celebrity, you don't convey a message to the audience who actually hears it.

The difference is how you invite a YouTube fluster to participate in your TV ad and ask them to create their video for their channel.

**Tips for taking advantage of YouTube video features**

**36. Add in-stream call-to-action and encourage viewers to subscribe.** YouTube changed its policy in April 2017, and you now need 1,000 subscribers to post live video. That's why we're seeing more live video this year than ever before. You can post interviews or R&D sessions with users; you can show behind the scenes; share the latest news, events, etc. Tubularinsights requires that whatever opportunity you choose online, be sure to practice before you post it. Live video sessions also require advertising in advance. Otherwise, no one will see the live video, and your efforts will be wasted. Do not forget to add an in-stream call to action, as well as visual that verbal that urges viewers to subscribe.

**37. Add an item to share with your video.** Now, it is very important and useful. If you are looking for high and varied traffic to your videos, you need to create videos to share. You can try to make your videos entertaining, educational, or catchy. also, Viewers are more likely to share videos with these features with friends and family.

**38. Tag your content and video.** If you're the original creator of the content, you need to tag it with your name and logo and a link to your website. Also, Branding is very important because it gives you credibility. Also, if your videos add value, tons of visitors will share them with others. Or downloaded elsewhere, you will still get credit and traffic for your brand.

**39. Create stunning YouTube thumbnails.** Even if this is a small detail in appearance, YouTube thumbnails can increase or decrease your clickthroughs. My favorite analogy is author Maria Jose:" The YouTube thumbnail is the cover of a 21st-century book. "

Thumbnails are small clickable photos that visually depict each video. They also have a task to do: click and paste. Thumbnails should entice people to click, and then stay watching them.

**40. Create compelling video titles.** I know, it sounds obvious, but that's how people decide what to look at, and creating compelling headlines isn't as simple as it sounds. You want something descriptive enough for someone to want to look, but not long enough to cut it when it shows. You should make it exciting, but not so exaggerated that it looks like spam. Try to include keywords in irresistibly clickable studies and adjectives.

**41. Include branding images.** The importance of a brand in marketing can never be overestimated. Branding helps build loyalty. Including tagged news, series will help your loyal viewers recognize your work right away, so you don't lose them to your competitors.

"Also, this kind of Branding is important to ensure that viewers remember the video, which is especially handy when they have to refer to it. Even if they forget the actual content and name of the video, remembering your brand will help viewers get to your channel.

**42. Add real people to your videos.** The beautiful images and scenery are nice, but the video needs a face. People are thirsty for human interaction, and if you want someone to listen to what you have to say, the message must be from someone, preferably someone who can smile naturally, and act relaxed in front of the camera.

A personality person can eliminate all problems and show the world that your team is made up of the right people with the real-life outside of work. It makes the video message less similar to the marketing pitch than the conversation side.

If you're not really comfortable in front of the camera, look for someone in your organization.

**43. Keep your video short.** When I started working in video marketing, I noticed that there was a well-known rule of thumb: your marketing videos shouldn't be longer than three minutes.

"Why so? Well, because engaging with videos is tightly tied to the length of the video. Likewise, your potential customers' ability to watch the entire video and understand what you're trying to sell them.

"... The average number of views of a video drops dramatically after the first 2.5 minutes. The first tip is to create clear and unambiguous video marketing. Otherwise, you won't get close to the first pages of YouTube with a long boring video.

"Explanatory videos are the best types of engagement. they present a brief introduction to introduce the problem for the first few seconds, then offer a possible solution to the problem, and finally introduce the brand and explain why people should choose this product from the competition to solve their problem.

**44. Optimize video audio.** "You might have heard this before, but it remains true. The sound of the video is more important than the video itself. Users may apologize for the lower picture quality, but they have little patience for bad sound.

"In an uncertain?

"Go to YouTube now and see the comments. While the professionals on YouTube create great videos, most of the videos uploaded to YouTube are bad, and viewers express their dissatisfaction with the comments.

"Remember, these users have time to book comments. In most cases, click the back button and select another video. "

**45. Optimize your video and playlist for viewing time.** Industry expert Mark Robertson who confirmed that since October 2012, YouTube's algorithm had prioritized videos that have a longer or longer viewing session than videos that get more views. So, if people watch your videos - and suggested videos - after the first view, the videos will rank more likely in YouTube search results and related videos.

So, use YouTube Analytics to see which videos are successful in retaining viewers. Keep a close eye on the length of the time report and the audience retention report. Keep viewers watching each of your videos using powerful editing techniques to maintain interest and generate interest in each video. Your subscriber base, because subscribers are your most loyal fans and will be notified of new videos and playlists to watch. Finally, create a longer viewing session for your content with playlists and create a regular schedule to encourage viewers to watch a series of your videos instead of videos.

**46. Place the hook in the first set of the message.** You only have a few seconds to attach your message. During these precious moments, your brand message must be heard. Before publishing content, it is important to ask yourself," Can a viewer have a compelling glimpse of what they are going to watch?", even better, genuine, make sure your message in the first explosion has the hook they need to follow.

**47. Try streaming videos.** Early in the buyers' journey, especially for B2B, live streaming can be used as an advantage to improve SEO. YouTube live streaming can really increase your organic ranking because live videos are more, and search engines reward you. It's like generating new content, which is similar to news and search engines, especially Google, as new content that is relevant and useful.

**48. Use a little humour.** Have you ever wondered why funny YouTube videos get so many hits in such a short amount of time? It's because people like humour. We all like to laugh. Several YouTube channels have known a huge hit by injecting humour into their videos. Your there's no need to make the audience laugh from behind - just a little humour blinking does.

**49. Use tags correctly.** One of the biggest mistakes hindering the organic growth of YouTube videos is the misuse of tags. Identification on YouTube works differently than blogging. If you've never borrowed Beware of YouTube tags, now is a good time to start. You can even go back and edit any old ones. your tags.

**50. Use YouTube tools.** Start by using the tools available directly on YouTube. well, for example, provide a detailed and accurate title and description for each of your videos and attach relevant tags (keywords) directly.

# CHAPTER FIVE
# TACTICS FOR AN EFFECTIVE YOUTUBE MARKETING STRATEGY

**YouTube marketing strategy**

Regarded as the second largest search engine in the world (behind Google), YouTube is a precious opportunity for marketers to discover and connect brands and organizations via video. YouTube's marketing strategy should include:

- Audience studies
- Creative content
- partnerships
- Links to your website
- Calls to action
- consistency

In content marketing, video is affordable and new, and it speaks volumes. According to the State Inbound 2017 report, video content is the biggest distraction on the market. Consumers want more than ever to learn and connect with brands through video content, and brands listen.

The results of any video marketing are undeniable - 52% of marketing professionals cite video as the best ROI-type video. For many businesses, the simplest part of creating a video is deciding where to publish it. Since uploading videos to YouTube is by far the most popular video hosting site, it's a clear choice.

However, among all the great benefits of video marketing, only 9% of small businesses are on YouTube. Why? It is the second-largest search engine behind Google and is used by 1.3 billion people worldwide. The main reason business owners cite the lack of a YouTube content strategy is that they simply don't understand enough how to produce video content.

Here are six tactics for an effective YouTube marketing strategy:

**1. Do your research**

it is the first step in any content marketing strategy. Just like if you weren't writing a blog before knowing what your audience wants to read or how blog writing works, you are sharing the lead on video content mainly without any information is not the wisest.

The best way to do this when developing your YouTube marketing strategy. Is to see what your competition is doing. What type of video content do they produce? How successful is their video content? And Are there gaps in the content they produce? See what already exists and what succeeds or fails before you start creating your content.

**2. Create creative and useful content**

When you create content for YouTube, it's important to consider why people interact with video content more than any other type of content.

Indeed, they find video more personal and attractive than blogs, wallpapers, and e-books and seek the entertainment value of video combined with the use of conventional formats.

What does this mean for the creator of the video? One thing to always try to keep in mind is that you have to keep your content interesting. Even if people prefer to watch a video tutorial, if you create an interesting video on the use of a product, the customer will probably reject the video and, in some cases, the product.

You have an endless variety of video subjects to choose from. You can create content to use the product, success stories of those who have used it, corporate culture videos, presentation videos - if it can be presented in a creative and useful way, it's worth the effort—worth studying.

I was wondering what type of content people would find useful? Here's an awesome book from HubSpot that tells you what kind of content is filling the gaps in your content strategy.

**3. Partnership with others**

Well, YouTube is dominated by a unique form of celebrity that has only existed in recent years - YouTuber. These stars are building huge sanctions around their channels that can attract millions of followers and billions of prospects.

While there is a common misconception that YouTubers only attract thousands of millennial audiences, thousands of popular age-oriented content providers disagree. Everyone is interested in YouTube stars -

while stereotypical YouTuber vlogs are about beauty, video games, or fashion, many are making videos on home organization, parenting, repair automotive, and anything that might interest the consumer.

Try contacting YouTubers who create videos for your industry or resonates with the customer you want. It's a very effective way to draw attention to your brand and content and will benefit both parties. When you collaborate with someone with an audience similar to yours, cross-interaction is both organic and lucrative.

**4. Link to your website**

While it may sound simple, it's actually one of the best ways to drive traffic to your website. Well, there is actually two ways to do this: you can add a video comment that immediately brings users to your site by clicking on it, or you can add a link to the description area below the video.

5. Create a call to action

While adding CTA additions to traditional buttons is not an option in YouTube marketing, you still need to create a call-to-action for your users. What do you ask them to do at the end of each video?

Well, the answer should depend on the stage of the funnel the video is directed to. In the case of an introductory video, ask the people to like it and subscribe to more content on your page.

**6. Be consistent**

Naturally, the YouTube channels of many companies are more difficult to manage than, for example, a blog - YouTube videos can quickly collect production costs, and the scripts, filming, and editing can take a long time. However, YouTube should be treated the same as any other part of the content strategy.

In other words, if you are not consistent, you will not see results.

YouTube marketing is like any other marketing, and if you plan to do it, you have to be thorough. Make an introductory video of your channel, so subscribers know how often you are going to publish - and once you are on the beat, stay tuned.

However, consistency doesn't stop at how often you post videos - you also need to be consistent with their quality. If you start posting well-produced, thoughtful videos and soon start posting poorly described and poorly written content, you will see a drop in the following. When you upload your first video, make sure that the following videos retain their original quality, unless they have improved. To build the next one and see the results, you have to be consistent.

**YouTube marketing tools**

The power of visuals cannot be denied. Not only does visual content better connect with the audience, but it also leaves a more lasting impression than text. And if it's in video format, the effects are even better.

Videos are capable of conveying emotions. No wonder it is easier for people to understand them. And for the same reason, marketers are more inclined to use YouTube marketing today. A well-made video can be very helpful in promoting your brand and increasing conversions.

However, creating a video is not exactly a child's play. It is much more complicated than creating textual content. But does that mean you should turn away from it? Absolutely not.

Here is a list of 11 YouTube marketing tools you need to get started this year.

# BEST YOUTUBE MARKETING TOOLS

With these tools, you can not only easily create videos but also put them in front of your target audience.

1. **BuzzSumo**

The biggest challenge most content providers face is proposing topics for their content. Something relevant to your audience. Something trendy. Why else would anyone be interested, right?

BuzzSumo is a customized solution to these problems. Thanks to its social search function, you can identify the type of content currently in trend on YouTube. With plans starting at $ 79 / month, it's a great tool for finding inspiration for your videos.

2. **GoAnimate**

GoAnimate is a platform that allows you to create animated videos with simple, easy and hassle-free. With a plan of $ 39 a month, you can create professional-looking videos with simple drag-and-drop operations.

You can add sounds, change backgrounds, characters and props with one click. Creating videos couldn't be simpler.

3. **Canva**

Canva is a tool that allows you to create beautiful, professional images for your content. Their interface is quite simple and intuitive, allowing you to create beautiful banners in a variety of layouts and fonts.

The best part of Canva? You can pretty much use it for free, although a paid version is also available for more advanced features. And a larger library from which you can choose photos and photos.

4. **CoSchedule**

Many content producers focus so much on core content that they forget some of the basics. For example, the title of your content is just as important, if not more so. After all, it helps you find your content in searches.

CoSchedule helps you create compelling headlines by using the right keyword combination to maximize traffic to your content. So be sure to use this free tool and find the perfect title for your videos.

5. **Bulk suggest Tool**

This tool can help you find keywords or tags that you can use in your videos. Just type in a keyword, and it will show a list of suggestions for the most popular phrases that start with it. This tool uses Google and YouTube's "Suggest" databases and is completely free.

6. **keywordtool.io**

Now you know how important it is for your YouTube video to show up in searches. It is practically the only way to get real visibility in your video. And where there is research, you need to find the right keywords.

The YouTube Keyword Tool is a free application that helps you find the right keywords for your videos. It helps you find what people are looking for on YouTube.

7. **VidIQ**

vidIQ is a YouTube Certified Partner to help you add an organic dimension to your videos. It allows you to add your tag collection up to 10 times. They have a basic version that you can use for free. They also have plans for more advanced features starting at $ 7.50 per month.

8. **Hootsuite**

Hootsuite makes it easy to manage your YouTube workflow. You can schedule videos and share them on all your social platforms using it.

It even helps you manage multiple YouTube accounts, regulate video comments, and save time. Their plans start at $ 19 a month.

9. **Agora pulse**

the tool can be very useful for managing your YouTube channel. With plans starting at $ 49 / month, it ensures you can interact with your audience in real-time. You no longer have to worry about missing comments on your videos.

10. **BirdSong Analytics**

It is a very useful tool that allows you to analyze any YouTube channel for engagement or review SEO elements. It can be very useful in analyzing competitors.

With plans at $ 5.99, it provides you with detailed reports to help you analyze this data offline.

11. **BRAND24**

BRAND24 is a tool that allows you to gather social information about your brand. You can use your mention in real-time and see what people are saying about you.

Well, It is a great tool to help you understand your audience's feelings about your videos. Whether positive, negative or simply neutral. You can order their free version or even use the paid version, which costs $ 49 per month.

# THE TOP TEN MISTAKES PEOPLE MAKE IN YOUTUBE MARKETING

YouTube has so much to offer, and its potential to meet your marketing needs is limitless. Unfortunately, marketers who attack the channel often develop busy approaches that are not considered in a start-up attempt or worse; they overload analysis and paralysis in trying to understand everything before starting.

1. **Trying to do too much**

YouTube is a search engine, community, ad platform, content item, subscription service, and more. It is unlike any other digital platform and is constantly evolving and changing. As a result, marketers are not able to easily identify YouTube as one thing or another, confusing when using it as a marketing channel.

Anything is possible on YouTube. It is not the goal of every marketer to be The YouTube strategy is because the boss wants them to check the box, but rather because they have a YouTube strategy that meets the needs of the company. You can use YouTube selectively if necessary. Nothing says you should do everything in this book.

By assessing your business needs, the resources available, and all the different marketing techniques you can use, you can decide that you don't need to use YouTube yet.

Successful marketing consists of responding to a company's needs, without marketing activities in all possible channels or supporting a sense of false perfection.

If you are convinced that YouTube is the tool you want to use in your marketing, the best way to avoid making the mistake of trying to make too much is to choose a path. You can be

- An advertiser who displays ads on YouTube
- A sponsor who shows your ads in specific locations or works with influential YouTubers
- A content producer that lets you create your videos
- A supplier where the content you create is your company's main goal

In the unlikely event that you decide not to use YouTube for marketing, At least set your channel to register it. Because you're not actively using YouTube, you can use one simple video or channel image to direct people to other places where they can find you. People search YouTube and expect to find you, so at least a minimal presence in place.

2. **Do not specify success criteria.**

Regardless of the marketing channel in question, not defining success criteria before starting is a common mistake. A marketer may have an idea of the campaign they want to run, as well as a rough idea of what success looks like, but the more specific you are, the more successful your campaign will be.

Marketers need to determine the specific KPIs they use to measure a platform like YouTube and ensure that these KPIs are correct to achieve business goals. I have repeatedly seen the CEO requesting marketing team for providing several video views and channel subscribers, but the question to ask yourself is "why is it important?" If views or subscribers make sales, these are likely to be good indicators of success, but if they don't achieve your business goal, you're wasting time.

Think about what you want YouTube to offer your business and set the appropriate metrics. For example, if you want YouTube to help increase brand awareness, you want to maximize the number of people you reach most cost-effectively. To increase sales, you need to make sure that the ads you use on YouTube are forcing people to click and buy.

By knowing what you need to do on YouTube and defining these success metrics, you'll save time by creating videos that do nothing for your business. At the end of any campaign, the big boss asks you, "What has it done to the company?" Marketers who spend a lot of time and money developing videos that don't meet the right success criteria are destined to lose their jobs.

3. **Forget the audience**

While emphasizing YouTube's potential as a marketing channel, don't fall into the trap of thinking it's a traditional marketing mode where you can use a megaphone to simply shout out messages. Your potential audience may ignore your ad if it isn't interesting or moves to watch or do something else. Marketers need to work harder than before to deliver the truly awesome advertising and video content their audience wants to see.

Marketers easily make the mistake of sticking to thinking about marketing strategies, business jargon, reports, data, processes, offices, and more, forgetting that you end up trying to talk to a real person and show them that you have something to offer them. It all depends on the audience, and ignoring their needs and desires can lead to ad and video ad content that just doesn't resonate with them.

Identify a unique and compelling understanding of your target audience and then focus on creating your creation. You will find that you have created something that resonates with them.

4. **Without creating YouTube**

The challenge for marketers is the growing need to make marketing channels more creative than ever.

The marketing channels were once only television, print and radio. New digital platforms are now appearing every few years while existing digital channels are evolving. For example, YouTube video requirements are different from Facebook and Instagram and will change as YouTube creates new ad formats. It's hard to be a marketer! You have some time to think about and keep up to date. However, the advantage is that your marketing efforts can be more effective and efficient than before.

Marketers, with whom I have worked, are forced into the trap of thinking that they can download TV ads on YouTube and it works just fine, or that the video made by them on their websites is good enough to be sent to YouTube, and social media. The best creative performance results are obtained with the channel or platform in mind. Of course, creating deeds designed specifically for each platform or channel requires more work, but it's worth it. Make sure, when you create a video ad on YouTube, you keep in mind what makes your ads work on the platform.

5. **Paid media thinking is optional**

Perhaps the most common mistake that I have met with existing customers is that it allows you to upload videos to YouTube, and they will find a magically free to the public. Sure, it's possible that anyone can find the video, but with millions of YouTube videos, it's more likely that it will disappear into the ocean and will never be seen.

Using paid media can seem daunting, especially for small marketing groups and people with a smaller budget, but you can spend a few hundred dollars and see results. YouTube offers a lot of control so you can make sure your paid media budget works for you. If not, disable it.

6. **Copying others**

Copying others is a real bane. I have had many clients who have seen another advertiser's successful campaign and said: "I want it". Sure, just copying an idea from another advertiser can work, but it often isn't. Great creation and content are original works, not just copying and pasting.

I see the same mistake when I meet people who say they want to be on YouTube. I ask them what they would like to do with the videos, and the answer is always "Oh, probably just makeup instructions". Flash-information! No one wants to see your makeup guide. A lot of people already do a great job of making zombie-taco makeup guides, so don't just copy someone else. Instead, think of something you can create uniquely. Excellent marketing stands out when it is original and compelling. So do not copy another person's work.

7. **Skip the basics of quality video production**

In the past, for example, picture and sound quality were not as important as they are today. When online videos were born, the quality wasn't the best, but now people watching YouTube videos expect a certain level of quality.

A friend who is on YouTube recently made a video with some problems with his voice. It really didn't seem like a big deal, so he uploaded the video, but then blazed into fan comments. It turns out that people really want a basic level of quality, so make sure all the videos you create are

- Is focused, clear and high definition
- It has a clear and seedless sound
- It has a smooth and professional configuration

Gone are the days when the webcam is turned on, and videos are made because professional devices are now available to everyone. It's an easy mistake to think that YouTube doesn't require professional quality, but when a 14-year-old at home makes movie-level videos, it raises the bar higher for everyone.

8. **Do it once, share it once**

If you make a video but post it in one place, you lose the opportunity. Of course, while I think you need to customize your video creation on YouTube. (and adapt it differently to other channels), you can find ways to make simple adjustments and customizations to your video so you can publish it in as many places as possible.

I have been working with marketers, who do a great job in creating YouTube videos, even using the effective paid media to support the campaign. Still, I forget that they can take advantage of many other possible distribution channels to reach a wider audience.

For example, once you've uploaded a video to YouTube, you can

- Publish it on your blog and embed it on your website
- Connect it to your social networks
- Send it to customers in your next newsletter
- Play it at events or shops

Ask yourself the question "Does the video in its current version work on another channel?" If your video works just as well elsewhere, post it! If adjustment helps, take this extra step. For example, if you actually want to play a video you made in a store, you might not want the audio to always play, so you can edit the video by adding subtitles.

9. **When you give up too early**

I admit that this is a big question because I ask you not to give up, even if things may seem difficult. YouTube is one of the most complex forms of marketing.

Channels to approach - after all, that's why I wrote this book. I had many clients and friends who have wanted to give up, and my advice is to stick with it.

Savvy marketers know when to change their plans and turn away from unsuccessful channels. However, YouTube needs at least a year of hard work before deciding to reduce, review or reject an effort. Marketers should start small, be consistent and persistent.

"Oh, he tried the YouTube thing, and it didn't work," said a friend of mine, referring to a mutual friend who wanted to be a YouTuber. It's not that YouTube couldn't have worked for him; it is so that he gives up too early and does not know what he is doing correctly. It's a shame to hear that because I know YouTube can work incredibly well. People who think it doesn't usually need additional support and advice to start seeing results.

10. **Slow optimization**

Correct speech: do not even interfere with the use of YouTube in your marketing if you do not intend to engage in optimization. This advice also applies to most other digital channels. Their biggest advantage is that everything you create and publish generates information that you can use to iterate and improve. You have to

- Test, test, test! Try different ideas and see what works best. For example, test thumbnails and captions to see what more people are clicking.
- Use all available YouTube features. They make sure that you optimize your chances of finding it. Part 5 covers all the features that YouTube offers for your channel, video publishing and community management.
- Check your analyzes regularly and develop ideas for the next task. Your information is your gold mine, revealing an idea of what works and what doesn't.

**Reasons to Do YouTube Video Advertising**

Not Until a few years ago, the use of video in digital marketing was questioned by marketers, as slow network connections and the very limited ability of smartphones to display video material limited its capabilities. Because of this, the video was largely missed by website visitors.

As technology advances, the video has become a very effective way to communicate online, and its use has exploded:

- Currently, 70 hours of video are uploaded to YouTube every minute of the day.
- YouTube watches 4 billion hours of videos every month.

With YouTube Video Marketing, you get your videos in front of a larger audience, and you can target your audience to just the audience you want. So you can reach more people with a more specific message.

Here are five benefits that videos and YouTube marketing bring:

**1. Video conveys emotion**

The sounds and views of videos convey emotion and message better than any other form of content. Video ads move their viewers far more than just text or image ads.

**2. Video is an additional way to reach your customer**

The mere fact that we humans learn in different ways - by reading, seeing, hearing, and doing - means that video reaches a different audience than your textual content. In the video, the message is also conveyed on several levels. And thus, the delivery of the message is also more efficient.

Google video advertising is not limited to www.youtube.com but also appears on the Google Display Network. Google's display network reaches 98% of Finnish Internet users.

With YouTube marketing, you can reach people on different devices and in different places. Watching a video while sitting in a coffee shop in the city is a very common way to kill time. If by chance the video advertises discount sales of new spring shoes at a nearby store, the coffee shopper's next destination may change.

**3. You only pay when the video is actually watched**

Although YouTube in-stream videos that run as ads on top of the actual video will start automatically, as an advertiser, you won't have to pay anything for this unless the user watches your video for at least 30 seconds.

The five required seconds before a user can watch the video they are looking for are free for the advertiser. Make sure your videos convey your brand's message as effectively as possible in the first 5 seconds.

**4. Videos are much more than just commercials**

The use of the video should not be limited to advertising on YouTube.

- You will always be able to build your channel on Youtube with videos.
- You gain visibility on social media.
- Your video may go viral and get a huge amount of "free" visibility.
- Good videos have also been proven to increase a website's conversion rate - in other words, a video on a website increases sales.

**5. YouTube video advertising is measurable**

The greatest thing about digital marketing is its measurability and targeting. All the benefits of digital marketing also apply to videos. You can calculate the effectiveness of your video ad campaign from the click from your AdWords video campaign to the final purchase contact on your website.

## Finally

The more people's reasons for buying have been researched, the clearer it has become that emotions are the biggest factor in the buying decision. Although a person often justifies a purchase for himself by being sensible, before that, the purchase decision has already been made for emotional reasons.

Video is a very effective way to appeal to emotions and thus get the message across. When you invest in a video. Be sure to also invest in getting the video in front of your target audience.

# 16 TIPS FOR YOUTUBE MARKETING

What makes a YouTube channel special, and what added value does it bring to its viewers? If the answer to these questions is already ready, marketing will be easier. Video marketing requires a lot more channels than just YouTube. We put together tips for marketing your YouTube channel.

## 1. The graphic look of the channel online and offline

If you want to invest in channel branding, you should also invest in a graphic look. For example, business cards, flyers, and stickers, as well as a branded tilter, should be designed to be uniform. This way, recognizability works to the advantage of the channel.

The business card and other print material should include the YouTube name, URL, and channel channels. And has a striking slogan been developed for the channel that can be used in print and even in shirts? A font large enough, a simple design, and easy-to-read text are important things to consider when designing. The same fonts and colours can also be used for blogs and videos.

## 2. Some profiles

Social media is the best way to grow a channel. For example, Twitter and Facebook can be harnessed for marketing use. Instagram is also in heavy use by betters and vloggers. Some guarantee instant visibility of videos. Every tweet, status update, and the post can result in watching videos. When setting up accounts, it's a good idea to consider whether it's a convenient way to market your videos through personal profiles or create your profiles or pages on your YouTube channel. Of course, you can also link a personal profile to a YouTube channel's profile if you wish.

You should take the time to talk to your followers. People appreciate being taken into account. In addition to the comment field for videos, Twitter is a good place to chat. Tweeting and hard-working conversation also show up outside of your followers. Other fake users will see the conversations and may well be interested in and subscribing to the channel's videos.

A Facebook page or group can be used to create a discussion forum for followers. A closed group requires an invitation, allowing the atmosphere to become intimate. An open group, on the other hand, has a lower threshold to join. The advantage of the page is that anyone can like the page, and the publications can also be spread outside the immediate audience.

Some, you should also remember to use hashtags. Hashtags help viewers find new ones to follow, and through that, new audiences are lost on the YouTube channel as well. Hashtags are used, especially on Twitter and Instagram. Relevant hashtags are selected for publications so that those who use hashtags can find content that interests them.

Viewers can be asked to share videos on Some. With each division, the channel finds new viewers. Sharing can also be rewarded or used as an incentive for competitions.

You should also actively comment on other YouTube videos. Both the author of the video and the viewers will then know about the channel. Every time good feedback is given and commented on, the comment gets likes. Likes raise comments in the comments field.

## 3. Email Marketing

Email lets you send messages directly to followers and let you know about new videos at any time. Email marketing can be formatted as a regular newsletter with news and videos from the last month or week. One email can potentially get plenty of new views for your videos.

Emails are supplemented by an email signature that contains channel information and links to some channels. Each time you send an email, the channel appears at the end of the message.

## 4. Youtube ads

Is there an advertising budget for videos? If so, you can create video ads on YouTube through Google Ads (formerly AdWords). Such True View ads will appear to YouTube users before the video is shown (15-30 second ads, also which can be skipped after 5 seconds). When you advertise on YouTube, you only pay for views over 30 seconds, or if your video is shorter than 30 seconds, you only pay for views for the entire promotional video.

You can target YouTube ads. However, you like it. The first few seconds of a video ad will determine the fate of the ad, as users will only see the end of the ad if they are interested right from the start.

## 5. Youtube video optimization

You can also get more views by optimizing your YouTube videos and adjusting a few settings. You can find more information about optimization in our optimization book.

## Search Engine Optimization

Keywords and phrases improve the search engine visibility of the video and make the video available on Google and other search engines. Keywords should be relevant and reminiscent of searches within a topic. Optimization helps people find a channel. Keywords are used in the title, video description, file name, and video keywords (tags). It's worth remembering that too many keywords will not benefit anyone.

## Capturing preview images

Images have a big impact on search results. You can create a separate preview image for the videos and stand out from the crowd with images. You can create a preview image for each video. Fonts should be readable even in small sizes. The image should be associated with the video so that viewers stay on the channel.

## Embedding videos

You can either allow or block the embedding of videos. Enabling embedding will make it easier to share content on blogs or websites. When someone wants to embed a video, all they have to do is copy the link from *Share*. Each embedding spreads the videos more widely.

## The title,

Each title should be striking, descriptive of the content of the video, and include keywords. If the title is not related to the content, the videos will not be watched until the end! Keywords in the title help people find the video, so the best title is captivating and has some keyword in it.

### Playlists

YouTube Playlist is a customized list of videos. When someone watches one video from the list, they are automatically redirected to the next video. You can create a list from existing videos and direct people to the list instead of a single video, for example.

## 6. Blogging

Blogging also helps you gain followers outside of YouTube. Every time you can write a new blog post, you are more likely to get new traffic from search engines, and the traffic will generate Video Views. For best results, attach videos to the end of each blog post or the sidebar. Videos can be attached using YouTube's embed feature. The code is just copied and pasted in the appropriate place!

Another help with the blog is YouTube's ***subscribe*** feature. The feature can be found through the Google Developers channel. So you can add an embedded button to your blog or another page that allows new website visitors to start following your channel with a single click. If for some reason, the poem doesn't pulse when the blog should be updated, you can always write a blog post based on the videos. It also leads to visitors who are primarily looking for text-based information.

Also, commenting on blogs is one way to gain visibility. There are usually two required fields for commenting on blogs. In addition to the name and email, you can mark a web page when commenting. You can paste a channel address here. Commenting, of course, works best on related blogs.

## 7. Forums and social websites

In the forums, you can participate in the discussion whenever the topic is in any way related to the topic of the YouTube channel. By providing quality responses and discussions, forum users peek at what the channel has to offer. However, unnecessary spamming should be forgotten. Most forums use a specific nickname to which you can link to the channel. The nickname may well be the same as the YouTube channel name.

Reddit is an example of a website where you can upload your content and find related communities (subreddit). Every community has a different feel, so you might want to explore them before uploading your videos. At best, the videos will spread. Users vote on user content, and the publications that get the most votes get a lot of traffic.

## 8. Kisat

People love races! What would a competition build around a canal sound like with something cool as a prize? The competition will give the channel more visibility and followers. The competition could include, for example, sharing videos on sommelier channels or commenting.

You can be creative with the prize. Could at least part of the prize be, say, a mention in the next video or a personal video for the winner?

## 9. Industry events

This marketing tool requires more investment, at least if the events of interest are abroad. However, appearing at events can be helpful. For example, the Finnish Tubecon is a big event for tubers. By participating in the events, you will, of course, have the opportunity to network with industry players. The events may give birth to awesome patterns of collaboration. At events, you can also hang out with your followers live, which is important for the continuity of the channel.

If collaborative patterns catch fire, a group with other YouTube video producers can be a nice way to stay in touch. In the group, you can share your knowledge and discuss the latest trends regularly. You can set up a group on any channel, as long as it is natural and pleasant for the whole group to use.

Speeches at events provide an opportunity to bring out your expertise. Events related to the topic of the channel are, of course, the best for such expert marketing. For example, if you make videos related to taxation and finances, a suitable event could be related to finances. If you also want to use your speeches for marketing your YouTube channel, you may want to choose events where your audience reminds you of your channel's audience.

If a marketing budget is available, you may also want to consider renting a trade show or event booth. Renting a booth is also an opportunity to network with people interested in the channel. Besides, appearing at trade fairs is an opportunity to gain media visibility.

## 10. Collaboration videos and brand collaboration

Collaboration is a great way to grow your audience. Co-Videos are two or more parties co-production, which usually also strongly related to thc mcntion of partncrs and Linking its channel.

Through collaboration, you can also reach the Followers of your partners. One way to implement collaboration videos is to divide the collaboration into several parts. It allows anyone involved in video production to publishing part of the entire production on their channel. Of course, cooperation can also be done without a specific project.

Companies are often very open to collaborative ideas. Brand cooperation benefits both parties. Through the videos, the company reaches new target groups and the benefits from the company's marketing machinery and customer base.

## 11. Leaves

Writing in magazines allows you to appear as an expert. Readers worth pursuing are people who belong to the channel's target group. The channel name must, of course, be mentioned with each entry. To publish books, you need to find a magazine that fits the content produced by the channel. It's easier to get readers to watch videos if they're already interested in the topic. There is also an opportunity for the local newspaper to market the channel. Reporters are constantly looking for stories and interviewees.

## 12. Podcast

The podcast makes it possible to reach a new audience. Besides, the podcast provides additional content for existing followers. The topic of the podcast may be close to the topics of the YouTube channel. For example, if you describe workout tips and moves, you can supplement your videos with a podcast that covers the latest exercise trends, workouts, and diets. Podcasts naturally mention the name of the YouTube channel and encourage listeners to subscribe to the channel's videos.

## 13. Workshops and webinars

The YouTube channel should profile itself as an expert in their field. The workshop helps with profiling. For example, a vlogger describing makeup tutorials could organize a makeup workshop. After the workshop, participants are sure to look for makeup guidance on the channel the next time they need help.

A webinar is a great way to brand your channel. The webinar develops conversations with followers and networking with influencers. The webinar actually offers much the same benefits as a traditional workshop, but when the event is online, it is more accessible. At the very end of the webinar, you can answer the participants' questions and thus strengthen the relationship with the followers.

## 14. Regularity

The more videos, the more routes there are to the channel, and the more search results the channel will show. Regular video publishing is important. If you post from time to time and when it hurts, Followers will quickly disappear. Regular and consistent content production also has a positive effect on follower numbers in the longer term.

## 15. Trendy Youtube tags

You often come across the word *tag* on YouTube. *The best friend tag* or *five questions tag* are examples of video *topics flickering* on YouTube. Tags are keywords that can be attached to a video during the optimization phase. Certain keywords, or tags, trend in the videos of several tubers at the same time, and many publish videos under the same tag and in the same style. Grabbing the tag trend will help bring more audience to your channel when viewers are looking for videos that have the tag mentioned. When a viewer finds one video with a tag and watches it, other similar videos will also appear in the sidebar. It's also worth noting that it's a good idea to use the same basic tags from time to time in your videos, even if some keywords are momentarily trendy. It's easier for users to find multiple videos from the same author when they use the same keywords.

## 16. Q&A videos

It is important to maintain a conversational connection with the subscribers of the channel. A good way to get viewers excited and discuss is Q&A. Viewers post questions, and the channel administrator responds with a video. Often, questions are left in the YouTube comment box, but nowadays, you can also see a lot of styles that combine several different Finnish channels. Followers can ask,

# CHAPTER SIX
# HOW DO YOU LEVERAGE YOUTUBE ADS TO GROW YOUR MARKETING AGENCY

---

Well, how to get the best return on investment from YouTube ads? YouTube ads are a weird beast, and YouTube's creative landscape is constantly changing. However, YouTube ads can help you grow your office quickly if you stick to your buyer persona and drive the ideal customer.

In this section, we discuss:

- Why you need 2 YouTube channels.
- The difference between YouTube and Facebook ads.
- 3 Steps to Creating Better YouTube Ads.
- Why 5 seconds could make or break your ad.

Tom Breeze (A.K.A, King of YouTube Ads) who manages visibility - the most effective consumer campaign on YouTube! Tom has already been on the podcast, and he gave an excellent overview of performance-based models. I invite you to read this section if you have not already done so; It's one of my favorites.

Tom has looked at some of the most critical YouTube advertising strategies and how he and his office place YouTube ads that engage and generate results.

Let's dive in!

**Why you need 2 YouTube channels**

Tom talked about sharing your organic YouTube channel and your ad-based YouTube channel. It may sound strange at first, but since the two require different things to succeed, it makes sense to separate them.

When you upload videos to your organic channel, you want a lot of impressions and engagement (subscribers, comments, shares, etc.) so that you can improve your channel's ranking in the YouTube algorithm.

When you show ads, you want prospects, but you don't want a lot of engagement (and you probably don't want a lot of engagement.) Here's another channel useful.

Sharing them gives you the freedom to track different metrics in each account with the risk of overloading your YouTube ranking with either.

# THE DIFFERENCE BETWEEN YOUTUBE AND FACEBOOK ADS

Tom explained the main differences between YouTube and other types of ads. You already have the attention of your viewers on YouTube. They are already there to see and buy. Facebook, TV, Instagram, and other creative outlets require that you be entertaining and engaging to grab viewers' attention.

You don't want too entertaining ads on YouTube. When you show preview ads (the ones you can ignore after watching 5 seconds before the video you really want to watch), you only pay if the viewer watches the ad for 30 seconds. You don't want anyone, also except potential buyers, to follow the entire ad because you're wasting advertising costs.

After all, you pay people who aren't your ideal customers and who don't match the nature of the buyer.

**3 Steps to Creating Better YouTube Ads**

YouTube ads can be boring. That's where I said it. When it comes to creating ads that feed customers into your channel, you need to use a little subtlety. Tom shared his agency's greatest advice on how to drive these critical clients without wasting money and time.

- You want to disapprove people within the first 30 seconds of your ad. You'll need to pay for the advance ads when they reach the 30-second mark. Make sure only your ideal customers reach this point in your ad.

- To Create different ads for each point your audience experiences. For example, suppose you have a social media marketing company. You want to create an ad that targets companies looking for help managing their Instagram accounts. At the same time, you want to show ads targeted to companies looking for help with social media stats on Facebook. If you create ads for each service, you will target your hyperlinks to people who need the service. That's why you only pay for the mains.
- Don't be too interesting! I know everyone has already said that all your ads need to be constantly interested, but for YouTube, compelling ads are a waste of money and people's time. Don't let people browse your entire ad because you've blown up your budget to create a hilarious creation. Be committed in a way that appeals to your ideal client, not everyone. Remember, also you already have their attention - you don't have to fight for it.

**Why 5 seconds could make or break your ad**

Here is good advice for everyone. By adding 5 seconds to the end of your ad, you can make or break a CTA. Tom remembers watching an interesting Saturday.com ad, but the ad ended before he was able to click on the CTA.

Tom's company did very well to test the countdown at the end of the announcement. This way, customers have time to click on this CTA, and it adds urgency. Remember that video ads don't like landing pages.

Well, People only have a certain amount of time to click on the CTA - give them enough time to click on it.

# THE MOST IMPORTANT TIP FOR THE FUTURE OF YOUTUBE ADS

The near future of YouTube ads lies in AI statistics. You want to track your conversion point. Gather as much good information as possible about each ad you submit. And You want to give the Google AI monster as much food as possible.

Well, The more Google knows about your ad and the people who use it, the better it will be able to target your ads to the right customers. The information has become the king of marketing - we all know it.

The near future of YouTube ad targeting (and ad targeting in general) depends on AI consuming as much information as possible.

Want to learn more about YouTube ads? Check out Tom's book Visibility, where he breaks down some of his office's proven strategies and gives advice - like how to find sales times and leverage different types of customers.

# CONCLUSION

With over billions of active users, YouTube is no longer just a video entertainment platform. Videos generate 157% more organic traffic from search engines. In this environment, YouTube is an important marketing platform that allows your brand to promote a continuous visual.

Inbound marketing techniques are essential to promote your YouTube channel and videos. Also, create content that shares an interesting story and provides valuable information to your viewers. Advertise this content on a variety of platforms, including social media, email, and your professional blog or website. Finally, optimize your content by including covers and displays with clear CTAs.

YouTube is a platform that may seem confusing at first, but it makes it easier to share and read the content. Your audience wants to learn, entertain and interact with your brand through videos. Follow the tips in this guide to optimize your YouTube marketing strategy.

CPSIA information can be obtained
at www.ICGtesting.com
Printed in the USA
BVHW041530110521
607048BV00007B/2245

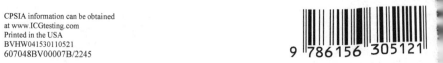